Elections without Order

Russia's challenge to Vladimir Putin

D0545710

Russians want both free elections and order. In the past decade Russia's political elites have supplied a great choice of candidates and parties. But order – a sense of predictability in everyday life and the rule of law – has been in short supply. This is the challenge that Russia presents to Vladimir Putin. This book is about Russia's attempt to achieve democratization backwards, holding elections without having created a modern state. It examines the multiplication of parties that do not hold the Kremlin accountable; the success of Vladimir Putin in offering a 'third way' alternative to the Communist Party and the Yeltsin Family; the new president's big but vague election mandate; the popular appeal and limits of Putin's coalition; and what the Russian people make of the combination of free elections and disorderly government. The authors draw on unrivalled survey data to show what Russians think of their new president and new regime.

Richard Rose is Director of the Centre for the Study of Public Policy at the University of Strathclyde. Author of more than forty books and hundreds of articles, he is a Fellow of the British Academy and an Honorary Fellow of the American Academy of Arts and Sciences.

Neil Munro is a Research Fellow at the Centre for the Study of Public Policy at the University of Strathclyde.

A society can move forward as it is, in spite of what it is, and because of what it is.

Albert Hirschman, *Journeys toward Progress*

Elections without order

Russia's challenge to Vladimir Putin

Richard Rose and Neil Munro

Centre for the Study of Public Policy
University of Strathclyde, Glasgow

PUBLISHED BY THE PRESS SYNDICATE OF THE UNIVERSITY OF CAMBRIDGE
The Pitt Building, Trumpington Street, Cambridge, United Kingdom

CAMBRIDGE UNIVERSITY PRESS
The Edinburgh Building, Cambridge CB2 2RU, UK
40 West 20th Street, New York, NY 10011-4211, USA
477 Williamstown Road, Port Melbourne, VIC 3207, Australia
Ruiz de Alarcón 13, 28014 Madrid, Spain
Dock House, The Waterfront, Cape Town 8001, South Africa

http://www.cambridge.org

First published 2002

Printed in the United Kingdom at the University Press, Cambridge

Typeface Plantin 10/12 pt   *System* LaTeX 2$_\varepsilon$ [TB]

A catalogue record for this book is available from the British Library

ISBN 0 521 81609 2 hardback
ISBN 0 521 01644 4 paperback

DEDICATED TO

All the peoples who survived the consolidation of the Soviet Union and to those who survived its subsequent fall and the rise of the Russian Federation – and remembering those who did not.

Contents

Figures

Tables

Introduction. The reality of Russia

Elections are about what people want; government is what people get. In the Soviet era, there were elections without choice. The Communist Party told people who to vote for and election results were literally too good to be true. In the past decade Russians have voted in five free elections, and in the year 2000 Vladimir Putin won a much bigger and much less controversial election victory than did George W. Bush. Elections to the Duma, the chief house of Parliament, return more than half a dozen different parties and Duma members are more effective in obstructing executive initiatives than are MPs in the British House of Commons.

Yet something is missing in how Russia is ruled. From the prescriptive view of democratic theory, what is needed is more democracy. But from the point of view of Russians, what the country lacks is order. The order taken for granted in a democratic modern state cannot be taken for granted in Russia, because it is not a modern state. The legacy of Russia's past is that of despotism and totalitarianism. The Federation established by Boris Yeltsin has rejected that tradition and institutionalized free elections, but the means used have not established a Western system of government.

What is normal in the West is not *normalno* in Russian politics. The great challenge facing Vladimir Putin is not how to win re-election; it is how to bring order to Russia. Ordinary people experience disorder when their savings suddenly become worthless because of inflation, or when they receive excuses rather than wages after a month's work. The disorder of everyday life is implicit in mortality statistics that show a big rise in death from avoidable causes, such as drunkenness, accidents and murder. Disorder is evident in the violence that erupts when the *mafiya* enforces its code, and in the corruption producing enormous wealth for 'kleptocrats' who have used political connections to secure privileges worth billions of dollars.

The goal that Vladimir Putin has repeatedly proclaimed is profoundly ambiguous: to achieve 'the dictatorship of law'. Emphasis can be given to the term dictatorship, for which there is ample precedent in Russian

1

history, or to government according to the law, for which Russian precedents are few and discouraging. The challenge to Vladimir Putin is whether he will be able to get Russia out of the trap of disorder without springing the trap of dictatorship, or whether life will continue much as before, with government on the basis of elections without order.

The meaning of order

Order is about things being in their expected place, so that people can go about their daily lives without unexpected or unpleasant surprises. In classical times Greeks categorized architectural columns into different orders, and set out rules for their use and harmonious relations. The medieval Catholic Church had many different orders, each distinctive yet integrated in a hierarchy leading up to the pope. In the eighteenth-century Enlightenment, philosophers believed in a natural order of things, a term broad enough to embrace the movement of the solar system and political order. Today, traffic rules about driving on the right or the left are examples of the state imposing order. The rules differ from country to country, but each is accepted without thinking by residents as part of the necessary order of everyday life.

Ordinary people value order because it provides a secure framework for everyday life. Personal property is safe, or if it is stolen the police will pursue the thieves rather than be in league with them. Profitmaking firms and people in work will pay taxes, and taxpayers will receive the benefits to which they are entitled. Public order does not make everyone rich or happy or equal. It provides a framework within which individuals and organizations can conduct their daily lives, rectify what is wrong and invest efforts in hopes of a better future.

Order is the prime responsibility of the state. Government contributes to order by the predictable provision of routine services. Electricity is continuously available rather than shutting off for hours at a time, and sewers dispose of waste rather than overflowing. The state lets people get on with their lives free of the interference that characterizes a totalitarian regime. In the marketplace, the economic dictum – you get what you pay for – is respected, as the goods one buys are weighed accurately. Wage-earners are paid on time rather than told to wait and see if they will be paid later. The German term *Ordnungspolitik* emphasizes the need for the state to guarantee the legal framework of the economy – for example, property rights, the enforcement of contracts and stable currency values – and to police economic activity to avoid anti-social outcomes. However, the state is a source of disorder if governors act arbitrarily or corruptly rather than according to the rule of law. If government is so weak that people do not pay taxes and organizations appropriate public property for

Table Int.1 *What Russians mean by order*

Q. *What in your opinion does the word 'order' mean? (More than one reply accepted.)*

	%
Predictability (mean mentions per person: 1.84)	
Political and economic stability of the country	45
Strict observance of the laws	35
Stopping the plundering and looting of the country	33
An end to power struggles, collapse of the country	32
Strict discipline	22
Possibility for all to get their rights	17
Socio-economic conditions (mean mentions: 0.26)	
Social protection of the poor	26
Tough enforcement (mean mentions: 0.17)	
Bringing in the army, security services to fight crime	13
Limiting democratic rights and freedoms	3
Slogan used on the path to dictatorship	1
Other	1
Don't know	3

Source: VTsIOM. Nationwide survey, 30 December 1999–4 January 2000. Number of respondents, 1,600.

private use, then there is no state, at least no state in the modern sense of that word.

There is a great demand for order in Russia. The meaning that ordinary Russians give to the word order (*poryadok*) emphasizes the predictability that citizens of modern states take for granted. Predictability requires that governors as well as the governed obey the rule of law, that governors do not bend or break rules in order to benefit their friends, steal state assets for private benefit or undermine the institutions of the state. In the week in which Vladimir Putin replaced Boris Yeltsin in the Kremlin, a VTsIOM (the Russian Centre for Public Opinion Research) survey of public opinion asked Russians what order meant to them. The replies were numerous and almost always positive (tab. Int.1). The most frequent definitions of order refer to political stability – strict observance of the laws; an end to plundering and looting of the country by governors; and an end to personal power struggles threatening the regime's collapse. A minority give order a social definition, such as the state protecting the poor from destitution.

The order that Russians want is not the repression associated with cries for law and order in Anglo-American societies. Russians have experienced that authority and they know it involves disorder. Only one in six associates order with actions contrary to democratic governance, such as using the army to fight crime or having a dictator limit rights and freedoms. However, Russians lack the confidence of Western liberals in the law as principally concerned with guaranteeing individual rights. When the third New Russia Barometer survey asked in 1994 whether Russians value order or democracy more, the replies showed that a big majority gave priority to order. The collapse of the Communist party-state has given Russians far more freedom from the state than ever before, but it has not brought about order. Order is the Russian priority because it is today in short supply.

Order does not require a democratic state, and starting with the Greeks many political theorists have portrayed democracy as encouraging disorder or even anarchy. Order requires a government that itself obeys the rule of law. Government contributes to disorder when it engages in arbitrary and lawless actions. In Russia the state has been doing this since tsarist times – and in response ordinary Russians have sought to avoid the state. The so-called order of Soviet times was not based on the rule of law, but on the unconstrained and overwhelming power of the Communist Party of the Soviet Union. As a critical citizen recalled, 'People now say that in the past we had order. Because we were afraid ... That's not order' (quoted in Carnaghan, 2001a: 17–18).

The disorderly transformation of the Soviet Union into the Russian Federation has maintained many disorderly practices that were part of the Soviet legacy – and added new ones. As the chief economist of the European Bank for Reconstruction and Development notes about doing business in Russia, 'The rule of law is the exception rather than the rule. Real negotiations start after a contract is signed' (Buiter, 2000: 25). One strategy for making authority effective is to mobilize institutions of law enforcement. In Russia today there are at least fourteen different agencies concerned with law enforcement, armed with extraordinary legal powers, guns and discretion in the way they go about their activities. However, the order of the modern state is not based on force or the threat of force, but on voluntary compliance with laws by both governors and governed.

A partly transformed society

In a society in transformation, the first few years are the most uncertain, for everything – the system of government, the value of money and even the boundaries of the state – is up for grabs. It is now commonplace to say that it will take a generation to transform Russia from what it was in the Soviet era to something new, whether the ideal is drawn from Russian or European traditions or a mixture of elements from both and novel features too. In the half-generation since the inauguration of the

Russian Federation, society has been partly transformed. For some years optimists have been proclaiming that Russia is almost there, whatever that destination is. Pessimists proclaim that Russia is going backwards. A third alternative is that governmental and popular responses to shocks are producing a society different from what went before and also different from what is recognizable in Western societies.

Whereas the challenges that politicians voice are usually rhetorical, the challenge of completing the transformation of Russia is palpable in every Russian household. That is why this book's subtitle emphasizes Russia's challenge *to* Vladimir Putin. We set out challenges as they appear to the less visible half of the Russian political system, the 140 million Russians living outside the Moscow Ring Roads, within which political elites debate what is to be done. While elites propose how Russia is governed, ordinary citizens can now dispose of governors they dislike.

Plan of the book

The tradition of Russian government is both undemocratic and disorderly. The power of the Kremlin appeared, in the ambiguous Russian word used to describe Tsar Ivan IV (*grozny*), as both awesome and terrible, because it was exercised arbitrarily. Under Joseph Stalin the Communist Party of the Soviet Union created a radically different yet equally lawless regime, a totalitarian state using whatever means necessary to assert its domination. After Stalin's death and the partial repudiation of his errors at the 20th Communist Party Congress in 1956, the grip of the party-state became less tight. While post-totalitarian liberalization was welcome, the subsequent stagnation of the regime did not promote the rule of law. The political forces that Boris Yeltsin mobilized to bring down the Soviet state created a vacuum. The Constitution of the Russian Federation was adopted in December 1993 while political smoke was clearing from a shoot-out between presidential and parliamentary forces.

Chapter 1 is an exercise in history backwards. It does not try to summarize Russian history. Its aim is to chart the process that created a disorderly regime of politicians, Soviet-style bureaucrats and plutocrats that is the legacy challenging Vladimir Putin. The presentation is succinct in order to highlight what is relevant to Russian government today. While this inevitably leaves out much that was important in the past, it does not ignore what happened before Vladimir Putin assumed office at the beginning of the year 2000.

Contemporary political science assumes that the worldwide transformation of political regimes is about creating a third wave of democracies

(Huntington, 1991). But to describe the Russian state as a new democracy is to prejudge three critical questions: what is a modern state? What is democracy? Can the one exist without the other? Chapter 2 answers these questions. A modern state is above all a *Rechtsstaat*, that is, a state governed by the rule of law. A modern state need not be a democratic state, as the history of Prussia demonstrates. Even today many states are not modern, as is illustrated by regimes from Albania to Zimbabwe. In a democratic state the government of the day is accountable to its citizens through free elections. While a modern state and free elections are often found together, it is a mistake to assume that the one necessarily guarantees the other.

In many Western countries the modernization of the state and the introduction of democratic elections occurred so long ago that the distinctive contribution that each makes to political rule is today forgotten. In countries such as Britain and Sweden, the establishment of the basic institutions of the modern state – the rule of law, civil society and the accountability of government to parliament – came a century before free elections with universal suffrage. Chapter 2 explains why theories based on the history of the first modern and democratic states are inappropriate to describe the problems confronting Russia. Lenin and Stalin rejected the modern state as a bourgeois institution and created instead an anti-modern state. In the absence of anything like a modern state, the Russian Federation was condemned to begin democratization backwards. Since then, elections confirm that in one respect Russia is democratic, but the lawless practices of the state's leaders show that it is not yet a modern state.

In the Soviet era public opinion was whatever party officials allowed to be said in public. The dissociation between the party-state's view of what people ought to think and what people actually thought led to the development of a split political personality, what Soviet novelist Vladimir Dudintsev described as living like two persons in one body (quoted in White, 1979: 111), the public person saying and doing what the state commanded, while the hidden person had different thoughts in the privacy of the home and among a very small circle of trusted friends. After becoming general secretary of the Communist Party in 1985, Mikhail Gorbachev promoted glasnost, open public debate, an innovation inconsistent with totalitarian and post-totalitarian Soviet practices.

Competitive elections now give Russians the chance to express themselves in ways that influence who governs. However, a ballot is a blunt instrument; it does not show whether a vote is cast because of agreement with a candidate or party's policies or because it is seen as the lesser evil. The claims of politicians to know what all Russians think should not be taken at their face value. Yet this sometimes happens. For example, after the 1993 Russian Duma election, Michel Camdessus, managing director of the International Monetary Fund, reported that President Yeltsin's reforms were widely supported in Russia. The evidence the IMF director cited consisted of assurances from the president himself; from selected members of the Duma; and from the patriarch of the Russian Orthodox Church.

Today, if you want to know what Russians think it is not necessary to rely on the words of commissars or of Kremlinologists who treat ordinary Russians as if they were putty in the hands of their leaders. We can rely on familiar social science methods, interviewing a representative nationwide sample of Russians. Ordinary Russians are able and willing to express opinions on all matter of things, especially if one asks questions that they relate to their own experiences. A unique feature of this book is that it draws on a decade of New Russia Barometer (NRB) surveys of the Centre for the Study of Public Policy at the University of Strathclyde. From its inception, the New Russia Barometer has sought to examine government from the 'underall' perspective of the Russian people through representative sample surveys in cities from Murmansk to Vladivostok, and in villages that collectively have more than four times the population of Moscow. Field work has been conducted by VTsIOM, founded by Tatyana Zaslavskaya and Yury Levada when glasnost made it both possible and necessary to take the views of ordinary Russians into account. Chapter 3 reports how Russians evaluated the old Soviet regime; how people coped with the challenges of transformation; and how they evaluated the new regime and undemocratic alternatives prior to Vladimir Putin becoming president.

Founding elections are certain to be different from the tenth or twentieth election held in an established democratic modern state. In the Communist party-state there were no independent institutions of civil society nor was there much organized dissent, as there had been in Poland or Czechoslovakia. When the first elections were held in the Russian Federation, political elites were challenged to supply parties from which voters could choose. An earlier book analysed the first free elections (White, Rose and McAllister, 1997). Chapter 4 examines the problems facing President Yeltsin and his entourage when Yeltsin's period of office approached its end and there was no party on which they could rely to nominate a successor to protect their fruits of office. The emergence of Vladimir Putin from political obscurity was the outcome of an increasingly desperate search for a friendly successor.

Political parties are necessary if voters are to hold their elected representatives accountable. Russian elections offer voters a much greater scope for choice than elections in the Anglo-American world. In December 1999, the proportional representation ballot offered 26 different parties, and in the 225 single-member districts the average voter had a choice of ten candidates. Both ballots explicitly offered electors the opportunity to vote against all candidates. Representatives elected to the Duma under one party label or as independents often join another party as soon as they take the oath of office. The eleven presidential candidates in 2000 were nominated by a variety of parties or none. Like Boris Yeltsin, Vladimir Putin was elected as an independent.

The outcome of an election depends on the choices that political elites supply as well as on how people vote. Each type of ballot offers incentives for political elites to offer voters different sets of choices. The result is that, instead of having a party system, Russia has four systems of parties. This makes it very difficult for voters to know which party or parties, if any, to hold accountable for the way Russia is governed. In addition, the appearance and disappearance of parties from one election to the next has created a floating system of parties. Citizens cannot vote to turn the rascals out when it is unclear which rascals are governing, and when some rascals refuse to face judgment at the ballot box. Chapters 5 and 6 show how Russia's political elites behaved in the competition for seats at the 1999 Duma election. Chapter 7 analyses how voters responded to the choices offered them. Two parties won votes with clear-cut appeals for and against transformation, the Communist Party and the Union of Right Forces. However, the majority of votes were cast for parties with a fuzzy-focus appeal to voters with contrasting political views or none.

Whereas Boris Yeltsin gained power by offering a radical alternative to a Communist regime, Vladimir Putin gained the presidency in much more ambiguous circumstances. Initially, he was the candidate supplied by the Yeltsin Family to protect its interests. However, his election as president owed much to being free of the unpopularity of President Yeltsin, because he was a new arrival on the political scene. The outbreak of the second Chechen War immediately after his appointment as prime minister in August 1999 propelled Putin into the public eye. The resignation of Boris Yeltsin at the end of the year gave a big boost to Putin's campaign for the presidency, since it made him the acting president. As chapter 8 shows, he ran an election campaign in which there was more emphasis on looking presidential than on policies. Observers likened the campaign to a coronation rather than a contest. Putin won the first-round presidential ballot with an absolute majority of the popular vote; the result appeared to be a landslide because his many opponents divided 47 per cent of the vote.

If Russia is to become a complete democracy, it must have order as well as elected officeholders – and that requires a different state from the one that Boris Yeltsin was able to establish. The legacy left to Vladimir Putin was a state that did not adhere to the rule of law. At times it can exercise arbitrary power with a great show of force, as the use of force to

Figure Int.1 COUNTRY OUT OF CONTROL.

Q. Do you think that Russia's leaders control the situation in the country or that the situation is out of control?

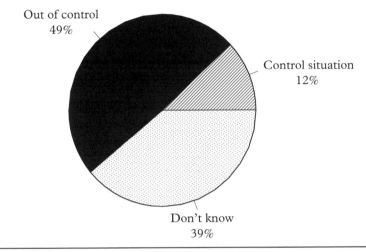

Out of control
49%

Control situation
12%

Don't know
39%

Source: New Russia Barometer VII. Nationwide survey, 6 March–13 April 1998. Number of respondents, 1,904.

suppress dissent in Chechnya shows. But the intermittent use of heavy force is not proof of effectiveness in all its activities. Only one in eight Russians thinks that Russia's leaders have the political situation under control (fig. Int.1). People divide into two large groups: those who think the situation is out of control, and those who do not know whether the government has things under control.

Order is best produced by a state that is both lawful and effective. By experience and temperament, Vladimir Putin is more of a bureaucrat than a personalistic leader in the manner of Boris Yeltsin. He is seeking to institutionalize a pyramid of power leading up to the Kremlin. Yet how much can one person do to change the legacy of generations of rule by a Communist party-state and a decade of Boris Yeltsin's efforts to repudiate it? Chapter 9 shows that Vladimir Putin has been outstandingly success-ful in his first two years in office in maintaining the popularity necessary to win re-election. It also shows he has used his position to strengthen the Kremlin's control of central agencies of government and regain influence on often wayward regional governments and the Duma. Events abroad have been favourable too, for high oil prices in world markets have ben-efited government tax revenues and produced hard currency earnings. Putin's cooperation with the United States following the terrorist attack of 11 September 2001 has improved Russia's standing abroad.

A decade after the foundation of the Russian Federation the probability that next year will be similar to this year is greater than that next year will see a return to the upheavals of the beginning of the 1990s. In his millennium address to the Russian people, Vladimir Putin (2000: 212) endorsed consolidation rather than radical change:

> Russia has reached its limit for political and socio-economic upheavals, cataclysms, and radical reforms. Only fanatics or political forces which are absolutely apathetic and indifferent to Russia and its people can make calls for a new revolution. Be it under communist, national-patriotic or radical-liberal slogans, our country and our people will not withstand a new radical break-up. The nation's patience and its ability to survive as well as its capacity to work constructively have reached the limit.

The prospect of consolidation raises the question: what sort of government is being consolidated? In chapter 10 we report what Russians think about the system of government over which Vladimir Putin now presides. The answers show Russia does not have a modern state, but an untrustworthy and unaccountable regime in which corruption is taken for granted. Free, competitive elections have been institutionalized, but in the absence of a modern state Russia remains a long way from the ideal of a regime that is both orderly and democratic.

Approaches to Russia

The conventional approach to Russia has been through the study of language, literature and history. Studies of Muscovite folkways emphasized continuity between the times of the tsars and the present (e.g. Keenan, 1986). The logic of historical determinism has been given new life by political science studies of democratization and political culture. Robert Dahl (1971: 47) has argued that evolution is the surest route to establishing democracy and that any attempt to move from a regime suppressing competition, as the Soviet Union did, to a democratic system will be 'a slow process, measured in generations'. Robert Putnam (1993: 183ff.) has theorized that the attitudes and behaviour that make democracy work take centuries to develop – and this implies that the obstacles to democratization may take a century or more to overcome.

The collapse of the Communist party-state and of the Soviet Union shows that great changes can occur with great speed. The fact that changes occurred almost simultaneously in many Communist states places into doubt whether the context of Russian history is as distinctive as Russian specialists often assume. Two Latin American scholars have sought to apply to Russia conclusions from their studies, arguing that post-Communist transitions are 'conceptually and theoretically equivalent' to democratization in Latin America (Schmitter and Karl, 1994: 185; Karl and Schmitter, 1995). In response, a scholar of Communist systems, Valerie Bunce (1995a, 1995b), has suggested that such experts stay at home until they are prepared to recognize that the Soviet legacy differs fundamentally from the legacies of undemocratic but non-totalitarian systems in countries such as Brazil and Mexico. Furthermore, Bunce rejects as Western ethnocentrism the assumption that all post-Communist leaders want to consolidate democratic rule – and developments in many successor states of the Soviet Union support her argument (cf. Charles King, 2000).

In the immediate aftermath of the collapse of the command economy, Western economists hurried to Moscow to offer advice that ignored the Russian context. Instead, they relied on theoretical models of a market economy. Lawrence Summers (1991: 2), then chief economist at the World Bank and now president of Harvard University, bluntly proclaimed: '*Respect the universal laws of economics*' (italics in the original). The World Bank and the International Monetary Fund, as well as many Russians, paid dearly for ignoring the fact that the economy in Russia does not operate with the mathematical elegance depicted in economic theories. As a Russian central banker has reflected, 'Life has proved to be richer and more complex than the theoretical notions that all of us were guided by' (quoted in Juliet Johnson, 2001: 253). A distinguished economist who has spent decades in countries that did not have modern market economies, Albert Hirschman (1963: 6), emphasizes the need to understand context in the epigraph to this book: 'a society can move forward *as it is, in spite of what it is, and because of what it is*' (italics in the original). Vladimir Putin (2000: 212) agrees more with Hirschman than with Summers.

The experience of the nineties demonstrates vividly that merely experimenting with abstract models and schemes taken from foreign textbooks cannot assure [*sic*] that our country will achieve genuine renewal without any excessive costs. The mechanical copying of other nations' experience will not guarantee success either.

The creation of the Russian Federation was not an end to history; the legacy of the past continues to constrain what its new rulers can and cannot achieve. Our approach combines a social scientist's concern with concepts relevant to many societies with a respect for Russian particularities. Doing so avoids the mistake of thinking that everything that happens in Russia has causes and consequences different from other countries, while recognizing that Russian responses to transformation have often not conformed to expectations of Western policymakers and social scientists.

Our intention is to show that crucial social science assumptions are not so much wrong as incomplete; they are contingent because they have been formulated in the context of states that are modern and democratic, conditions that are not universal. An understanding of the contingencies of time and place is a necessary condition for developing theories relevant to the worldwide transformation of political and economic systems that is now taking place.

New Russia Barometer questionnaires have been designed to find out how Russians are reacting to a society in transformation. Fundamental differences between Western countries and Russia have produced a very different questionnaire than what is familiar in a Western context, for our starting point has been to design questionnaires from 'the point of view of the actor' (Campbell et al., 1960: 27). NRB questionnaires are based on the belief that people will give the most meaningful and accurate answers to questions that refer to experiences arising in their national context. To ask people to express attitudes about what is remote from their experience is to invite blank responses or the creation of ephemeral 'non-attitudes' (Converse, 1964). Rather than assume that Russia's rulers have been trying to build a democratic political system that supplies what the people want, we ask Russians to say what they think of the regime that actually governs them, how it compares with the past and what they expect of the future. Instead of assuming that Western measures of poverty are just as relevant in Russia as in Scandinavia, we examine how Russians are coping with today's problems by applying skills developed in the non-market Soviet economy.

The NRB questionnaire was developed in collaboration with research institutes across post-Communist Central and Eastern Europe and what was then the Soviet Union. The first post-Communist questionnaire was written for surveys in Bulgaria and Czechoslovakia in spring 1991, and was revised for use in early autumn in Poland and across seven countries of Central and Eastern Europe. The first NRB questionnaire was written late in 1991 in collaboration with a group of Russians led by economists Viachyslav Shironin and Irina Boeva, who had every reason to want to understand what was happening to their own society. Since then, the Centre for the Study of Public Policy has been involved in more than 100 surveys across the post-Communist world (see *www.cspp.strath.ac.uk*). Questions asked in Russia have comparative as well as contextual application, for they are based on concepts relevant across post-Communist societies. Thus, it is possible to identify to what extent Russians have responded similarly or differently to transformation than have peoples from the Czech Republic and Hungary to the Baltic states and Ukraine (cf. Rose, Mishler and Haerpfer, 1998).

Because this book is about ideas, we have been careful to define key words to which many different meanings are given, such as democracy and the modern state. Working across languages and cultures makes us wary of the traps that arise in using the same word – for example, party – to refer to institutions that differ radically between Russia and established democratic states. Where Russian words are familiar in English, such as glasnost and perestroika, we have not italicized them. Where it is important to emphasize that a word refers to a phenomenon that is distinctively Russian, we have italicized the Russian word. For example, what is *normalno* in Russia is not what is normal in Britain or the United States. The transliteration of a 33-character Cyrillic alphabet into the 26 characters of the Roman alphabet is done differently by different academics. For example, the surname of the first president of the Russian Federation is spelled El'tsin by the leading British journal in post-Soviet studies and Yel'tsin by its American counterpart. In this book, we have followed the principle of spelling names in ways that will be familiar to our readers – for example, Yeltsin.

In the past decade the study of Russia has been transformed from being information-poor – with much of what was important written between the lines – to producing an enormous amount of information. The freedom of Russians to say and write what they want for an audience of their choice, domestic or international, has vastly increased the variety of information available, too. The worldwide web moves the latest, albeit often the most perishable, news to every corner of the world as soon as it is published in Moscow. Any summary of events since Mikhail Gorbachev began to change the Soviet Union would require a volume several times the length of this book. Any attempt to summarize the interpretation of these events in the scholarly literature would make the book longer still.

The challenge facing authors is to add to the understanding of what is known. We have sought to do so by drawing on concepts from the social sciences, the careful analysis of original survey data and a selection of publications from a vast scholarly and current affairs literature. Where information is available in multiple sources, including the daily and weekly journalism of Russia, we have not burdened the text with needless citations. The materials cited here are limited to what is immediate to our purposes.

The background of the authors gives this book a much broader frame of reference than is normal among specialists in one region. During a long professional career, Richard Rose has published studies of comparative politics and public policy on five continents. He first saw Soviet troops in Vienna when it was still under four-power military occupation and was familiar with East as well as West Berlin before the Wall came down.

Trips to the Soviet Union in the time of Leonid Brezhnev provided a practical introduction to the significance of a market economy by showing what its absence meant. The importance of order was brought home to him by two decades of research in Northern Ireland and by living in Italy when the Italian state was struggling to maintain order in the face of armed challenges from the extreme left and right. Working at the Wissenschaftszentrum Berlin when the Wall fell led to the development of the Barometer surveys reported here. Neil Munro brings to this book the experience of living on four continents, academic qualifications in Russian and Chinese as well as political science, formidable experience in analysing large computer data bases and familiarity with Russian at home as well as in the office.

We have tried to be honest and sympathetic in dealing with the realities of Russian life; that explains why we are neither extremely optimistic nor pessimistic. The approach owes something to Anton Chekhov, who applied his training in diagnostic medicine to write a timeless play, *The Cherry Orchard*. He did not label his play a tragedy, but a comedy or ode to Russian life. No doubt the orchard of Madame Raneskaya has long since been turned into a collective farm or a factory of the military-industrial complex. Yet Chekhov was concerned with characters of perennial relevance. While the society of which he wrote has been chopped down twice over, Russian life today still has its full cast of Chekhovian characters, not least its Lopakhins. The dedication reflects our appreciation of the old Russian saying, *Rossiyu umom ne ponyat* (You can't understand Russia with your head).

The full results of all ten New Russia Barometer surveys are published in the *Studies in Public Policy* series of the Centre for the Study of Public Policy (Rose, 2002b). All statistics in this book have been freshly calculated and may differ marginally from previous citations because of rounding or recoding. The cut-off date for the inclusion of materials in this book was 15 January 2002; updates of data from VTsIOM surveys can be accessed at *www.RussiaVotes.org*. Chapter 2 draws on an article initially published in the *British Journal of Political Science* (Rose and Shin, 2001). Chapters 5 to 8 on the Duma and presidential elections draw on materials initially published by Richard Rose in *East European Constitutional Review* (2000a), and by Rose, Munro and Stephen White in *Post-Soviet Affairs* (2000) and *Europe-Asia Studies* (2001). In each case, the materials presented here have been substantially revised for the purposes of this book.

We owe a special debt of gratitude to more than 20,000 people in Russia who have patiently answered our questions and to the staff of VTsIOM (the Russian Centre for Public Opinion Research), led by Professor Yury Levada and Alexei Grazhdankin, who have promptly and efficiently conducted the surveys analysed here. Funding for New Russia Barometer surveys VIII, IX and X comes from the British Economic and Social Research Council project 'Consolidating Russian Democracy? The Third-Round Elections' (ROOO238107), for which Richard Rose was the principal investigator. It was supplemented by funds from the ESRC 'One Europe or Several?' programme granted to Stephen White, Margot Light and John Loewenhardt to study relations between post-Soviet and European Union countries and from a Leverhulme Trust project on 'Coping with Organisations: Networks of Russian Social Capital', for which Richard Rose was the principal investigator. Useful comments on chapters of this book circulated in manuscript have come from Archie Brown, Alena Ledeneva, Augusto Lopez-Claros, Thomas Remington, Neil Robinson, Vladimir Shlapentokh and Lucan Way. In copyediting the manuscript, Karen Anderson Howes showed exceptional skills in both Russian and English. The authors are solely responsible for statements of fact and interpretation.

1   A disorderly legacy

The past is the logical starting point for any evaluation of change, but there is no agreement about *which* past is important in Russia today. The legacy of the past contains a plurality of protean traditions, and in total their implications are ambiguous. In the days of the Soviet Union, the Communist Party explicitly repudiated the tsarist past, and films and operas were carefully scrutinized by Joseph Stalin's cultural commissars to ensure that no unflattering parallels were drawn between terrible times under the tsars and Stalin's rule. Western Sovietologists were free to draw parallels emphasizing continuities and many did. Some went so far as to argue that there is an inherent tendency in Russian culture to accept authority and little or no desire for freedom in the Western sense. Stalin's successors have repudiated his legacy and had their own legacy repudiated too.

The treble transformation that created the Russian Federation shows that, even though the legacy of the past constrains choices, it does not determine the flow of events. Mikhail Gorbachev's efforts to reform the Soviet system were not so much a turning point as a breaking point, for a party-state that had enjoyed a monopoly of power for two-thirds of a century collapsed. The end of the power of the Communist Party of the Soviet Union caused the implosion of a non-market economy in which bureaucrats commanded what was produced. The attack on Gorbachev's reforms by Boris Yeltsin led to the destruction of the Soviet Union.

The launch of the newly independent Russian Federation at the end of 1991 was a voyage of discovery for all concerned. But governors inherit before they choose. The Federation started life with a Soviet-era constitution dating from 1978, and Boris Yeltsin was president because he had been elected to that office in the Russian Socialist Federal Soviet Republic when it was part of the Soviet Union. In eight years Yeltsin introduced a new constitution and established precedents for its use and abuse. Boris Yeltsin's achievements are now part of Russia's past, while the Russian Federation carries on. Vladimir Putin brings a fresh approach to the Kremlin, but the regime he now heads is marked by the legacy of his predecessors in the Kremlin. That legacy rules out as impractical or impossible many attractive alternatives, including the wishful hope that Russia should emulate free market America or social democratic Sweden. In the time of Lenin, Bolsheviks found it was impossible to leap straight from Russian backwardness to a socialist utopia. The 1990s showed that the burdens of a disorderly past made it impossible to achieve in a decade a rule-of-law state.

Disorderly rule under many regimes

The history of government in Russia has not followed the same path as in Europe. While nineteenth-century Russian tsars accepted changes in their regime, there was always a tension between Westernizers promoting modernization of the state in emulation of Prussia or France, and Slavophiles who rejected the Western idea of the modern state. Then, as now, Westernizers were in the minority (cf. Neumann, 1996).[1]

In Russia the tsar was not restrained by the legal obligations that created feudal order. The tsar's power was absolute in theory and often arbitrary in its exercise. When the princes of Muscovy threw off Mongol rule and united diverse principalities, they established the tsar as a ruler exercising authority with the backing of the Orthodox Church. Ivan the Terrible, who reigned from 1548 to 1584, further centralized authority by massacring *boyars* and nobles who had previously held the tsar in check. Ivan the Terrible's rule has been described as 'the most extreme example of arbitrary and capricious despotism to be found anywhere. Ivan's Russia shared few of the traits which characterize the modern European state' (Finer, 1997: 1409). Peter the Great (1682–1725) sought to make Russia the military equal of its European neighbours by importing its methods of warfare and industry. But Peter did not promote the rule of law; his idea of a strong state was a state in which he could rule absolutely, unrestrained by law.

The tsar was conceived as 'ruling by himself', enjoying absolute power free of internal checks and balances. Under the Fundamental Laws of the Russian Empire, the tsar's powers were deemed to be given by God himself, endowing the tsar with the combined authority of a caesar and a pope. While Western Europe was creating the modern state, tsarist

---

[1] For this reason, the term Western is used in this book to refer to a large range of countries, including Central European nations that have been interacting with Russia for centuries; the 15 states that are now in the European Union; and Anglo-American countries. Notwithstanding geographical dispersion and many other differences, Western countries all have an experience of markets and democratic rule that the Russian Federation still lacks.

rule involved a bureaucratic apparatus in which 'the law functioned as an administrative device, not as a set of rules to be obeyed by state officials' (Owen, 1997: 25). Government officials readily turned a blind eye to or even promoted violations of the law, such as anti-Semitic riots and the murder of Jews in *pogroms* at the beginning of the twentieth century (cf. Lier and Lambroza, 1992).

The new Soviet order

The 1917 Russian Revolution led to the creation of the world's first explicitly Communist regime. The Soviet Union was a party-state, in which the Communist Party of the Soviet Union (CPSU) claimed the power and the right to impose control from the top without the constraints of bourgeois legality. It rejected the idea of the rule of law in favour of an end-justifies-the-means doctrine of socialist legality. In the Soviet era, the rule of law 'was derided; Soviet legal dictionaries described it as an unscientific notion used by the bourgeoisie to mask its own imperialist essence and to inculcate harmful illusions in the masses' (Rudden, 1994: 369).

From 1922 to 1953 Stalin used his position as general secretary of the Communist Party of the Soviet Union to pursue the totalitarian goal of remaking society in every sphere, from the economy and agriculture to art and child rearing. While pure Communism, like ideal democracy, remained unattainable, massive efforts were invested in attempting to drive people toward that goal without regard for bourgeois constraints. The Communist Party was the organizational weapon for building a new society. Its ideological exhortations were reinforced by physical coercion from the state security services. The party threatened with internal exile, imprisonment in the gulag or summary execution those whose words, actions or social position made them appear to be potential enemies of the state.

In the 1930s Stalin's policy of forced collectivization of agriculture led to the killing of millions of kulaks, peasant proprietors who farmed independently of the state. The shortage of food resulting from Stalin's collectivization policy led to the death of millions more from famine. Stalin also purged the party of people whom he suspected of being inadequately loyal to him or of favouring Leon Trotsky, his great enemy. Before execution, many old Bolsheviks were psychologically intimidated and forced to make demeaning confessions. Their show trials were public events, but ignored by Westerners sympathetic to the new Soviet system. The founders of the British Fabian Society, Beatrice and Sidney Webb (1937), saw Stalin's Soviet Union as a new civilization and praised what they thought they saw. Before the Second World War began, millions of

Russians had been killed in pursuit of the new regime's goal; the only uncertainty is how many millions died (cf. Conquest, 1990). From the time of the Nazi–Soviet pact in August 1939 to the entry of Soviet troops into Berlin early in 1945, tens of millions more died, as Nazi and Soviet troops advanced back and forth across the bloody terrain from the Volga to the Elbe.

The defining attributes of the Soviet regime included the dominance of both state and societal institutions by the Communist Party; the centralization of power within the party and suppression of dissent through 'democratic' centralism; a command economy in which bureaucratic plans rather than market signals were meant to determine the production and allocation of resources; frequent invocation of Marxist-Leninist ideology to justify what the party did; and leadership of an international Communist movement backed up by the power and resources of the Soviet state as well as by appeals to ideological goals relevant across national boundaries (Brown, 1996: 310ff.).

The Communist party-state was not distinctive because it was undemocratic, for most systems of government for most of the history of the world have been that. It was distinctive because of the totalitarian scope of its claims to authority over individuals, which accepted no limits (see e.g. Koestler, 1940; Jowitt, 1992: 1ff.). Unlike most forms of undemocratic rule, a totalitarian regime is not indifferent to what citizens do and say at home or when with friends; it refuses to recognize a distinction between public and private life. The regime seeks to mobilize subjects to follow its lead in all aspects of social life. In pursuit of this goal, the party-state purged institutions of civil society and replaced them with party-controlled universities, trade unions, newspapers and broadcasting media. Actions inconsistent with totalitarian goals were treated as threats to or crimes against the state (Linz, 2000).

The Communist Party sought to inculcate its ideological slogans in all young people so that they could repeat them in public, whatever reservations people had in private. At work, there was a constant pressure to produce reports that showed fulfilment of production targets laid down by bureaucratic planners who had limited knowledge of what was actually happening. Even though there was no opposition party, elections were held to legitimate the one-party regime. There was no danger of the Communist Party losing, for local party officials were under pressure to produce unanimity. Between 1946 and 1984 the reported number of votes (as distinct from the number of people voting) was as high as 99.99 per cent of the nominal electorate; the percentage of votes counted in favour of candidates endorsed by the CPSU was as much as 99.95 per cent of the total, and never fell below 99.16 per cent of all votes counted.

When Nikita Khrushchev denounced Stalin's misdeeds in a speech to a closed party Congress in 1956, this heralded a post-totalitarian phase of Soviet rule in which rulers were more open to the discussion of differing points of view about the pursuit of party goals, as long what was said did not challenge the leading role of the party in the state. Totalitarian purges for the most part had destroyed any inclination among citizens to give organized expression to dissent, so the party-state no longer felt the need for the systematic use of terror. However, the post-totalitarian Soviet Union remained a one-party state. The choice of the general secretary of the CPSU by the party's Central Committee was effectively the choice of the head of government. In 1964 a full meeting of the Central Committee of the CPSU voted Nikita Khrushchev out of his post as party secretary, and thus out of power. His successor as party secretary, Leonid Brezhnev, adopted a far more cautious approach to political change.

By contrast to Khrushchev, Brezhnev showed a preference for collective decisionmaking within the one-party state. The Soviet elite welcomed the shift, for it made them more secure in the control of their particular part of the bureaucracy. It also made the regime as a whole more resistant to change. The institutions of the party-state gave the Soviet elite great influence on society, but the lack of accountability to institutions of civil society made the party-state ignore social changes and the need to adapt. A regime that had set out to transform Russian society had turned into a regime governing by 'institutionalized stagnation' (Roeder, 1993: ch. 6). The economy was even worse off, for the inefficiency and waste due to the allocation of resources by bureaucratic commands gradually led to economic stagnation instead of growth (cf. Winiecki, 1988; Kornai, 1992).

Changes in the post-Stalin period era were sometimes described as modernization, because of visible economic and social progress by comparison with the past. Increasing numbers of young people now received secondary education, industry was expanding and Soviet space achievements gave proof of scientific advance. But socio-economic modernization was not matched by political change. Brezhnev made this clear through a policy offering workers material improvements in their living standards without political rights. It was often assumed, consistent with Western theories about citizens voting with their pocketbook and with Bismarck's ideal of 'social welfare as authoritarian defence', that improvements in living standards would produce support for the Communist party-state, or at least maintain political quiescence. The policy was aptly described as 'welfare state authoritarianism' (Breslauer, 1978; cf. Flora and Alber, 1981). The longer Brezhnev remained in office, the more evident it became that the Soviet economy could not produce a rapid increase in living standards. Nor could it meet such basic human desires as longer life expectancy (see ch. 3).

There were doubts within the political elite about whether post-totalitarian policies had gone far enough in adapting the party-state to changing circumstances, both domestic and international. However, as long as these doubts were not publicly debated, the regime was secure. As a leading Russian political scientist later explained, 'Gorbachev, me, all of us were double-thinkers, we had to balance truth and propaganda in our minds all the time. It is not something I'm particularly proud of, but that was the way we lived' (Georgy Shakhnazarov, quoted in Montgomery, 2001).

The masses of the population took double-think for granted too. People lived in an hourglass society in which elites and the masses kept themselves to themselves as best they could, and the party's public expression of mass opinion was at variance with what people said to their most trusted friends (Shlapentokh, 1989; Rose, 1995b). The post-totalitarian party-state did not expect to prevent all expression of dissatisfaction; its goal was to atomize opposition, confining it to the expression of dissatisfaction within informal groups of a handful of individuals. A Soviet sociologist explained his objection to referring to the Soviet Union as an industrial society: 'this was not because there was no industry there – of course there was – but because there was no society' (quoted in Goble, 1995: 25). When individuals were forced to deal with officialdom, they sought to exploit it. Yury Levada (2001: 312f.) described as 'Soviet peculiarities' the cultivation of a cunning mentality, in which an individual 'adapts to social reality, seeking out loopholes in its normative system, or ways of turning the current rules of the game to his own advantage, whilst at the same time – no less importantly – constantly trying to find a way to get around those rules'.

The Soviet party-state encouraged a morality in which it was normal for people to say things they did not believe, and do things that they felt were wrong – and to teach their children to dissemble too (cf. Clark and Wildavsky, 1990). In one of its first surveys in 1989, VTsIOM asked Soviet citizens whether they ever had to act unjustly or improperly. Three-fifths said that this was the case, and a fifth gave an evasive answer. The most frequently cited reasons for acting against one's principles were that 'it was necessary' or 'pressures at work' from the collective or from management (tab. 1.1). The persistence of this legacy was shown when VTsIOM repeated the question a decade later. In the Russian Federation, as before, ordinary people continue to feel that necessity, or the need to look after family and friends, sometimes made them act unjustly or improperly.

Table 1.1 *Wrongful behaviour as a part of life*

Q. Did you ever have to act in a way you thought improper or unjust?

	1989 %	1999 %
When it was necessary	24	32
Pressures at work	22	19
Own weakness	13	15
For family and friends	9	25
Difficult to say	21	20
No	17	12

Source: VTsIOM Bulletin 1/2000, 23.

The Soviet system was part of the socialization of today's leaders of Russia. Boris Yeltsin grew up at the time of 'everyday Stalinism' (Fitzpatrick, 1999). Both his father and uncle served months in a prison camp for the 'crime' of being kulaks. Vladimir Putin was born the year before Stalin died, and was socialized politically in the days of Leonid Brezhnev. In explaining his youthful ambition to join the KGB, Putin (2000: 41) said, 'I didn't think about the Stalin-era purges. I was a pure and utterly successful product of Soviet patriotic education.'

The collapse of the party-state

The death of Brezhnev in 1982 triggered a turnover of generations in the political elite. The Central Committee's chosen successor, Yury Andropov, died after only 15 months as leader, and his successor, Konstantin Chernenko, lived only 13 months in post. The much younger Mikhail Gorbachev was promoted to the post of general secretary of the CPSU in March 1985. The intention of Gorbachev was to reform the Soviet state rather than end it, for he was a career party bureaucrat accustomed to working within the party. In a 1987 speech on the seventieth anniversary of the Russian Revolution, Gorbachev claimed to be applying 'the historical experience of Bolshevism and the contemporaneity of socialism' (quoted in Jay, 2001: 151). His idea of what that experience implied was radically different from that of his predecessors. Gorbachev believed that the party-state needed big changes, and he set about introducing reforms. But his efforts opened up divisions within the party-state that he met by escalating pressures for change, while Communist conservatives, radical critics and opportunists of many stripes simultaneously opposed and undermined his efforts (see Gorbachev and Mlynar, 2002).

Perestroika (reform and restructuring) was intended to stimulate a stagnating economy. Gorbachev's visits to Western European countries opened his eyes to the achievements of market economies. However, he proceeded without a clear idea of how the Soviet Union could forge a third way between a bureaucratic command economy and a market economy. Moreover, the Soviet economy faced the challenge of marshalling military and industrial resources to compete with the American rearmament programme of President Ronald Reagan. Shortly after taking office Gorbachev launched a programme of accelerating Soviet military strength in order to 'maintain parity with NATO by all means necessary because it holds down the aggressive appetites of imperialists' (quoted in Shlapentokh, 2000). But Gorbachev also began discussions with Reagan about ways to avoid a rearmament race that the Soviet Union's leadership worried that it would lose. President Reagan was ready to negotiate from strength.

Gorbachev introduced glasnost (openness) as a means of encouraging public debate about the means of reform. However, his efforts to restructure the party-state made him many enemies among those whose jobs, habits and beliefs were threatened by changes in the institutions that were the source of their power and privileges. When the debate licensed by glasnost began questioning the Communist Party's monopoly of power, many party officials wanted to respond by crushing criticism, while Gorbachev moved in the opposite direction. He proposed a halfway house to free elections, a system in which a multiplicity of candidates who accepted fundamentals of the Soviet state could compete. A multi-candidate election for the Soviet Congress of People's Deputies in March 1989 led to the defeat of some traditional Communists and produced victories for opponents of Gorbachev, including advocates of independence in the Baltic states. In February 1990, Gorbachev proposed and the Central Committee approved an amendment to Article 6 of the constitution abolishing the monopoly of power of the Communist Party of the Soviet Union. Although Gorbachev introduced the post of Soviet president, he did not want to face popular election. Instead, he became president by vote of the Congress. This deprived Gorbachev of popular endorsement for a programme that was increasingly under attack within the Communist Party. Although unopposed, Gorbachev received the vote of only 59 per cent of Congress delegates (Brown, 1996: 202ff.).

In Communist-controlled states of Central and Eastern Europe, openness and restructuring undermined the Soviet power bloc, allowing political elites and protest groups to demand national independence and the withdrawal of Soviet troops. There were past precedents for demonstrations against Soviet imperialism: they had occurred in East Berlin,

Poznan and Gdansk, Budapest, and Prague. What was new was the unwillingness of Gorbachev to jeopardize his domestic reforms and negotiations with the West by using a show of force or gunfire to suppress dissent and demonstrations. The fall of the Berlin Wall in November 1989 effectively marked the end of Soviet control of its satellite states. In 1990 free, competitive elections ended the rule of Communist parties backed by Moscow throughout most of the former Communist bloc.

In republics of the Soviet Union distant from Moscow, the meaning of perestroika was stretched to breaking point. In Estonia, Latvia and Lithuania, all forcibly incorporated into the Soviet Union during the Second World War, openness gave national movements the opportunity to demand the right to secede and regain national independence. In other republics of the Soviet Union, officials who had previously carried out directives from the centre now faced conflicting cues. Opportunistic apparatchiks turned their attention to looking after their future in circumstances in which the CPSU was no longer a credible authority. As Steven Solnick has emphasized (1998: 7), 'Soviet institutions did not simply atrophy or dissolve but were actively pulled apart by officials at all levels seeking to extract assets . . . These officials were not merely stealing resources *from* the state, they were stealing the state itself.' What Mikhail Gorbachev had intended as the restructuring of the Soviet state ended with its break-up.

The disorderly creation of the Russian Federation

Whereas the Communist Party under Brezhnev had become gerontocratic or even sclerotic, Boris Yeltsin was different. He started his political career as a party official, and his energy and ambition caught the eye of party superiors. Mikhail Gorbachev promoted Yeltsin from his native Sverdlovsk to Moscow, and gave him a series of appointments in the party apparatus. Nonetheless, Yeltsin attacked Gorbachev's reforms at a Central Committee plenum in October 1987; he claimed they did not move fast enough and far enough to meet the needs of ordinary people. Gorbachev denounced the speech and Yeltsin became a political outcast. In February 1988 Yeltsin was deprived of his status as a candidate member of the Politburo. In spite of party efforts to end Yeltsin's political career, he used the introduction of multi-candidate elections to demonstrate his popular support. In the March 1989 election for the Congress of People's Deputies of the USSR, Yeltsin won 89 per cent of the vote against a candidate backed by party officials. In retrospect, Gorbachev regretted not having sent Boris Yeltsin to serve as the Soviet ambassador to 'some banana republic' (polit.ru, 2001; Jack, 2001a).

Once pushed outside the party-state apparatus, Boris Yeltsin became a charismatic politician in the literal sense, using personal qualities to carry out an aggressive campaign that led to the destruction of the Soviet Union. As he said in a memoir, 'Sometimes it takes a sharp break or rupture to make a person move forward or even survive at all' (Yeltsin, 1994: 149). Yeltsin was not a theorist of economic reform or of liberal democracy, nor was he seeking to create new state institutions; he was first of all an enemy of Gorbachev's party-state, and he attacked it with whatever institutions and opportunities came to hand. In the words of a Kremlin advisor on public relations, Gleb Pavlosky, President Yeltsin 'did not build a state; for ten years he led a revolution' (quoted in Rutland, 2000: 342).

The populist content of Yeltsin's criticisms won him a following. The formal federalism of the Soviet Union enabled Yeltsin to turn the previously subordinate Russian Socialist Federal Soviet Republic (RSFSR) into an insubordinate institution. In March 1990 Yeltsin won more than 80 per cent of the constituency vote in an election to the Russian Congress of Deputies. In May 1990 Yeltsin was elected chair of the Russian Supreme Soviet and used this office as a platform to speak for 150 million Russians. Yeltsin proclaimed that Russian laws had precedence over Soviet laws. Although Yeltsin's position as the chair of the Congress legitimated his claim to represent the Russian people, it did not give him executive authority. While the Communist Party could not produce unanimous votes in the Russian Congress, it was the only disciplined party there and Yeltsin had neither the organizational base nor the inclination to build a coalition of support. To enhance his personal authority, Yeltsin pushed for the creation of a post of directly elected president of the Russian Republic. This proposal was carried by an overwhelming popular vote at a referendum in March 1991. In June, Yeltsin won the presidency with almost three-fifths of the popular vote in a six-candidate race.

Push came to shove in August 1991, when leading hardline Communists placed Gorbachev under house arrest in the Crimea and the Soviet vice president assumed power on the grounds of Gorbachev's temporary incapacity. Gorbachev refused to resign from office but remained out of sight. Boris Yeltsin very publicly denounced the measures as an illegal *coup d'état*. He made an emotional televised appeal in front of the White House, then the home of the Russian Republic's parliament. The coup of the hardliners failed spectacularly, and encouraged party and state officials from the Baltic to the Central Asian republics to hasten the dissolution of the Soviet Union. On 8 December 1991 Yeltsin joined with the leaders of Belarus and Ukraine to proclaim the dissolution of the USSR. Two weeks later Gorbachev met Yeltsin to agree that the

Soviet Union would cease to exist at the end of December. By comparison with the creation of the Soviet Union by Lenin and Stalin, the creation of the new Russian Federation was virtually bloodless.

The abrupt break-up of the Soviet Union occurred without plan. Unlike the situation in ex-Communist states of Central and Eastern Europe, there was no prior constitution or usable past that Russia's new leaders could invoke as the basis for their new regime. Nor did the transition occur as the result of a round-table bargaining process as in Hungary and Poland. The simultaneous disruption of polity, economy and state was without precedent. As the only world he had known was collapsing, Mikhail Gorbachev said, 'We are making such a large turn that it is beyond anyone's dreams. No other people has experienced what has happened to us' (quoted in Rose, 1992a: 371).

The morning after

When the Soviet Union dissolved, the former Russian Republic became a sovereign state, the Russian Federation.[2] The changeover was symbolized by raising the tri-colour Russian flag over the Kremlin in place of the Soviet red flag. The Federation government operated under the RSFSR constitution that was adopted in 1978 and was subsequently amended more than three hundred times. Boris Yeltsin was the first president of the new Federation because he had been elected president of a Soviet republic. The Federation became the heir to the Soviet Army, and Yeltsin issued a decree naming himself commander-in-chief. Boris Yeltsin's immediate priority was to ensure the Federation's recognition internationally and in the near abroad, the other successor states of the former Soviet Union. International institutions such as the United Nations and the International Monetary Fund were prompt in accepting the Federation as a member. Post-Soviet successor states[3] joined together in the Commonwealth of Independent States.

Ordinary Russians were ready to leave behind the ideological symbols of the Soviet era. In the first month of the Russian Federation the first New Russia Barometer asked what people felt about familiar

---

[2] In Soviet times, every citizen had a nationality entered on his or her internal passport. At the creation of the Russian Federation, people with any nationality recognized by the former Soviet Union and resident in Russia were automatically granted citizenship there. Since four-fifths of the population of the Russian Federation is Russian by both nationality and citizenship and no other nationality constitutes a large ethnic bloc, in this book the term Russian is used to refer to all citizens of the Federation.

[3] Here and subsequently, Estonia, Latvia and Lithuania are excluded from the category of post-Soviet successor states, since they were independent countries prior to occupation following the Nazi–Soviet Pact of 22 August 1939 and incorporation in the Soviet Union as a consequence of the Second World War.

Table 1.2 *Feelings about basic Russian values, 1992*

Q. We often hear the following words. What feelings do they evoke?

	Positive %	Neutral %	Negative %
Freedom	78	17	4
One and indivisible Russia	75	20	5
Christianity	73	24	3
Glasnost	63	21	16
Capitalism	25	46	28
Socialism	24	42	33
Perestroika	21	33	45
Marxism-Leninism	16	46	37

Source: New Russia Barometer I. Nationwide survey, 26 January–25 February 1992. Number of respondents, 2,106.

Soviet symbols. Less than a quarter expressed a positive feeling toward Marxism-Leninism or socialism. A plurality were neutral about both these Soviet symbols, and also about their arch-enemy, capitalism (tab. 1.2). Perestroika, a reality not a symbol, had just as few friends and produced even more negative feelings.

Four symbols evoked a positive response from the majority of Russians. Freedom was the most positive symbol of all, evoking a positive response from 78 per cent of Russians. Although only 21 per cent favoured perestroika, 63 per cent endorsed the openness introduced by glasnost. Big majorities were also positive about the traditional patriotic idea of 'one and indivisible Russia' and about Christianity. A factor analysis showed that Russians tended to divide along two dimensions, and to divide unequally. A total of 75 per cent tended to feel positive about freedom and glasnost, as against 8 per cent negative and 17 per cent neutral. The second dimension, involving socialism and Marxism-Leninism, showed 25 per cent positive, 36 per cent neutral and 40 per cent negative.

While Russians did have political and economic values, there were no institutions to represent their beliefs. Boris Yeltsin was prepared to accept and exploit this situation. Yeltsin deployed *vlast*, a Russian term connoting raw power rather than constitutional authority. Michael McFaul (2001: 17) describes this type of power as the 'capacity to prevail over opponents in an anarchic context, that is, a setting in which rules do not constrain behaviour'. This was the situation that Yeltsin faced when he rose to power, for his dispute with Mikhail Gorbachev was not a disagreement about how to apply laws, but a power struggle about whose laws would apply.

Personal charisma can be an asset in winning elections, but is insufficient to establish a modern state. Building institutions requires the skills of a bureaucratic politician, and these skills Yeltsin conspicuously lacked. At the rhetorical level, he endorsed Western models of democracy and markets, thereby winning praise and money from Western leaders and distancing himself from political enemies who favoured retaining Communist institutions. But Yeltsin preferred to assert personal authority rather than attempt the patient and difficult task of creating modern institutions of governance amidst the wreckage of the Soviet Union. He did not rely on party loyalists or on bureaucrats; instead he relied on the antithesis of a modern state, a coterie of personal advisors to carry out his orders and protect his political interests. In exercising personalistic rule, Yeltsin could be generous and he could be capricious – and he could not be held accountable to political institutions limiting his discretion. George Breslauer (2001: 39) explains why Yeltsin preferred to behave this way: 'Personalism is a form of rule in which the leader is not held accountable – formally, regularly and frequently – to institutions that can substantially constrain his discretion.' However, personal authority is effective only if impersonal organizations and impersonal market forces bow to personal commands rather than subverting, rejecting or ignoring them.

The immediate institutional problem was the absence of a constitution designed for the new state. Even worse for the president, the constitution inherited from Soviet days declared the Congress of People's Deputies the supreme authority. The Congress had been elected in March 1990, when there was competition between candidates but the Communist Party was the only organized political party. Yeltsin could not appeal to fellow party members in the Congress, and many of its members were inclined to oppose the reform programmes of both Gorbachev and Yeltsin.

The ambiguous relationship between the president and Congress was 'a matter of political struggle rather than constitutional law' (Sakwa, 1996: 118). The Congress granted President Yeltsin extraordinary powers to issue decrees, but only on a temporary basis. It retained significant powers that could be used to block changes, and the will to use its blocking powers. Traditional Communists disliked everything Yeltsin stood for. There were criticisms of economic policies on technocratic and on social democratic grounds. There were disappointed democrats who thought that Yeltsin was riding roughshod over their rights as elected representatives, and there were politicians disappointed by not receiving patronage from the new president. When Yeltsin named economist Yegor Gaidar as his choice for prime minister in June 1992, the Congress refused to confirm the appointment. In December 1992, Yeltsin secured the

Congress's approval of a compromise candidate for the prime minister-ship, Viktor Chernomyrdin.

While both Yeltsin and leaders of the Congress of Deputies agreed about the need to create a new constitution, there was a basic conflict about the division of powers between them. Under the law, the Congress was due to remain in office until March 1995. It enacted a constitutional amendment stipulating that any attempt by the president to dissolve the Congress would also deprive him of his authority. Yeltsin counterattacked by decreeing a plebiscite on 25 April 1993. Constitutionally, the vote was not a referendum nor were the questions measures that could be placed on the statute book. The vote was a massive opinion poll soliciting back-ing for the president. In response to the question *Do you have confidence in the president?*, 59 per cent voted yes, 39 per cent voted no and 2 per cent spoiled their ballots. In response to a question asking for support for the unspecified economic and social policies of the Yeltsin government,[4] 53 per cent voted yes, 45 per cent voted no and 2 per cent spoiled their ballots. A question about holding an early election for deputies showed two-thirds in favour, while a question about early elections for the presi-dency showed 49 per cent in favour, 47 per cent against and the median voters spoiling their ballots (see White, Rose and McAllister, 1997: 82). The Congress of Deputies ignored the results, which had no legal validity, and intensified its opposition to Yeltsin's government.

The conflict came to a head when President Yeltsin dissolved the Congress of Deputies on 21 September 1993, and called a December election for a new parliament. The action violated constitutional clauses and the Constitutional Court ruled that Yeltsin's actions were grounds for impeachment. The Congress met in emergency session and voted to depose Yeltsin as president. It named as acting president Alexander Rutskoi, recently dismissed by Yeltsin as vice president. Rutskoi called for a new election of both parliament and president. In response, Yeltsin ordered deputies to vacate the White House. Instead, deputies barri-caded themselves inside the building and arms were issued to supporters of Rutskoi. On 3 October pro-parliament demonstrators sought to seize the state television centre and were repulsed by armed police from the Interior Ministry.

After weeks of effort, President Yeltsin finally succeeded in getting the military to move against the deputies. Tanks were placed around the

---

[4] Here and elsewhere the term government without an adjective is used to refer to the insti-tutions and activities of state that continue when the presidency changes hands, while the terms 'Yeltsin government' or 'Putin government' refer to measures and actions associated with the president of the moment.

White House at dawn on 4 October. The outcome was so uncertain that, as Yeltsin later recalled, 'The people in the Kremlin – me among them – feared ending up in the role of the August coup plotters' (quoted in Colton and Hough, 1998: 7). Gunfire broke out, government forces stormed the building and Rutskoi surrendered. Official statistics reported that more than 145 people had been killed in the bloodiest street-fighting in Moscow since 1917. By demonstrating his superior force, Boris Yeltsin lived up to the Russian notion that power is not given by the law but taken.

Having literally shot down the last defenders of the Soviet-era constitution, Boris Yeltsin moved quickly to promote a strongly presidentialist constitution. The new document gave the president unambiguous power to issue decrees, to declare martial law or a state of emergency; and to call elections and referendums. A new bicameral parliament was proposed, with the Duma representing the national electorate, and an upper chamber, the Federal Council, representing the regions. The Duma's approval was required for the confirmation of a prime minister, but if this was withheld three times then the Duma could be dissolved by the president and face a new election. The Duma could vote no confidence in the prime minister, but the president could ignore the vote. If the no-confidence vote was repeated within three months, the president could either dismiss the prime minister's government or dissolve the Duma. Formally, the constitution gave the Duma impeachment powers, but only through a tortuous process. Although the new constitution established a separately elected legislature and executive, it was not a system of checks and balances like the American Constitution. Instead, it resembled a Latin American document, for it protected the president from interference by the Duma and made the Duma subject to his influence through the threat of unilateral dissolution.

In the December 1993 constitutional vote, the reported turnout of voters was 53 per cent, barely enough to satisfy the legal requirement that half the electorate take part. The 56.6 per cent reported in favour of the new constitution was sufficient for adoption. However, political opponents challenged the validity of doing so on three grounds. The vote had not been called in accordance with the existing law on referendums; the turnout figures and vote in favour of the constitution were said to be produced by fraud; and the failure of the Central Electoral Commission to publish full details of the count were assumed to justify suspicions of fraud (see White, Rose and McAllister, 1997: 99ff.). When Russians were asked what they thought the new constitution would accomplish, the median group, 36 per cent, were pessimistic supporters;

Figure 1.1 PESSIMISTS GAVE 1993 CONSTITUTION ITS MAJORITY.

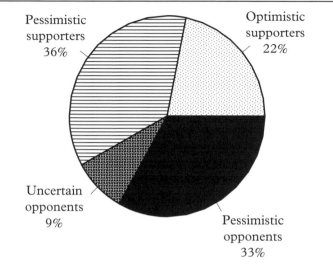

Pessimistic supporters 36%

Optimistic supporters 22%

Uncertain opponents 9%

Pessimistic opponents 33%

(Fourfold classification based on how people voted in the December 1993 referendum on a new constitution and whether they thought it would ensure a lawful and democratic state.)

Source: New Russia Barometer III. Nationwide survey, 15 March–9 April 1994. Number of respondents, 3,535.

they had voted for the constitution but did not expect it to make Russia a rule-of-law state (fig. 1.1). The second largest group were pessimistic opponents who had voted against because they thought the constitution would not guarantee the rule of law. Only 22 per cent believed that the new constitution would become the foundation for the rule of law.

The Duma election held at the same time as the vote on the constitution was the first time that Russians could choose between competing parties. While President Yeltsin did not organize a party to contest the election, Russia's Choice was created in October 1993 to support the Kremlin's programme. It was led by Yegor Gaidar, then first deputy prime minister and very prominent as a proponent of pro-market reforms. The election result was a big setback for the reformers, and also for President Yeltsin. The biggest share of the proportional representative list vote, 21.4 per cent, went to the Liberal Democratic Party headed by a demagogic nationalist, Vladimir Zhirinovsky. The party fully committed to the government's reform programme, Russia's Choice, won only 14.5 per cent of the vote, only a few percentage points more than the Communist list. While the constitution gave the president substantial powers independent of the Duma, the electorate gave the president a Duma in which his opponents were in the majority.

An economy with too much money and not enough order

The command economy of the Soviet era was based on bureaucratic rather than market power. The first hundred pages of Janos Kornai's (1992) classic account of a socialist economy are about the organization of power. The power of the economy's commanders was such that factory managers were compelled to give the appearance of meeting plan targets. To do this required hoarding labour; the waste of cost-free energy resources; 'fixers' with connections to obtain supplies; bursts of intense effort known as storming; and, if all else failed, bribery and fraud. Because the Soviet Union was rich in raw materials commanding a high price in world markets, such as oil, gas, diamonds and gold, it could secure hard currencies through exports. Within this opaque economic system, party and ministry officials could divert substantial resources for their own benefit, and in parts of the Soviet Union criminal gangs controlled some economic services.

In the Soviet era, there was little concern with conventional Western concepts of property and ownership, for the party-state could effectively command what it wanted. But as the economy began to stagnate under Leonid Brezhnev there were not enough resources to fund welfare benefits for citizens and maintain investment. In consequence, the state turned to a variety of forms of borrowing money. The timing and extent of borrowing was influenced by political calculations of both Soviet and Western governments. Western support of changes initiated by Mikhail Gorbachev was shown by loans totalling $92 billion in the last four years of the Soviet Union (Tikhomirov, 2001: 263).

As the power of the party-state waned, officials increasingly exploited public office for private gain. In the last phase of Gorbachev's rule, new types of *biznesmen* emerged, using skills cultivated in the Soviet economy to make real money – and bank it in real foreign banks. When the first New Russia Barometer asked at the beginning of 1992 about the image of people making money, their character had been clearly established (fig. 1.2). Russians making money were viewed not only as helping the economy grow and creating jobs, as in standard market textbooks, but also as using foreign connections and dishonest, as in standard accounts of behaviour in Soviet times.

Figure 1.2 POPULAR IMAGE OF RUSSIA'S NEW RICH.

Q. With economic reform, some people have been able to make more money. Which of these words do you think applies to people who are now making a lot of money?

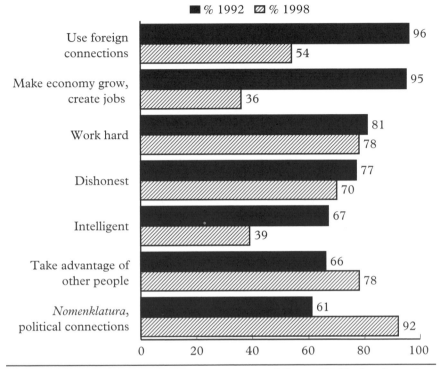

Source: New Russia Barometer I. Nationwide survey, 26 January–25 February 1992. Number of respondents, 2,106. New Russia Barometer VII. Nationwide survey, 6 March–13 April 1998. Number of respondents, 1,904.

Trials and errors

The collapse of the commanding power of the party-state pushed the non-market economy into free fall. Just as early Bolsheviks had proclaimed the abolition of capitalism without a practical plan for running a non-market economy, so the Federation's new government was confronted with the urgent and unprecedented task of creating a market in the wreckage of an economy that fed and housed 150 million people. The uncertainties of economic transformation intensified shortages that had long plagued the command economy. Within the government there was no agreement about what to do. At one extreme were market Bolsheviks arguing that extreme circumstances required a great leap of faith, abolishing controlled prices and privatizing state-owned assets quickly in hopes of creating a market economy. At the other extreme were ministries and state-owned enterprises experienced in running a command economy and averse to giving up familiar practices in unfamiliar times. Social democrats as well as state enterprise interests warned that a rapid move to the market would bring about massive unemployment and that the mass unrest that was forecast to follow would threaten disorder or a Communist-led counter-revolution. Boris Yeltsin stood above the debate, telling an interviewer, 'I do not claim to be able to discuss the philosophy behind economic reform' (quoted in Breslauer, 2001: 35).

A pro-market economist, Yegor Gaidar, was placed in charge of creating a market economy. A policy of shock therapy, that is, moving rapidly to the market whatever the cost, was deemed necessary to fill the economic void. However, the Gaidar team did not have the power to administer a thorough shock, for it was subject to multiple political constraints from stakeholders who could see the costs but not the benefits of radical measures. In the event, the policies administered were those that could overcome political obstacles rather than the policies prescribed by Western textbooks which treated politics as irrelevant (cf. Shleifer and Treisman, 2000). In 1992 official statistics reported that prices rose by more than 2500 per cent and the official economy contracted by 14 per cent. The base for such trend calculations was a notional estimate of what the previous year's economy would have been had it been a market economy. Nonetheless, the direction of change was correctly signalled, and the magnitude was undoubtedly great. The costs of transformation ended Gaidar's brief tenure in the prime ministership; he entitled his subsequent memoir *Days of Defeat and Victory* (1999). The new prime minister, Viktor Chernomyrdin, came from the gas industry of the old command economy. This background gave him a network of allies with whom he could work in dealing with the exigencies of economic transformation.

Deficiencies of official statistics tended to exaggerate the costs of transformation. Some entries that appeared as costs could even be regarded as benefits, for example, the drop in arms exports of $17 billion between 1988 and 1992 and the 60 per cent reduction in the production of defence materials between 1991 and 1993 (Lopez-Claros and Zadornov, 2002: 106). The fall in demand for Russian-produced goods due to competition with Western-made goods was a textbook example of a market signalling to Russian producers that they should make what customers wanted and not what bureaucrats commanded.

Demonetization insulated Russian households and enterprises from inflation to a significant extent, for households could grow food for themselves and rents were reduced to almost nothing. Enterprises with little hope of surviving in a market economy because they were subtracting rather than adding value to the national economy turned to tactics reminiscent of Gogol's novel *Dead Souls* (Gaddy and Ickes, 1999; Seabright, 2000). They created a virtual economy in which suppliers were paid with promissory notes, and promissory notes given them by customers were treated as real receipts. Barter, a common practice in the command economy, was also used in place of cash transactions. Workers could be paid in kind or not paid at all, and this was accepted when the alternative was to be declared unemployed. If these tactics failed, regional banks could be prevailed upon to extend credit rather than risk a city's largest employer pushing thousands into the category of officially unemployed, and connections in Moscow were also invoked to maintain enterprises.

The conspicuous consumption of rich new Russians in Moscow and, to a lesser but equally conspicuous extent, in other cities showed it was possible to make big money in a time of economic turbulence. As the joke had it, Moscow became like New York: 'In New York, you can buy anything with dollars and nothing with rubles; here it is the same.' Government favours were chief among the services that were bought and sold.

The new regime sought to end state control of the economy by privatizing state assets, but there was no private sector that could buy these assets at a fair market price. Every adult was given a voucher to buy a few shares in privatized enterprises, but this did not make citizens into stakeholders, for many quickly sold or traded their vouchers for tangible goods they could enjoy here and now. Yeltsin-style privatization ended up being private inasmuch as the transfer of wealth occurred without the constraints of public scrutiny or accountability. Privatization without a private sector transferred valuable state assets into the hands of those with political connections in the old *nomenklatura*, the elite of the party-state. In the new economy, many activities were carried out under a roof supported by both private and public pillars, and offering benefits to all who sheltered under it (cf. e.g. Aslund, 1995; Blasi et al., 1997; Hedlund, 1999).

The government continued to need revenue to meet the everyday expenses of the state, and it could no longer rely on the methods used in the Soviet era. However, Russia's new rich companies did not want to pay taxes routinely. Nor have ordinary Russians been anxious to learn about taxation. When the 1998 New Russia Barometer asked employees what percentage of their wages was deducted as taxes, 54 per cent replied that they did not know. In the worst of times, the gap between taxes due and taxes collected has approached half the revenue due according to the law.

Like its Soviet predecessor, the Yeltsin government looked abroad for loans. In optimistic periods, officials argued that loans were a good economic investment, and in bad periods the government argued that loans were a political necessity to save Russia and, by implication, Western allies from something far worse. International financial institutions such as the International Monetary Fund (IMF) and the World Bank gave loans. Energy enterprises were told to pay taxes in return for political protection for the hard currency profits they gained from exporting oil and gas, and energy firms were ordered to subsidize loss-making enterprises by allowing them to run up big debts for unpaid supplies. Instead of collecting all the taxes notionally due, the state covered its deficits by borrowing money from banks at very high rates of interest. This enabled tax evaders to profit twice, once from nonpayment of taxes and again from loaning money to the state to cover the resulting public deficit.

Whereas a modern state concentrates on extracting taxes from private enterprise, Russian businessmen have extracted benefits from the state. Benefits have included exemption from paying taxes and licences to pursue profitable activities. The National Sports Foundation was given tax exemption for the import of alcohol, tobacco and luxury cars from abroad, a boon worth an estimated $3 billion to $4 billion a year. Similar benefits were given to entrepreneurs hiding behind such names as the Afghan War Veterans Union and the Humanitarian Aid Commission. Lucrative privileges attracted the attention of gangsters. The chair of the Moscow Society for the Deaf and the chair of the All-Russian Society for the Deaf, both beneficiaries of import duty exemptions, were killed by gunmen (Klebnikov, 2000: 230ff., 250). The state also granted profitable licences for commercial television. Peter Aven, a former Gaidar minister turned banker, has described the system thus:

To become a millionaire in our country it is not at all necessary to have a good head or specialized knowledge. Often, it is enough to have active support in the government, the parliament, local power structures and law enforcement agencies. One fine day your insignificant bank is authorized to, for instance, conduct operations with budgetary funds. Or quotas are generously allotted for the export of oil, timber and gas. In other words, you are *appointed* a millionaire (Reddaway and Glinski, 2001: 603; italics added).

The climax in the private exploitation of public resources was the 'loans for shares' scheme to which the Yeltsin government agreed in August 1995. It handed over enterprises with tens of billions of dollars of revenue to oligarchs, a group of politically connected multimillionaires and billionaires. The scheme was complex. In the first instance, the bankers offered loans sufficient to cover much of the government's 1995 budget deficit. In return, they gained the right to manage on very favourable terms enterprises such as Norilsk Nickel and oil and energy companies, which for the moment remained nominally state-owned. In the months following the summer 1996 presidential election, the government was to repay the loans or auction the enterprises on terms enabling the new managers to gain full ownership by hook or by crook.

A critical political feature of the loans-for-shares timetable was that oligarchs would gain ownership only if Boris Yeltsin's bid for re-election was successful, since any other politician would repudiate the agreement, keeping the properties in state hands or awarding them to its friends. The oligarchs, who also put money into major media institutions, went all-out to discredit Yeltsin's opponents and urge support for their financial benefactor. In summer 1996, Yeltsin won re-election in a run-off against Communist Gennady Zyuganov. Soon after, the oligarchs took ownership of billions of dollars of state assets. An account of the sale of the century by Chrystia Freeland (2000: 180) concluded that the businessmen were not to be blamed for pursuing an opportunity for great wealth: 'The real problem was that the state allowed them to get away with it.'

In theory, the rapid, even illegal, enrichment of a small number of rapacious entrepreneurs could be justified if they abandoned the pursuit of quick profits in order to become what Mancur Olson (2000) has called stationary bandits, that is, people who give up the high-risk business of seizing assets and invest their sudden wealth in conventional ways, thus promoting economic development and augmenting their riches legally. However, this did not happen. Instead, Russia's new rich kept much of their new wealth abroad in dollar accounts. From 1995 to 1999, the net amount of capital exported by Russians was more than $65 billion, three times the amount of money loaned by international financial institutions (Lopez-Claros and Zadornov, 2002: 109). Furthermore, Russia's oligarchs discouraged foreign companies from competing with them by investing in Russia. A former Russian government official and Yeltsin appointee to the board of the IMF, Konstantin Kagalovsky, explained that foreign investors had no chance of enforcing their property rights in disputes with Russian firms because politically pliable judges were bound to interpret vague laws in favour of Russian oligarchs. He added that this was the case, because 'I wrote the laws myself, and took special care with them' (Freeland, 2000: 176).

While the oligarchs gained permanent control of great assets, the Yeltsin government was left with the problem of annually raising money to cover a budget hole that grew as interest on past debts increased and the assets the state had to offer became fewer. The government borrowed at increasingly high rates of interest from Russian banks and from foreign banks that accepted debts denominated in rubles because the short-term profits were so high. On 27 May 1998 the Russian Central Bank raised interest rates from 30 per cent to 150 per cent. Fearing that Russia's problems would add to global instability arising from Asia's financial crisis, the IMF pressed the Yeltsin government to reduce its government deficit. The Kremlin turned to the Clinton White House, which had repeatedly turned a blind eye to CIA briefings about the extent of financial maladministration and corruption by the Yeltsin government (Klebnikov, 2000: 325). Lacking the authority to loan United States government funds to Russia, President Clinton put pressure on the IMF to do so. Although IMF officials were aware of what was going on in Moscow, in mid-July a package of $22 billion in aid was given to Russia by the IMF, the World Bank and Japan. The Central Bank had to push up interest rates further as it became increasingly difficult to find the money to pay the interest on debts approaching $80 billion.

On 17 August 1998 the government announced a moratorium on Russian companies paying debts to foreign companies, and suspended payment on short-term domestic bonds until the end of the year. The ruble was also devalued, and in foreign exchange markets it soon dropped to one-quarter of its former value. Moscow's default on foreign borrowing cost the IMF both credibility and cash. The comment from Anatoly Chubais, then first deputy prime minister for economic reform, and now the head of Russia's electricity monopoly, was, 'Today in the international financial institutions, despite everything we've done to them – and we cheated them out of $20 billion – there is an understanding that we had no alternative' (Reddaway and Glinski, 2001: 600).

While foreign investors were surprised by what happened to them, ordinary Russians were not. When the spring 1998 NRB survey asked about the image of Russia's new rich, more than three-quarters thought Russian businessmen took advantage of other people and 70 per cent thought they were dishonest (fig. 1.2). The big change by comparison with six years earlier – a drop from 95 to 36 per cent – was in those thinking that Russian businessmen helped make the economy grow. A detailed analysis of capital flows by Vladimir Tikhomirov (2001: 279) came to the same conclusion, 'A large part of the US $169 billion net financial flows that entered Russia between 1992 and 1999 was actually spent (or rather misspent) on keeping the bankrupt Soviet economy afloat and on creating the so-called stratum of new Russians, a few *nouveaux riches* who spent their money supporting Western economies by buying expensive Western consumer goods, Western banking services and real estate in Western countries.'

The optimist could describe the Russian economy as undergoing the 'creative destruction' that Joseph Schumpeter (1952) had posited as an integral part of the process of economic growth. However, the creativity of entrepreneurs was not directed at increasing the nation's productive assets; it was aimed at finding ways to re-allocate to themselves wealth that was already there. The result was not only the destruction of the state's fiscal capacity but also of any claims to the integrity of the state. For example, Alfred Kokh, a minister involved in the loans-for-shares swap, believed that he should be rewarded like a medieval court favourite by being paid a commission on all the money he brought into the state. The figure he suggested, 3 per cent, would have yielded him an income of $60 million in 1997. When a Western journalist noted that officeholders in modern states were also rewarded through a sense of honour, Kokh replied, 'What do you mean by honour? You won't get far on honour alone' (quoted in Freeland, 2000: 282f.).

The legacy: debt and corruption

In his last major speech to the Duma, President Yeltsin admitted, 'We are stuck halfway between a planned, command economy and a normal, market one. And now we have an ugly model – a crossbreed of the two systems' (quoted in Gaddy and Ickes, 2001a: 103). In the light of his work in Russia for the European Bank for Reconstruction and Development, Joel Hellman (1998: 205) described this crossbreed as a 'partial reform equilibrium' in which those who initially gained great benefits from the lawless privatization of state assets now have a vested interest in maintaining the status quo. New rich Russians do not want to continue the process of reform; they want to stop it in order to protect their wealth from competitors and from prosecution by the state. The concentration of wealth in their hands gives rich entrepreneurs more influence on the Kremlin than that of the tens of millions of scattered citizens who have felt the costs of the oligarchs' gains.

The debts left behind by decades of excess do not go away (fig. 1.3). In a vain attempt to buy reform, the Gorbachev government piled up tens of billions of dollars of debts to foreign lenders. In the closing days of the Soviet Union, Boris Yeltsin volunteered that an independent Russian Federation would take responsibility for Soviet debts. After three years of complex negotiations involving counterclaims by other successor states on Soviet properties at home and abroad, this was agreed. Agreement made it easier for the Russian Federation to finance its inherited debt and to seek new foreign lending (Tikhomirov, 2001: 265ff.; Robinson, 2001). The Yeltsin government added to this debt burden, borrowing an additional $51 billion from abroad. While most of the goods and services on which borrowed money has been spent are gone, the debts remain.

Figure 1.3 A LEGACY OF DEBTS.

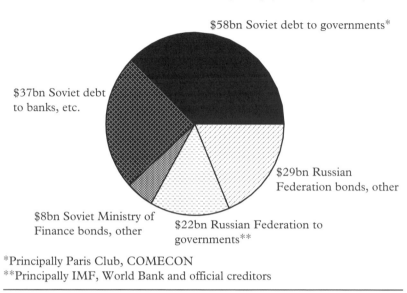

Russian external debts, beginning of 2000 (US$154bn)

$58bn Soviet debt to governments*

$37bn Soviet debt
to banks, etc.

$29bn Russian
Federation bonds, other

$8bn Soviet Ministry of
Finance bonds, other

$22bn Russian Federation to
governments**

*Principally Paris Club, COMECON
**Principally IMF, World Bank and official creditors

Source: Lehman Brothers.

While Vladimir Putin could rhetorically offer the Russian people a 'new beginning', he could not escape the legacies of a disorderly past. On taking office at the beginning of the year 2000, he inherited $154 billion in foreign debts, equivalent to almost four-fifths of Russia's gross domestic product in the previous year. Inflation has devalued many of the government's domestic debts, albeit at the expense of Russians who gave the government credit. However, the devaluation of the ruble in 1998 has increased the burden of debts that must be repaid in hard currencies.

A defining attribute of a modern state is that it is able to collect the taxes needed to provide essential services. As Sergei Kirienko, a former prime minister, has declared, 'If the state does not learn to collect taxes, it will cease to exist' (quoted in Gregory and Brooke, 2000: 453). Like its predecessors, the Russian Federation is not, or at least not yet, a modern state that can tax and spend efficiently and honestly. The reality facing Vladimir Putin is that he is president of a regime that is democratic and disorderly. It is democratic in that the chief offices of state are filled by free elections. But it is disorderly because affairs of state are not subject to the rule of law.

2   Democratization backwards

Free elections are good for blowing away the claim to rule of an undemocratic regime, but in the absence of a modern state they leave a void.
The problem of Russia is not a problem of elections; it is that it lacks a
modern state. For more than a century, the government of Russia has
met the minimal definitional requirements of a state: its institutions mo-
nopolize the power of coercion within a given territory. But Russia has
not been governed by a modern state, that is, a state that exercises its
authority according to the rule of law. As the Russian folk saying has it,
'The law is like a door in the middle of the field. You can go through
it if you want, or you can go around it.' Post-Soviet states are heirs to
an anti-modern legacy. A World Bank (1997: 5, 35) survey found that
Russia and other post-Soviet successor states ranked below the states of
sub-Saharan Africa, Latin America, the Middle East and South and East
Asia in the predictability and lawfulness of government.

The rule of law is the central characteristic of the modern state. It
establishes order by setting out what governors and governed are free to
do and imposing constraints on both. However, a big majority of countries
introducing free elections in the past two decades have done so in the
absence of a modern state. A strong state is not the same as a modern state;
the Soviet Union and Hitler's Third Reich have demonstrated as much
by wielding punishing powers in an arbitrary way. Nor need a modern
state be strong in the sense of active involvement in the affairs of society.
The laissez faire government of Britain in Victorian times did little, but
it was modern in carrying out what it did according to the law. Boris
Yeltsin sought to be a strong president, but not a modern president. He
was an autocrat who, without regard to formal constraints, manoeuvred
and acted in unpredictable and arbitrary ways to achieve his goals.

Elections are of central importance for a democratic regime, and a
minimalist definition treats elections as a sufficient as well as necessary condition of democracy. For example, Przeworski and colleagues
(1996: 50) stipulate that 'democracy is a regime in which government
offices are filled as a consequence of contested elections'. In the past

quarter-century competitive elections have spread to dozens of countries around the globe. However, introducing elections where the rule of law is absent is democratization backwards. Elections are free and fair only if they are conducted in accord with the rule of law, and the outcome is democratic only if the winner is constrained by the rule of law. However, Freedom House (*www.freedomhouse.org*) reports that, while at the end of the year 2001 there were 121 countries holding competitive elections, in 35 of these cases elections were held in countries that could not be described as free.

In the strict sense, democracy is an abstraction describing values or qualities of a political regime. The presence or absence of elections is often treated as a sufficient indicator of a regime being democratic. But doing this commits what Karl (2000: 95) calls 'the fallacy of electoralism'. To call an electoralist regime a new democracy obscures both its weaknesses and its potential for development. To define democracy without regard to the character of the state makes democracy an abstraction divorced from governance. To ask Russians whether they endorse the values of a democratic political culture is to separate the study of attitudes from governance, for many Russians do not consider that their system of government is democratic (cf. Gibson, 2001; and below, fig. 3.6).

A completely democratic state must meet two conditions: it must be a modern, rule-of-law state and the government must be chosen by free elections. If only one of these conditions is met, then a regime is incompletely democratic (Rose and Shin, 2001). Differentiating regimes on two dimensions – the rule of law and free elections – distinguishes four types of contemporary regime. Britain and the United States are examples of democratic modern states, while Singapore is a prominent example of a state that upholds the rule of law but does not hold free elections. From Afghanistan to Zambia there are many examples of lawless regimes without free and fair elections. The Russian Federation exemplifies the fourth alternative; it has free elections but the rule of law is often breached. The critical distinction between electoralist regimes and rule-of-law regimes is ignored when attention is focused exclusively on only one characteristic. Both Russia and Singapore are incompletely democratic political systems, but for contrasting reasons: Russia because the state does not govern by the rule of law, and Singapore because it fails to hold free and fair elections.[1]

The widespread introduction of free elections on many continents in the past two decades has been described as the 'third wave' of

[1] This distinction is missed by organizations such as Freedom House (*www.freedomhouse. org*) and Transparency International (*www.transparency.org*), which each specialize in evaluating regimes on only one of the criteria of a completely democratic modern state.

democratization (Huntington, 1991). But this label contains fundamental errors. It assumes that a new regime can only move toward democracy, thus substituting an idealistic teleology for a realistic political sociology. It also assumes that a modern state is already in place. On occasion, this is so. For example, when Ireland gained independence in 1921 it had in place modern institutions of government that were developed under Westminster's rule. However, in the absence of a modern state a regime with free elections must give priority to state-building. Yet, the leaders of new regimes are often more concerned with building their own power than with institutionalizing a rule-of-law state that imposes constraints on the power they claim by virtue of election.

The fundamental challenge facing leaders of a new regime is to consolidate their authority. A regime's authority can be described as consolidated when all the political elites in a country, including the military and bankers as well as politicians, accept that it is 'the only game in town'. Democratic consolidation, with governors committed to promoting the rule of law and free elections, is only one type of consolidation that can occur (cf. Diamond, 1999). From Libya to the People's Republic of China, there are countries where the only political game in town involves neither the rule of law nor free elections.

Social scientists and policymakers confronted with regimes outside their experience are inclined, as Leon Trotsky predicted, 'to seek salvation from unfamiliar phenomena in familiar terms' (quoted in Jowitt, 1992: 124). This can result in Russia being referred to as a new democracy and the challenge facing Vladimir Putin as that of completing the consolidation of democracy. Whatever temporary reassurance such phrases may bring outsiders, they can lead to misunderstandings and disillusionment. The challenge facing Vladimir Putin is not that facing the eighteenth-century American Founding Fathers, nineteenth-century English campaigners for the right of working class men to vote, or twentieth-century female suffragettes. The great political challenge facing Putin is to build a modern state without using the dictatorship of law to suppress free elections.

Creating modern and anti-modern states

The first modern states did not have automobiles, large numbers of university graduates or democratic aspirations. They became modern by developing the rule of law, recognizing the right of individuals and organizations to form civil society institutions and accepting accountability to elites. The first modern states, the Kingdoms of France and of Prussia, were not democratic states but enlightened despotisms. The leading theorist of the modern state, Max Weber, saw Imperial Prussia as a good example of a modern state; he did not regard democratic elections as a necessary condition of a modern state (Weber, 1947; Cohen, 1985).

For centuries the rulers of Russia have been concerned with building a state that has the administrative capacity to enforce their will on subjects, to protect its boundaries from foreign invasion and to raise the taxes needed to meet these minimal responsibilities. The vast territory of the tsars was an obstacle to making the state effective. The nineteenth-century development of the telegraph and railway showed that distances were not the only obstacle to creating a modern state, for the arbitrary practices of the tsar remained an obstacle. The Soviet Union was able to put a sputnik into space. However, harnessing the resources of modern science did not make the Soviet Union a modern state, for technological development does not depend on the lawfulness of government.

Modernizing the state not a Russian tradition

The modern state is above all a *Rechtsstaat*.[2] Laws specify what public officials ought to do as agents of authority and laws control how bureaucrats implement the decisions of governors. The rule of law meant that the king and the king's servants could not act arbitrarily. The need to restrict the powers of the state is the foundation of the American Constitution too. James Madison proclaimed: 'In framing a government which is to be administered by men over men, the great difficulty lies in this: you must first enable the government to control the governed; and in the next place oblige it to control itself' (Hamilton et al., 1948: 337).

When the rule of law applies, individuals and organizations know where they stand, for rules are not waived or enforced according to who you are, whom you know or what you pay officials. The laws are applied the same for everybody at all times. Within the limits of the law, individuals are free to act as they wish; outside these limits people face predictable sanctions. Consistency and impersonality are fundamental characteristics of the rule of law. This makes it the foundation of modern bureaucracy, for bureaucrats administer government 'by the book', that is, according to rules. Long before modern means of communication came into being, bureaucratic institutions enabled the state to maintain domestic order, settle disputes in courts, promote public health and collect taxes to finance these activities. The growth of government in the past century has built on the bureaucratic foundations of the early modern state.

[2] The word is cited in German rather than English, for German distinguishes between *recht*, in the English sense of 'rightful', and *gesetz*, in the English sense of 'lawful'. A similar distinction is made in French and other languages, including Russian *pravo* (right) and *zakon* (law).

In the first modern states laws discriminated between categories of subjects, such as men and women, property owners and the property-less, and adherents of the state's religion as against other Christians and Jews. Franchise laws identified more people who could not vote than those who could. The great majority of adults lacked the right to vote. Article I of the United States Constitution stipulated that slaves should count as only three-fifths of a person for purposes of representation, and women did not have the right to vote. In Europe, the right to vote was given to members of estates representing the nobility, the clergy, urban leaders and other elites. Irrespective of how few the number of elec-tors were, each estate had a substantial number of seats in the national parliament.

In Russia, the tsar ruled without the constraints of law. In the early eighteenth century the Procuracy was established to enforce the tsar's edicts on subordinate public officials and subjects. 'Until the emancipa-tion of the serfs in 1861, the vast majority of Russians had no civil rights, were subjected to the violent and arbitrary rule of their lords, and had no recourse to the state for basic legal protections' (Sachs and Pistor, 1997: 5). The Soviet state followed Karl Marx in dismissing legal con-straints as a means of protecting the privileges of the ruling class. Lenin proclaimed that 'all law is politics' and that law should be 'a weapon of the state' (quoted in Gordon B. Smith, 2001: 108). The state security apparatus investigated and prosecuted people deemed to have violated edicts of the party-state, and there was a presumption that anyone ac-cused of a crime against the state was guilty. Even in the time of glasnost, when government was headed by a lawyer, Mikhail Gorbachev, many regulations were not published but circulated on a restricted basis within ministries. Rules could thus be ignored until a situation arose when se-lective enforcement served the party-state's interest (Huskey, 1990).

The development of *civil society* depends on the rule of law recogniz-ing the right of business associations, trade unions, churches, the media and other institutions to organize independently of the state. In Western Europe, institutions of civil society existed for a century or more before every adult had the right to vote. These institutions fostered elitist politi-cal parties that competed in elections held on a restricted franchise. Civil society organizations were also created to campaign for the right to vote (cf. Lipset and Rokkan, 1967). By contrast, in pre-1914 tsarist Russia the 'lack of independence of civil society' was an obstacle to creating a Duma representative of organized elite interests (Emmons, 1983: 1f.). Organizations that expressed interest in political affairs were usually small in membership, and often infiltrated by the tsar's police.

The Soviet state treated the idea of civil society as a bourgeois device en-couraging false consciousness. Whereas tsarist censors had been content with prohibiting the publication of works that were deemed subversive, the Communist system sought to direct what artists and scientists wrote, whether a symphony or a biology text. Under Stalin, the party-state pursued a totalitarian campaign to purge organizations of any potential to be independent of it. Leaders of nascent institutions of civil society – universities, the press, chambers of commerce and trade unions – were deprived of office, forced into exile, imprisoned or even executed, and party loyalists were placed in charge. Institutions nominally the same as in Western countries were under the control of political commissars. The regime's totalitarian ambition was to mobilize citizens of all ages. The party-state even encouraged children to spy on parents. Unfree and uncompetitive elections were held to mobilize a nominal show of unanimous support. In a standard reference book on the Soviet Union, the concept of civil society is discussed under the heading 'Social control and social development' (Brown, 1994b: 459).

In the post-totalitarian era of Soviet society, individual expressions of dissatisfaction, frustration and even dissent were tolerated. Dissidents were sometimes allowed to speak their minds to Western journalists, since Westerners would interpret this as a mark of the tolerance of the party-state while Russians would not know what had been said unless they heard the interviews in forbidden broadcasts of Radio Free Liberty or read *samizdat* publications, which circulated secretly. When the first elections were held in the Russian Republic, there were multiple candidates but no political parties that voters could hold accountable. Nor did the Communist Party openly split and offer voters a choice between hardliners and dissidents. Introducing institutions of a market economy has aptly been described as *Starting Over* (Simon Johnson and Loveman, 1995), for Russia had not had the semblance of a market economy for three generations.

A government subject to the rule of law can be held *accountable* for its actions by courts. It can also be held accountable by an assembly with members representing interests of the nobility, clergy and selected professions or guilds (Myers, 1975). From the seventeenth century onwards the English Parliament successfully held the Crown accountable, even though the House of Lords consisted of hereditary peers and the House of Commons was elected by esoteric franchises and constituencies. The first modern states were pluralist in giving multiple interests opportunities to represent diverse views, even though membership of parliament was not determined by universal suffrage.

The Russian tradition was of accountability *to* the tsar rather than by the tsar. In the sixteenth century Ivan the Terrible created the *oprichnina* (realm apart) to enforce his will through a reign of terror directed at subordinate officials. Peter the Great's subsequent reform of the state was based on a military model that subordinated the nobility to the monarch in a carefully graded table of ranks. The first elected Duma (council or parliament) was authorized by the tsar only after the abortive revolution of 1905. However, the franchise law 'showed mistrust of all social groups' and was 'so arbitrary in its terms that it lacked a precedent in any country' (Eugene Anderson and Anderson, 1967: 335). The Russian Federation has elections and parties – but the prime minister and Cabinet are not accountable to Parliament. This was very evident when the party of Prime Minister Viktor Chernomyrdin did badly in the 1995 Duma election: nonetheless, President Yeltsin kept Chernomyrdin in office until 1998.

The fundamental assumption of the Soviet state was that there were no conflicts of interest requiring expression through competitive elections. The Supreme Soviet, notionally a Parliament, met only a few days a year to rubber-stamp decisions already taken in conclaves of the party-state. The complexity of Soviet government did institutionalize competing claims for resources between ministries and between networks of elites in the party and the state (Skilling and Griffiths, 1971; Roeder, 1993). But disagreements within the ranks of the rulers of the party-state did not make the government accountable to the Russian people.

The anti-modern legacy

To understand the process that has created the Russian Federation we must know where it is coming from. In a third-world country, the starting point for modernization is a population divided into a rural group distant from the national capital; a marginal urban sector of poor people and petty entrepreneurs; and a small elite who run the modern sectors of the state and economy. In such circumstances, political and economic development is about shifting people and activities from the traditional and marginal sectors of society to an existing but small modern sector.

The Soviet legacy is less favourable for building a modern state, because the pervasive reach of the totalitarian party-state eliminated both traditional village ways of life and the modernizing elite emerging in a few Russian cities before 1917. When the party-state collapsed, there was no modern sector that could be the foundation for creating a modern state. Worse than that, the discredited Soviet regime left behind an arbitrary and corrupt *nomenklatura* in control of the state. The Russian Federation inherited a much greater industrial capacity than a developing country could claim, and Russia's natural resources gave it energy supplies so plentiful that it could be grossly inefficient in energy consumption. Human capital was substantial, for academic, technical and vocational education was widely available, encouraging sympathetic commentators to describe the Soviet system as modern (see e.g. Hough, 1988). However, such a description confuses the material embellishments of a modern society with its substance.

The Soviet goal was not to catch up with the West but to create a radically different society. Western ideas of a modern society were rejected, whether based on the classic liberalism of John Stuart Mill or on social democratic values. The orthodox Communist position was that late capitalist industrial societies carried within them the seeds of their own destruction; the more they developed, the sooner they were doomed to collapse through internal contradictions. Marxism-Leninism was trumpeted as the modern method for development and the Soviet Union was its prime exponent. In the words of Nikita Khrushchev to a gathering of Western diplomats in Moscow in November 1956, 'Whether you like it or not, history is on our side. We will bury you.'

Scholars sought labels to describe the Soviet phenomenon. Alec Nove (1975: 626) aptly noted, 'We may be facing a qualitatively new phenomenon for which our customary categories (whether derived from Marx or from Parsons) may require substantial modification.' The Polish economist Jan Winiecki (1988) described the Soviet system as 'pseudo-modern', because of its reliance on non-market mechanisms. Martin Malia (Z, 1990: 298ff.) said the contrast between Soviet ideology and reality created a 'surreal' society. But such negative labels do not tell us what the Soviet system was – and thus what its legacy to the Russian Federation is.

The Soviet system appeared modern because it was complex, but in reality it was anti-modern (tab. 2.1). A modern society is transparent; organizations are open about their activities and information flows freely. In the Soviet system censors controlled the flow of information and much that happened was veiled from the public. For example, the disastrous nuclear explosion at the Chernobyl power station in 1986 was not publicly admitted until more than two weeks after it happened. In a modern society, laws and rules are followed by officials in charge of organizations as well as by their subordinates. Rules could be bent or broken in pursuit of goals endorsed by the party-state, such as meeting a production target laid down by economic planners – or at least producing a document saying that this had been done. The use of connections and bribes for personal gain was commonplace too.

In a modern society the feedback of votes is a signal of approval or disapproval of government and prices signal what goods and services ought to be produced to meet market demands. For all the readiness of Soviet technocrats to talk about cybernetics, the system did not allow for

Table 2.1 *Comparing modern and anti-modern societies*

	Modern	Anti-modern
Processes	Transparent Laws and rules followed	Controlled or opaque Bending and breaking rules, exchanging favours, bribes
Decisionmaking	Votes, prices Rational calculation	Ideology dictates Fanciful calculation
Outcomes	Effective Efficient	Usually but not always effective Inefficient

Source: Derived from Richard Rose, 'Uses of Social Capital in Russia: Modern, Pre-Modern and Anti-Modern', *Post-Soviet Affairs*, 16, 1, 2000, 33–57.

measuring feedback. Ideology dictated what people should really want and commanders of the planned economy dictated what goods and services the economy produced. In an economy of favours, valued goods were often allocated through *blat* (that is, connections; see Ledeneva, 1998). Calculations made in a modern society cannot be made in an anti-modern society. The problem was not a shortage of information but a surplus of disinformation, since economic and electoral data gave misleading accounts of what people actually wanted. The absence of data for rational calculation thus led to fanciful decisionmaking, whether anti-modern governors believed what ideology produced or cynically decided to make up evidence to justify what they wanted to do.

After a generation of internal terror and war against Nazi Germany, the Soviet system had become effective in feeding and clothing its subjects; producing consumer goods that Russians had never had before; and maintaining a military establishment across a bloc of countries from the Pacific Ocean to Germany. While it lasted, scholars often described the Soviet state as an 'omnipotent state', because the Communist Party claimed to control many political and economic institutions limiting the power of governors in modern states (Connor, 1988: 9; cf. Ma, 2000). But effectiveness was achieved with great economic and political inefficiency. The concentration on top-down commands made little allowance for bottom-up feedback. Without knowledge of the consequences of commands, Soviet governors believed they were succeeding when the opposite was the case. The unrealistic targets of five-year plans encouraged factory managers to practise deceit and exaggeration in order to make it appear that everything was working all right – at least on paper. Elections allowed even less opportunity for citizens to signal what they wanted. The miscalculations of Soviet leaders became fatal when glasnost ended the party-state's monopoly of information and official views were challenged at the ballot box and in the marketplace.

The Soviet Union was not the only twentieth-century totalitarian regime: other examples include Nazi Germany, North Korea, Enver Hoxha's Albania, the People's Republic of China during the Maoist cultural revolution and the Khmer Rouge regime in Cambodia. However, the Soviet Union lasted much longer than any of these other regimes; for example, Stalin wielded totalitarian power more than twice as long as Adolf Hitler. The gradual relaxation in the pursuit of totalitarian goals following Nikita Khrushchev's denunciation of Stalin did not re-create the rule of law since it had not existed before Stalin. Nor could it replace nascent institutions of civil society destroyed by Stalinism.

The Soviet regime that collapsed in 1991 was not a *Rechtsstaat*; it was a post-totalitarian anti-modern state (Linz and Stepan, 1996). The system was a perverse example of Weber's (1973: 126) dictum that 'power is in the administration of everyday things'. From a modern perspective, the power of the Soviet party-state was evident in the *maladministration* of everyday things.

The Yeltsin administration confirmed its authority by winning elections, but it did not govern by the rule of law. When Pavel Krasheninnikov was dismissed as minister of justice, President Yeltsin publicly criticized him for not pursuing investigations of the Communist Party assiduously enough, and privately criticized him for not finding grounds 'to liquidate the party'. One Kremlin official told the outgoing justice minister, 'You have one problem; you always cite the law' (quoted in Brown, 2001a: 564). When Boris Berezovsky, a backer of Boris Yeltsin, was threatened with prosecution on corruption charges after falling out with President Putin, he charged that the move was politically motivated, because 'No one who was active in Russia over the last ten years respected the law' (quoted in Jack, 2001a; see also Klebnikov, 2000).

Western leaders, headed by President Bill Clinton of the United States and Chancellor Helmut Kohl of Germany, preferred to ignore the Soviet legacy and assume that, even if they were not just like us, they were enough like us to do business with. This was an expensive act of misplaced faith. Intergovernmental agencies, led by the International Monetary Fund and the World Bank, loaned billions of dollars to Russia and commercial lenders followed. To give the illusion to visitors that all was going well, financial statements were created to conform to Western expectations and interests. In the cynical words of one Russian official, 'Programmes were drafted just to be shown to IMF officials. They were, so to speak, an export commodity. Nobody really intended to implement them' (quoted in Reddaway and Glinski, 2001: 597; see also Wedel, 1998).

The institutional challenges facing post-Communist rulers have been described by Western political scientists as 'rebuilding the ship at sea' (cf. Elster et al., 1998). The phrase is reminiscent of the task facing Germans in 1945, the rebuilding (*Wiederaufbau*) of an economy, a polity and a morality after the destruction of Hitler's Third Reich. In the Russian Federation, the idea of rebuilding is overly optimistic. The task facing its governors is far greater, for Russia never was a modern state. It is more accurately described as *building* a modern state while battered by the storms and threatened by the rocks that are legacies of an anti-modern Soviet regime and of the actions, for good and ill, of the Yeltsin government.

Realizing the democratic potential of modern states

The most favourable starting point for democratization is a modern state. Given the rule of law, representative institutions of civil society and accountability to elites, a regime can become democratic by expanding a restrictive franchise until every adult has the right to vote. However, becoming modern does not guarantee that a state will also become democratic. At most, we can describe modern states as having the prerequisites for becoming democratic. It is much easier to extend the right to vote when there are already competitive elections with a restrictive franchise than to introduce party politics, competitive elections and a democratic franchise all at once.

The leaders of the first states to become modern were not promoting democratization. It is anachronistic in the extreme to claim that Frederick the Great of Prussia and Napoleon were trying to promote democracy when they took steps to modernize their states. Today, the leaders of regimes in many developing countries are seeking to modernize their state to promote their political power, economic development and wealth rather than to give their population the right to choose their governors.

The evolution of modern states into democratic states was not the choice of a single leader or the result of a pact among political elites. It occurred gradually through an accumulation of events. In England the initial foundations were laid in the seventeenth century when Parliament established that the king was accountable to its laws by rising in arms, placing King Charles I on trial, and then beheading him. His royal successors accepted a degree of accountability to a Parliament representing privileged estates. The British Reform Act of 1832 began the process of rationalizing the franchise, but it gave the right to vote to only 2 per cent of adult males. Almost a century after competitive elections became the norm, a democratic franchise was established at the end of the First World War. In Scandinavia, the Netherlands and Belgium an undemocratic rule-of-law state was likewise established centuries ago (Rustow, 1955; Daalder, 1995).

In countries that we now think of as long-established democracies, it took generations to complete the realization of their democratic potential (cf. Bartolini, 2000). More than a quarter of a millennium passed between the time the English Parliament first challenged the absolute authority of the king and the introduction of universal suffrage. The American Constitution was adopted in 1787 but it was accepted as binding only after the defeat of the Confederate states in 1865, and universal suffrage was not effectively guaranteed until the Federal Voting Rights Act in 1965. There were 35 presidents in the period between the inauguration of George Washington and the presidency of Lyndon B. Johnson.

Many modern European states have experienced interrupted development, moving back and forth between democratic and undemocratic regimes. Before the First World War, regimes from Spain to Finland endorsed the rule of law, licensed institutions of civil society and accepted political accountability to elites. Universal male suffrage was introduced, but the completion of democracy was aborted. Free elections were abolished and some form of undemocratic regime, whether Nazi, fascist or a military or civilian dictatorship, was introduced. The great majority of these new regimes fell before the Second World War.

After the Second World War, defeated countries had the opportunity to attempt redemocratization, and the military presence of victorious allies imposed pressures to do so. Where there were already the foundations of a modern state, redemocratization often proved successful. The Federal Republic of Germany became a prime example under the leadership of politicians socialized in the democratic Weimar Republic or in the kaiser's *Rechtsstaat*. In Austria, politicians similarly socialized in the Habsburg *Rechtsstaat* or a failed interwar democracy invoked the country's 1920 democratic constitution as the basis for governing after 1945. Major parties in both countries had originated in the civil society of undemocratic regimes; the German Social Democratic Party was founded in 1871, and the Austrian Socialist Party in 1889. In Spain General Franco won power in a bloody civil war. But unlike Nazi Germany and Soviet Russia, Franco's regime did not pursue the totalitarian suppression of civil society. In the lengthy concluding period of his rule, Franco sought to strengthen modern institutions of the state, the economy and society. This led to the peaceful introduction of democratic elections after his death in 1975.

The early establishment of administrative institutions of a modern state has enabled a few developing countries to succeed in democratization. India is an extreme example; poverty is widespread, adult literacy is incomplete and Indian society is divided by language, religion and ethnicity. Nonetheless, for more than a century India has had many institutions of the modern state. Beginning in the middle of the nineteenth century British officials began introducing modern courts, the rule of law and modern forms of public administration. For example, Mahatma Gandhi, the father of Indian independence, was admitted to practise law in London in 1889. The Indian National Congress, founded to campaign for independence in 1885, has been the most successful party in a half-century of free elections since Indian independence.

In the absence of institutions of the modern state, democratization is difficult. The point is illustrated by the post-independence history of many former British colonies in Africa, where there was not the time, resources or inclination to build modern institutions as in India. The initial constitutions of newly independent African countries provided some form of representative government. However, attempts to introduce democratization backwards quickly failed. The regimes broke down and were replaced by one or another form of undemocratic rule. Even though public opinion surveys in many African countries indicate that the idea of democracy is widely recognized and endorsed by citizens, the absence of the rule of law and other institutions of a modern state are great obstacles to democratization (cf. Bratton and van de Walle, 1997; Bratton and Mattes, 2001).

Contrasts in post-Communist contexts

To treat the transformation of countries in the former Soviet bloc as part of a third wave of democratization reaching from Portugal to Thailand is trebly mistaken (cf. Huntington, 1991; Brown, 2000: 181ff.). In the first place, the starting point of post-Communist countries is distinctive, a post-totalitarian legacy differing from less pervasive forms of undemocratic rule that preceded regime change on other continents. Second, post-Communist countries created new regimes in response to a common and abrupt shock: the collapse of the hegemony of the Soviet party-state. Third, the contrasting ways in which post-Communist countries have been transforming themselves show that instead of forming a single wave, they are running in more than one direction. Some post-Communist regimes are not trying to become democratic and are succeeding.

The Communist legacy meant that all post-Communist regimes began democratization backwards in 1990, but some were much more backward than others, because of differences in previous histories. The transformation of the boundaries of states and the murder or displacement of tens of millions of people during the Second World War make the attribution of histories to peoples and places approximate (cf. Rose, 1996b). We can nonetheless note that before 1914 modern institutions of the Kaiser's *Reich* and the Habsburg Empire covered lands that now constitute much or all of the Czech Republic, Hungary, Poland, Slovakia and the Baltic states. In the interwar period these states were fiercely anti-Soviet but experiments with democratization failed, except in Czechoslovakia. Lands that had been part of the tsar's empire or the Ottoman Empire were much less subject to modernizing political influences. In Central Asia and the Caucasus, the Soviet Union promoted socio-economic development but pursued its goals through anti-modern methods.

In Communist times Moscow offered a common template for undemocratic governance and anti-modern rule. Countries of Central and Eastern Europe were subjected to Communist rule for four decades after the Second World War, and this lasted almost twice as long in the Soviet Union.[3] In Central and Eastern Europe, Communist parties were imposed by Soviet military force in collaboration with Communists operating as agents of Moscow. Anti-modern institutions were introduced there and the party-state followed a totalitarian line in eliminating independent institutions of civil society and making citizens vote in unfree and unfair elections. The government was accountable to the party, not the people, and national Communist parties were subject to unsolicited advice and directives from Moscow. The Warsaw Pact binding countries into a military alliance with the Soviet Union was used to justify stationing Soviet troops throughout the region. COMECON (the Council for Mutual Economic Assistance), dominated by Moscow, enforced trade relationships on non-market command economies. Censorship and control of passports and visas restricted individual contact with democratic states.

Countries differed under Communist rule. The German Democratic Republic was economically the most prosperous but politically among the most repressed, as the state security system encouraged friends and family members to spy on each other. Street demonstrations against Soviet domination by Czechs and Slovaks, Poles and Hungarians were put down by Soviet force. Bulgaria was a loyal satellite that benefited economically by following the Moscow line. In Romania Nicolae Ceausescu maintained totalitarian repression and a cult of the leader long after Moscow had repudiated Stalinism. In the Soviet Union there were substantial

---

[3] Here and subsequently, Communist and post-Communist regimes refer to successor states of countries of the Soviet Union or integrated in its military alliance, the Warsaw Pact, and its ruble-oriented economic bloc, COMECON. Although nominally Communist, Yugoslavia and Albania were outside Moscow's orbit, and so too were non-European regimes such as the People's Republic of China. The Baltic states of Estonia, Latvia and Lithuania, forcibly integrated into the Soviet Union as a consequence of the Second World War, are treated here as part of Central and Eastern Europe.

differences in social and economic conditions between Russia and the Central Asian republics, but there was substantial migration, including movement of Russians into non-Russian republics. The Communist Party of the Soviet Union was a major force for integration.

When the Communist bloc collapsed, 21 post-Communist regimes were created in its wake. The successor states of the Soviet Union started with fewer assets and more handicaps than Central and East European countries. Post-Communist regimes have differed substantially in the extent to which they have created institutions of the modern state and introduced free elections. The achievements of the Russian Federation are neither the best nor the worst to date.

Today, economic gain rather than political repression is the most common motive for post-Communist public officials undermining the rule of law. The Perception of Corruption Index compiled annually by Transparency International (TI) evaluates more than 90 countries. The Index pools a multiplicity of assessments of corruption from different sources, most of which concern wholesale corruption by high-ranking elected officials and civil servants in charge of mineral rights, the import and export of valuable products, the payment or non-payment of taxes and criminal prosecutions (*www.transparency.org*).

The extent of corruption among post-Communist states varies greatly (fig. 2.1). Among Soviet successor states, Russia appears a little less corrupt than Central Asian states and Ukraine but much more corrupt than Baltic states. It is in the bottom sixth of countries, with a corruption rating the same as Pakistan. Russia, in common with most CIS states, shows less regard for the rule of law than Romania, the most corrupt post-Communist regime now seeking membership in the European Union. While no country seeking EU membership matches the integrity of its median member, Germany, three countries – Estonia, Hungary and Lithuania – are credited with more integrity than Greece, the EU state where standards are lowest.

Post-Communist regimes are more likely to have competitive elections than public officials free from corruption (tab. 2.2). Across Central and Eastern Europe, elections are competitive, for no party wins as much as half the vote. In the median country, the biggest party secures less than a third of the vote. The use of proportional representation encourages more competition between parties than in Britain and the United States. In elections for the Russian Duma, the party winning the most votes has consistently been a party opposed to the Kremlin. Where presidential elections are held, the use of the two-ballot system ensures that the winner is the choice of more than half the voters, a condition frequently not met in the United States and absent in British parliamentary elections for two-thirds of a century.

Figure 2.1 RULE OF LAW IN POST-COMMUNIST REGIMES.

Transparency International (TI) Corruption Index
Maximum: 10   *Highest integrity*

	9.9	Finland: European Union top
	8.3	Britain
	7.6	USA
	7.4	Germany: EU median
Estonia	5.5	Italy
Hungary	5.3	
Lithuania	4.8	
	4.2	Greece: EU lowest
	4.1	Brazil: TI median
Poland, Belarus	4	
Czech Republic, Bulgaria	3.9	
Slovakia	3.7	
Latvia	3.4	
Moldova	3.1	
Romania	2.8	
Kazakhstan, Uzbekistan	2.7	
Armenia	2.5	
Georgia, **RUSSIA**	2.3	
Kyrgyzstan	2.2	
Ukraine	2.1	
Azerbaijan	2.0	
Tajikistan	na	
Turkmenistan	na	
	0.4	Bangladesh: most corrupt

Most corrupt

Source: Transparency International Perception of Corruption Index, 2001, *www.transparency. org*. Ratings for Armenia and Belarus are from 2000; Georgia and Kyrgyzstan are from 1999, as none are given for 2001.

Table 2.2 *Competitiveness in post-Communist elections*

		President Vote: 1st Round Leader	
Unfree or unfair	*OSCE assessment*	%	*Year*
Turkmenistan	Avoided[a]	99.5	1992
Tajikistan	Avoided	97.0	1999
Uzbekistan	Avoided	91.9	2000
Kazahkstan	Avoided	79.8	1999
Georgia	Free but unfair[b]	79.8	2000
Azerbaijan	Undue govt influence[c]	76.1	1998
Belarus	Undue govt influence	75.6	2001
Kyrgyzstan	Undue govt influence	74.4	2000
Competitive but disorderly			
Armenia	Undue govt influence	38.8	1998
Ukraine	Undue govt influence	36.5	1999

	Parliament Vote: Biggest Party		President Vote: 1st Round Leader	
Competitive and orderly	%	*Year*	%	*Year*
Moldova	49.9	2001	not elected	
Bulgaria	42.7	2001	36.1	2001
Hungary	42.1	2002	not elected	
Poland	41.0	2001	53.9	2000
Romania	36.6	2000	36.4	2000
Czech Republic	32.3	1998	not elected	
Lithuania	31.1	2000	45.3	1997
Slovakia	27.0	1998	47.4	1999
RUSSIA	24.3	1999	52.9	2000
Estonia	23.4	1999	not elected	
Latvia	21.2	1998	not elected	

[a]*Avoided*: OSCE did not send observer missions because it judged that political conditions did not allow competitive elections to take place. [b]*Free but unfair*: e.g. heavy bias in media coverage. [c]*Undue government influence*: e.g. falsification of vote counts; harassment of opposition candidates.

Sources: OSCE election reports of Office for Democratic Institutions and Human Rights, *www.osce.org/odihr/documents/reports/election_reports/* (2 November 2001); country results from a variety of national sources.

In ten successor states of the Soviet Union, elections are either unfree, unfair or both (cf. Karatnycky et al., 2001). The percentage of votes won by the leading candidate in the first-round presidential vote indicates the extent to which the regime harasses or suppresses opponents. Turkmenistan is an extreme example of the continuance of Soviet practices. In 1992 Saparmurad Niyazov won 99.5 per cent of the reported vote in a presidential election. This was followed by a referendum

in 1994 in which 99.99 per cent of reported votes endorsed the exten-
sion of Niyazov's position as *Turkmenbashi* (leader of the Turkmens) until
2002. In six other post-Soviet successor states, three-quarters or more of
reported votes in the first ballot favour one candidate, an indication of
official intolerance of opposition.

International observer teams of the Warsaw-based Office of Democratic Institutions and Human Rights (ODIHR) of the Organization of
Security and Cooperation in Europe (OSCE) provide additional evidence
of electoral manipulation. A sure sign of unfair elections is that the OSCE
does not send observers because the national government forbids their
presence or would so restrict their work that they could not freely examine what was happening on the ground. OSCE has avoided monitoring
elections in Kazakhstan, Tajikistan, Uzbekistan and Turkmenistan, where
presidential ballots give suspiciously large shares of the vote to the incumbent. In Georgia, internal and transborder strife has prevented elections
from being held throughout the country and election administration is
sometimes unfair. In three Central Asian countries to which monitors
have been sent, OSCE teams have found that undue government influence has given a big boost to the officially favoured presidential candidate.
While election results in Armenia and Ukraine show that no candidate
wins as much as half the vote in the first-round ballot, the conduct of
campaigns is subject to undue government influence.

The Russian Federation is exceptional among post-Soviet states in
consistently holding competitive and free elections for Parliament and
the presidency. The final report of OSCE observers of the 1999 Duma
election noted that election administration 'had improved significantly
with each successive election' (*www.osce.org/odihr/elecrep-rus.htm*). Russia
can claim that its electoral practices, although not its adherence to the
rule of law, are now up to the standards of neighbouring states in Central
and Eastern Europe.

Alternative outcomes

Theories of the consolidation of new democracies are honourable in intent but deficient empirically. They assume that leaders of every new
regime are, or ought to be, striving to make their country a complete
democracy. If this were the case, then many countries could be described
as failing to democratize. But this is not the case. The leaders of a significant number of post-Communist regimes have been trying to gather
power in their own hands in undemocratic ways, and some, such as the
Turkmenbashi of Turkmenistan, have been succeeding.

Studies of democratization have taken for granted the presence of a
modern state, or assumed that the rule of law and free elections always

Table 2.3 *Profiling post-Communist regimes*

	RULE OF LAW	
	More	*Less*
ELECTIONS *Competitive*	MODERN & DEMOCRATIZING Bulgaria, Czech Republic, Estonia, Hungary, Latvia, Lithuania, Poland, Slovakia	ELECTORALIST Armenia, Moldova, Romania, RUSSIA, Ukraine
Non-competitive	AUTHORITARIAN Belarus	ARBITRARY & UNDEMOCRATIC Azerbaijan, Georgia, Kazakhstan, Kyrgyzstan, Tajikistan, Turkmenistan, Uzbekistan

Competitive: No party or presidential candidate wins half the vote; tab. 2.2.
Less corrupt: Top half of countries in fig. 2.1.

Sources: Fig. 2.1, tab. 2.2.

go together. However, we can identify four different types of regime according to the extent to which they do or do not apply the rule of law and hold free elections (tab. 2.3). Where both are present, a regime is a completely democratic modern state. This status was reached a century or more ago in some Western countries, and up to a half-century ago in others. In Central and Eastern Europe there are a minimum of eight post-Communist regimes that not only hold free, competitive elections but also accept political and civil liberties and limit corruption close to or at the level found within the European Union. At the other extreme are seven regimes that are complete in the negative sense, being arbitrary and undemocratic, including five Central Asian '-stans', Georgia and Azerbaijan. In these regimes governance is arbitrary, for the laws of the state are bent or broken by officials corrupted by a desire for money, power or both, and rulers are not accountable in free elections. To describe these post-Communist regimes as new democracies or democratizing says more about the eyesight of observers than about the character of the regimes.

Two types of post-Communist regimes are incomplete because they lack one attribute of a democratic modern state. Belarus has a stronger claim to be a modern state than to be an electoral regime, for it limits corruption by its own officials better than most post-Soviet states. However, it does not hold free elections. In 1994 Alexander Lukashenko was elected president with 80 per cent of the vote in the second-round ballot. In 1996 the Constitutional Court declared a proposed referendum on presidential authority unconstitutional, but it was held nonetheless and Lukashenko's authority was strengthened. OSCE observers described the September 2001 presidential election as failing to meet international standards because of a catalogue of abuses, including allegations of kidnapping and murder of the regime's opponents.

The Russian Federation is a paradigm example of an electoralist regime. It has held enough competitive elections to demonstrate that there is no going back to the days of a one-party state. However, this is not sufficient to make a regime a democratic modern state. Even though every election offers Russians a multiplicity of parties, the names on the ballot do not represent civil society institutions; they are ad hoc labels of convenience created by political elites. The accountability of the government to the electorate is also weak. Although Vladimir Putin was popularly elected, he entered the presidency because Boris Yeltsin had first plucked him from obscurity for appointment as prime minister and Yeltsin then resigned, making Putin the acting president of Russia. Above all, the rule of law does not bind government officials. As Archie Brown (2001a: 567) notes, to call a regime without the rule of law a democracy 'devalues the very concept'.

The direction of change in modernizing and democratizing regimes is clear, while means are flexible. Post-Communist countries seeking to join the European Union want to return to Europe in an institutional as well as a metaphorical sense. The process of vetting applications for membership in the European Union can cause disputes, but friction arises because EU officials seek to assure existing member states that each post-Communist applicant meets the standards of a modern European state (cf. Vachudova, 2000; Pridham, 2001). For the rulers of arbitrary undemocratic regimes the goal is equally clear: it is to maintain their regime as the winner of the only game in town by being the only player, and the referee as well.

To describe Russia as a case of democratization backwards suggests that the leaders of the new regime do not know when or in what form a stable order will be achieved. The ambiguities of Vladimir Putin's statements reflect this uncertainty. President Putin's goal of promoting the dictatorship of law could lead to public officials subjecting themselves to the discipline of the law, as in a modern *Rechtsstaat*. Alternatively, it could lead to a constitutional dictatorship with elections irrelevant to the practice of government. A third alternative is that it could lead to frustration, if Vladimir Putin finds the challenge of modernizing an anti-modern state is too great.

3   What Russians have made of transformation

Russians have always lived in a very political economy. In the Soviet era political decisions were all-important, for the economy was subordinate to commands of the party-state. Decisions about where you worked, where you lived, and what you could buy were taken by public officials in the first instance. Few Russians could afford to appear apolitical, as the Communist Party regarded this as a political act. The turbulent transformation of a command economy into an imperfect market economy has forced every household to think afresh about politics and economics.

In Soviet times it was impossible to know whether there was a match between what the party-state supplied and what people wanted. As long as citizens complied with its demands, the party-state maintained its equilibrium. Thanks to the freedom of the Russian Federation, the old regime can now be evaluated retrospectively. Hence, this chapter's first section asks: how good were the old Soviet days – at the time and in retrospect?

The transformation of Russian society has given Russians such unaccustomed boons as being free to say what they think or, even better, to ignore politics and get on with their own lives without regard to what the party thinks. Insecurity has also increased. Russians have been shocked to find that the rubles they had saved when goods were in short supply can no longer buy goods now on offer in the market economy, because inflation has increased prices thousands of times. A majority of Russians are fearful of crime on the street or of their house being broken into, and worry about whether wages due will be paid at the end of each month. The second section of the chapter reports how people have been coping since transformation; the evidence shows big gains in freedom, but many economic costs.

Whether the new Russian regime is viewed positively depends on the standards by which it is evaluated. If the administration of Russia under President Yeltsin is compared with the way an ideal democracy is supposed to work, Russia will be found wanting. But comparing the new Federation with the Soviet party-state anchors judgments in realities familiar to Russians. Moreover, if the new regime is compared with alternative regimes, such as rule by a strong man or a reversion to the Communist system, Russians who regard the new regime as unsatisfactory can then show whether or not they regard it as preferable to undemocratic alternatives.

While the scope for choice has expanded greatly at elections and in the marketplace, the extent of choice differs between politics and economics. In the marketplace, Russians can choose between domestic and foreign products, and preferences differ with the product. On election day, the choice of parties is confined to what Russian politicians supply. The third section compares Russian responses to the new regime with realistic as well as idealistic alternatives. It shows a mismatch between the regime that Russia's political elites have supplied and the regime that Russians would like.

This chapter principally reports evidence from the seventh New Russia Barometer survey conducted between 6 March and 13 April 1998. By that time the impact of President Yeltsin's changes was very evident and public opinion was not affected by preparations for the following year's election campaign. By the standards of transformation, the situation was *normalno*, for a big majority of Russians were telling VTsIOM interviewers that they regarded the situation as tense or critical. In chapter 10 we compare replies in the seventh NRB survey to those in the tenth NRB survey in order to see how much or how little impact the Putin presidency has had on evaluations of how Russia is ruled.

How good were the good old days?

In the Soviet era the writing and rewriting of history made Russians sceptical of what was outside their own experience or what older family members were willing to tell them about experiences in Stalin's time. At the time the Soviet Union broke up, the median Russian adult was born toward the end of Stalin's rule; today, the median Russian was born a decade later and socialized after Leonid Brezhnev assumed power in 1964. Political indoctrination at school started by stressing the virtues of Lenin, lightly touching on Stalin's lengthy time in office and then praising the current leader of the glorious Soviet state. By remaining in office for 18 years, Brezhnev made himself a symbol of an era. That era can now be seen as the last normal period in Soviet life, since it was followed by Mikhail Gorbachev's disruptive initiatives.

In retrospect, many Russians see the time of Brezhnev as a golden era, for Soviet institutions were at their most stable and the relaxation of Stalinist pressures made the regime more bearable because it was

Figure 3.1 IN RETROSPECT, THE SOVIET REGIME LOOKS GOOD.

Q. Here is a scale for evaluating the political system. The top, plus 100, is the best and the bottom, minus 100, is the worst. Where on this scale would you put the political system we had before perestroika?

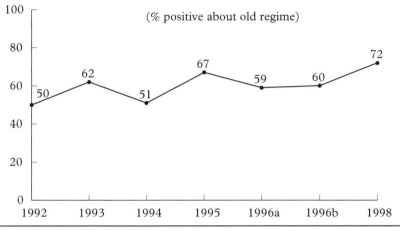

Source: New Russia Barometer I–VII, 1992–8.

post-totalitarian. To assess what Russians think about this period, the New Russia Barometer asks for an evaluation of the pre-perestroika regime on a scale in which plus 100 is the best and minus 100 is the worst. Consistently, a substantial majority give the old Soviet regime a positive rating (fig. 3.1). Moreover, the proportion giving a positive rating has been rising; in 1992 only 50 per cent were positive about the old political system, but by the seventh NRB survey 72 per cent were positive about the Brezhnev-era regime, 9 per cent neutral and 18 per cent negative.

However, an examination of what actually happened under Brezhnev emphasizes that the system had many undesirable characteristics:

Patron–client relationships, which had always been a feature of Soviet political life, flourished as never before, while corruption grew in response to the lessening of the fear of retribution and to the loss of belief in the ultimate goals of the system. If the Brezhnev era was both politically and socially the most stable of all periods of Soviet history, it was also the most cynical (Brown, 1994a: 125).

For a Russian who wanted to see progress (and Mikhail Gorbachev was one example), the stagnation that characterized the Brezhnev era was a source of frustration. Moreover, the political hardening of the arteries that characterized the era stored up troubles that contributed to the subsequent collapse of the Soviet regime (Winiecki, 1988; Roeder, 1993).

Evidence about living conditions in the Brezhnev era is bedevilled by multiple deficiencies in Soviet statistics; they range from non-reporting of data to misleading or false reporting. For example, the measure of output in the Soviet economy, net material product, was not intended to be nor was it the same as gross domestic product (see Marer et al., 1992). Official statistics of the Soviet economy were often interpreted as evidence of economic strength, and Soviet sympathizers viewed the guarantee of jobs for all as evidence of economic success rather than as a sign of enterprises inefficiently hoarding and wasting labour. Given the limitations of Soviet economic data, for a measure of wellbeing under Brezhnev we turn to statistics about life and death.

While Russians led a quieter life in the Brezhnev era, they did not live longer (fig. 3.2). According to official Russian statistics, shortly after Brezhnev arrived in office the average Russian man could expect to live 64.3 years, and the average Russian woman 73.4 years. By 1981–2, when the geriatric Brezhnev died in office, official statistics reported that Russian male life expectancy had *fallen* by 2.3 years and that of Russian women had risen by only one-tenth of a year (Boutenko and Razlogov, 1997: 9; cf. Anderson and Silver, 1986; Meslé et al., 1992).

The cost in human life of Brezhnev-era stagnation is shown by comparing trends in Russia with advanced capitalist societies. In 1965 there was a difference of 3.8 years between the life expectancy of Russian men and its average in eight major Western societies, including the United States, Germany, Japan and Sweden. By 1970 the gap had widened to 5.5 years, because life expectancy had risen in modern societies with markets and democracy while it had fallen in Russia; by 1975 the gap had widened to 7.4 years. By the time Brezhnev died, the average Russian man had a shorter life than when Nikita Khrushchev had left office; by contrast, men in Western societies were living more than three years longer. During the Brezhnev period the gap in male life expectancy between Russia and the West more than doubled to 9.5 years.

Material measures of growth show that Russians were making progress, yet simultaneously falling behind their neighbours. Immediately after the Second World War a car was a luxury good throughout Europe; for example, in the Federal Republic of Germany in 1950, there were only 13 cars per 1,000 people. With increased prosperity, car ownership has steadily risen in Western Europe. Within command economies the rise in car ownership was dramatic too. Between 1960 and 1989 car ownership increased more than 40 times in Hungary, 30 times in Poland and 11 times in Czechoslovakia and in East Germany. For decades after the Second

Figure 3.2 RUSSIAN MALE LIFE EXPECTANCY IN THE BREZHNEV ERA.

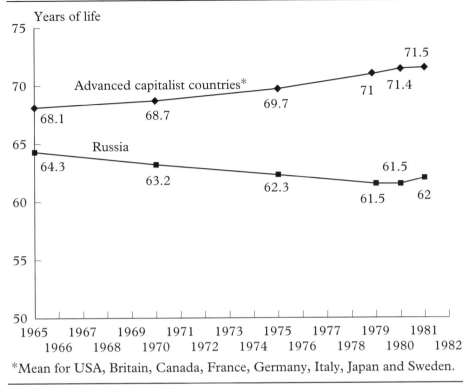

*Mean for USA, Britain, Canada, France, Germany, Italy, Japan and Sweden.

Source: Irene A. Boutenko and Kirill E. Razlogov, *Recent Social Trends in Russia, 1960–1995*, Montreal: McGill-Queen's University Press, 1997, p. 9; OECD, *OECD Health Systems: Facts and Trends, 1960–1991*, Paris: OECD Health Policy Studies no. 3, vol. I, 1993, table 3.1.2. Because of inconsistencies in years in reporting OECD data, the nearest year is taken when compiling averages.

World War no figures were published about car ownership in Russia and the few who regularly used a car often took one from an official car pool. When car ownership statistics were first published in 1980, there were 30 cars per 1,000 Russians, less than half the number in Poland and even fewer than in East Germany. At the time the Berlin Wall fell, car ownership in Russia had risen to 58 per 1,000, but remained less than half that in Poland, a quarter the level of car ownership in East Germany and one-seventh that in West Germany (cf. Boutenko and Razlogov, 1997: 7, 20; Rose, 1999b: 187ff.). The widening gap in living standards was not due just to a lower starting point, for in the same period Japan had been transformed from a poor and defeated dictatorship to a modern state with far healthier citizens (Eberstadt, 1999).

Even when nominal Soviet growth rates appeared high, the quality of the goods produced by monopoly firms in a command economy was usually lower than in competitive markets. For example, when the fourth New Russia Barometer survey asked in 1995 whether people would prefer a Russian or a Japanese colour television set, the question had to be posed in terms of buying a Russian set or paying twice as much for a Japanese colour television set. Even so, more than two-thirds of Russians under the age of 60 said they would rather pay twice as much in order to watch television on a Japanese set.

Coping with a disorderly society

Russians have to work hard to cope with a disorderly political economy when the alternatives are destitution or death. In trying to cope, people draw on skills developed in the Soviet era and learn new tricks to meet the challenges and opportunities of transformation. Most Russians are much more concerned with the exigencies of everyday life, such as getting enough to live on and occasional treats, than with deciding how to vote every fourth year.

Freedom but not much law

In an established democracy, individual freedom is grounded in the supremacy of laws that give citizens rights and confer restrictions on governors. By contrast, in Russia freedom is grounded in the weakness of a state unable to enforce laws. While a weak state avoids interfering with individual activities and offers much scope for the non-payment of taxes, it also increases the likelihood of crime in the streets and theft in government ministries.

The first freedom – freedom from the state – was gained by citizens of most Western countries a century before gaining the right to vote (Berlin, 1958). However, in tsarist and Soviet times Russians did not enjoy freedoms taken for granted in countries where civil society flourished under the rule of law. Unlike efforts to transform the economy, reducing repressive actions by public officials is not expensive in money terms – but it does deprive officials of power. In pursuit of the goal of destroying the power of the Communist Party, the Yeltsin administration repealed most of the repressive laws and practices of the Soviet era.

In a civic democracy participation in politics is valued, but in a post-Communist society freedom is the right *not* to be involved in politics. This choice did not exist when the Communist Party made political participation compulsory. To measure the extent to which people feel freer due

Table 3.1 *A greater sense of freedom from the state*

Q. Compared to our system of government before perestroika, would you say that our current system is better, much the same, or not so good as the old system in the following respects:

	Better %	Same %	Worse %	Difference better–worse %
Everybody has freedom of choice in religious matters	79	16	5	74
One can join any organization one likes	75	18	7	68
Everybody has a right to say what they think	73	21	6	67
Everyone can decide individually whether or not to take an interest in politics	66	27	7	59

Source: New Russia Barometer VII. Nationwide survey, 6 March–13 April 1998. Number of respondents, 1,904.

to the change in regimes, the New Russia Barometer asks people to compare their current freedom to engage in everyday activities with what it was in the Soviet era. Consistently, Russians report a much greater sense of freedom today; in the seventh New Russia Barometer an average of 73 per cent said they had greater freedom from the state than before (tab. 3.1). A total of 79 per cent feel freer than before to decide for themselves about religion; 75 per cent feel freer than before to join organizations of their choice; 73 per cent feel freer to say what they think; and 66 per cent feel freer to decide for themselves whether or not to participate in politics. Hardly anyone believes the state has more control of their lives than before, and across four indicators an average of one in five think the new regime has made no change in freedom from the state.

Transformation has also caused people many troubles, and consistent with the logic of political accountability Russians blame their rulers for this. In the NRB survey immediately after the 1996 presidential election, 74 per cent blamed the government for economic problems, 65 per cent blamed President Yeltsin and 60 per cent blamed Yegor Gaidar, the minister most identified with promoting the market. By contrast, only 8 per cent blamed Jews, and 22 per cent blamed foreign governments for their economic problems.

Casting blame is not enough; in a democratic political system citizens should also be able to influence those held accountable for bad government. But Russians have been very sceptical about the extent to which the new regime is responsive to their views. In the seventh NRB survey, only 4 per cent said that people like themselves can influence the state of affairs in Russia as a whole. Even more striking, 46 per cent thought that ordinary people have less influence on Russian government now than in Soviet times, while only 9 per cent said they had more influence; 45 per cent felt that popular influence on government had not changed.

Even though Boris Yeltsin twice won popular majorities at election time, he and his officials were distrusted by an overwhelming majority of citizens. In the 1998 NRB survey, only 14 per cent trusted the president, 13 per cent trusted the Duma and 7 per cent trusted political parties. The distrust was also reflected in only 7 per cent thinking that the national government, most of the time, looked after the interests of people like themselves. Similarly, only 13 per cent thought that local government usually looked after their interests.

Distrust of government is grounded in observations of the regime's behaviour. Like alcoholism, crime and corruption were chronic problems in the Soviet era. From time to time, the Communist regime announced crime-busting crusades, and people accused of crimes were normally convicted and imprisoned. Party officials too were occasionally singled out for punishment for corruption. The high standard of living enjoyed by top party and government officials was regarded as *normalno*. The powerful lived differently from ordinary people because they were privileged.

A majority of Russians are now fearful of crime. When the seventh NRB survey asked if people feel safe when out on the streets, 57 per cent said they did not. When people were asked whether they worried about thieves breaking into their house, 51 per cent said that they did. Moreover, people feel less secure than in Soviet times. A total of 53 per cent felt less safe on the streets than before and 36 per cent reported no change, while only 11 per cent feel safer on the streets than in the Soviet era. The fears that Russians have of crime are based on personal experience as well as media reports (fig. 3.3). In the previous two years, 17 per cent had been a victim of a street theft or had had a family member robbed on the street. In addition, 7 per cent had had their house broken into and some had been robbed both on the street and at home. At home, 23 per cent had friends who had been victims of crime on the street and 30 per cent had had a friend whose house had been burgled. Altogether, a fifth of Russians had been victims of crime or had had a family member victimized and a third had had friends who were victims of crime. A majority of Russians are directly or indirectly affected by crime.

The collapse of the Soviet regime demoralized law-enforcement officials as well as other state employees. Simultaneously, the wild privatization of the economy created a demand from the newly rich for private security firms offering armed protection against competitors and

Figure 3.3 EXPERIENCE OF CRIME.

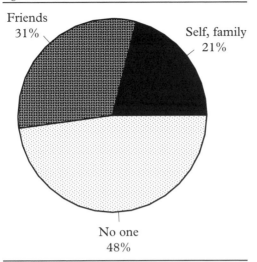

Friends
31%

Self, family
21%

No one
48%

Source: New Russia Barometer VII. Nationwide survey, 6 March–13 April 1998. Number of respondents, 1,904. Combined replies to questions on experience of street crime and burglary.

criminal gangs. Private security firms recruited tens of thousands of people with commando-style training in Soviet armed forces and the police. The new rich also sought protection from the law, offering employees in law-enforcement agencies the opportunity to augment meagre salaries by selling immunity from tax investigations or prosecution. In Moscow the deputy head of the office responsible for investigating crime estimated that from 60 to 80 per cent of all state-employed criminal investigators received bribes (Gordon B. Smith, 2001: 119; see also Frisby, 1998; Shelley, 2001).

When citizens assume bribes and connections are necessary to get things done, the rule of law is undermined by their behaviour as well as by that of public officials. Confronted with corrupt governors who do not enforce the law or who actively cooperate with corrupt businesses and organized criminal gangs, ordinary people lose a sense of obligation to obey the law. If everybody is doing it, it takes a strong conscience to be different and obey all laws. When the New Russia Barometer asked about tax evasion, 56 per cent said there was no need to pay taxes, for the government would never find out if you didn't pay. An additional quarter thought that, if officials did find out that a person was evading taxes, the official could be bought off. Only 17 per cent believed the Russian government collected taxes honestly and effectively. In desperation the government created an armed tax police in the belief, stated by then prime minister Sergei Kirienko, 'If the state does not learn to collect taxes, it will cease to exist' (quoted in Gregory and Brooke, 2000: 453).

When public officials fail to deliver services with the predictability and impersonal fairness of Weber's 'vending machine' bureaucracy, most Russians are not passive. When asked what a person should do if a government office fails to issue a required permit, only one-fifth say that nothing can be done. Few believe that writing a letter or telephoning to inquire what is happening is sufficient to get public officials to act. The most common strategy, endorsed by 38 per cent, is to use connections to get action, and 32 per cent recommend giving officials a bribe or a present to get what they want.

While appreciating freedom from state interference in everyday life, Russians know that it is not freedom under the law. When asked how close the national government comes to the idea of a law-governed state (*pravovoe gosudarstvo*), 71 per cent say the country is not governed by the rule of law, 24 per cent think it is to some extent law-governed and only 5 per cent believe it very closely approximates this ideal. To paraphrase an old Soviet-era expression about wages and work, most Russians believe that 'The government pretends to enforce the law, and we pretend to obey it.'

Getting by – with or without money

When the Russian Federation came into being, the Soviet-era saying that socialism was the longest path from capitalism to capitalism was no longer a joke. During Boris Yeltsin's years in office, official statistics about the Russian economy showed an extremely gloomy picture, as the gross domestic product contracted instead of expanding. Since each year's decrease was added to what had gone before, the cumulative effect was enormous. From the start of 1992 to the end of 1998 the official gross domestic product was reckoned to have contracted by two-fifths (fig. 3.3). While all post-Communist countries showed some contraction in their official national product, the decline in Russia was far greater than that in Central and Eastern Europe. In Poland, for example, the official economy, as measured in zlotys, contracted by 7 per cent between 1990 and 1991 and then started expanding steadily. In Russia, after a sharp fall between 1991 and 1995 the economy began to decline much more slowly.

The move from a command to a market economy was bound to lead to increases in the nominal price of goods, because in the Soviet economy barter, connections and shortages rather than prices controlled supply

Figure 3.4 ECONOMY CONTRACTED WHILE PRICES ZOOMED.

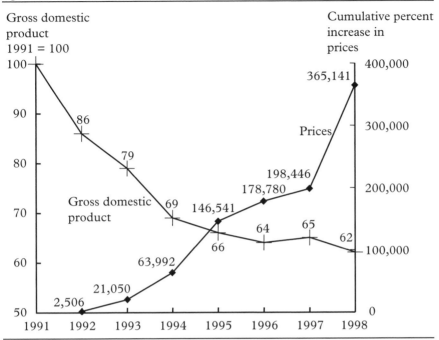

Source: EBRD, *Transition Report Update, April 2001* (London: EBRD, 2001), p. 15; EBRD, *Transition Report 2000* (London: EBRD, 2000), p. 205.

and demand. In the first year of the Russian Federation, prices went up by an estimated 2500 per cent. In the second year, prices only (!) went up by 875 per cent. However, because the effect of inflation is cumulative, this meant that goods costing one ruble at the beginning of 1991 cost more than 21,000 rubles by the end of 1992. The annual rate of inflation then began to slow down, reaching only 48 per cent in 1996, and remaining in double digits since then. But ordinary Russians did not regard this as good news, for each year's annual inflation rate is added to price increases that went before, and people remember what prices were before inflation took off.

No Russian household has been immune from the economic effects of transformation. Russians have been more likely to go unpaid while nominally in employment than when nominally unemployed. This perverse effect has arisen because many enterprises have responded to transformation by engaging in elaborate barter arrangements in an effort to keep active. Barter is used to avoid the need to pay cash for supplies and customers are allowed to offer goods instead of cash for payment. When an enterprise is short of cash, workers are not paid when they should be or are offered goods that the factory has produced itself or obtained through barter. In the seventh New Russia Barometer, 63 per cent reported that they had had wages delayed or not paid at all during the past year. Among those paid late or not at all, loss of earnings was most likely to occur among public employees, such as teachers, nurses and workers in state-owned enterprises. Even in the new private sector about half were sometimes paid late or not at all.

Amidst the turbulence of transformation, debates about the merits of competing policies for turning Russia into a market economy had no more meaning to ordinary Russians than Soviet disputes about the theories of Lenin or Hilferding. For the great majority of Russians, the priority has not been to get rich but to get by, that is, to cope with transformation's consequences. For a household the critical issue is whether it can get through the year without borrowing money or spending savings. In an inflationary period, savings soon disappear. However, while most Russians reckon that they can borrow money from their friends, this cannot be done indefinitely. Nor can everyone in a society be borrowing money at the same time, and in cities where the largest employer is not paying its workers, friends might lack money too.

When the first NRB survey asked people if they had managed to get through 1991 without spending savings or borrowing money, 62 per cent said that they had done so. When the same question was asked in 1998, virtually the same proportion, 63 per cent, had got by, including 10 per cent who reported saving money. When the same question is asked in Britain or in Austria, four-fifths report that they can get by without borrowing or spending savings in a year, while a fifth, such as students, the unemployed, the sick or partners in a messy divorce, do not. In a market economy the great majority of people who get by do so from earnings in their regular job. This is not the case in Russia: people need to juggle a portfolio of economies to get by.

The secret of coping with transformation is not to rely exclusively on the official economy. Official statistics about the Russian economy are half-truths, for they leave out many activities that Russians rely on to produce what they need. As in a command economy, people rely on a multiplicity of economies, official and unofficial. The household offers a form of social protection, for in the average household there are two people of working age and, therefore, two incomes if people are paid on time. If they are not, then one family member may receive wages while the other does not. If there is a grandparent in the house, this is the source of a third income, a pension. Nearly everyone is involved in social economies, exchanging help with friends. A minority are also involved in uncivil economies, earning cash in hand that is not officially recorded and taxed. Cashless social economies are more important than uncivil economies, because it is hard to earn money in the second economy when few people have money to put in your hand.

Russians differ in how they combine resources in order to get by. A majority, 56 per cent in the seventh NRB survey, tried to get by with a defensive portfolio, combining an official job with what can be produced without money in the household and with friends. One in seven were enterprising, combining income from the official economy with cash-in-hand earnings from uncivil economic activity. Anyone relying solely on the official economy was vulnerable; a sixth of Russians were in that category. The remainder were marginal, not relying on an unofficial or official money economy.

In the Yeltsin years, Russian households were feeling the pinch of trans-formation, and a majority found their living standards had fallen since the introduction of the market. But a fall in living standards does not necessarily make people destitute. Destitution is a matter of duration, the consequence of often doing without basic necessities, such as food, cloth-ing and heat and electricity. The most fortunate Russians have adapted, finding ways to avoid going without basic necessities during the year (Rose, 1995a). In the spring 1998 NRB survey, 23 per cent had adapted, never or hardly ever doing without basic necessities. For the majority, resilience is the best strategy: if you are pushed under from time to time, be sure to come back up. In total, 67 per cent are resilient, occasionally doing without necessities. If there is no money in the house to buy new clothes, then old clothes are patched until something better is obtained. If there is not enough money for meat on Sunday, then a meal can be made of potatoes and vegetables; if there is no money for meat the fol-lowing Sunday, one can try to get sausages from a friend, trap a rabbit or catch fish. In 1998 only 1 per cent of Russians often went without food, clothing and either electricity or heat, and people often going with-out two of the three basic necessities – food, clothing and energy – were 11 per cent of the sample.

The proportion of Russians prospering from economic transformation is greater than those who are without any standard consumer durable goods or are destitute. The seventh New Russia Barometer found that 18 per cent had at least three durable consumer goods – a colour TV, car, video cassette recorder or personal computer – compared to 13 per cent who had none. Ownership of a VCR is particularly revealing of economic change, since they did not come into Russian shops until after the market was introduced. The 37 per cent of households with a VCR have sufficient disposable income to afford more than just the necessities of life.

Figure 3.5 IMPACT OF THE MARKET ON LIVING STANDARDS.

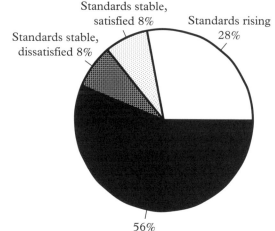

56%
Standards falling

Standards rising: Current economic situation much better or somewhat better now than five years ago. Standards stable, satisfied: Current economic situation the same now compared with five years ago AND respondent satisfied with current economic situation. Standards stable, dissatisfied: Current economic situation the same now compared with five years ago AND respondent not satisfied with current economic situation. Standards falling: Current economic situation a lot worse or a little worse now than five years ago.

Source: New Russia Barometer VII. Nationwide survey, 6 March–13 April 1998. Number of respondents, 1,904.

A half-dozen years after the move to the market commenced, its impact divided Russians (fig. 3.5). Even though subject to temporary shocks, 36 per cent found their family's standard of living rising or stable and satisfactory. On the other hand, 56 per cent reported that their living standards had fallen since the move from a command to a market economy, and an additional 8 per cent were dissatisfied because their standard of living was unchanged. In short, the median Russian was coping with transformation, but economically dissatisfied.

Regimes: matching supply and demand

In Soviet times there could be no mismatch between what the government wanted and what the people wanted, for the party-state determined both. Governors did not need to run opinion polls or focus groups to ask people whether they preferred guns or butter, or wanted to buy Soviet or Western goods. The party knew what was best; anyone who challenged the party line was, by definition, politically deviant. Mikhail Gorbachev opened up to public debate disagreements between leaders about what the party line ought to be. While this undermined the party's claim to know what the people wanted, there was no agreement about how Russia ought to be governed by a post-Communist regime.

In democratic theory government is demand-driven, providing what the people want. In established democracies, public opinion polls are frequently cited as evidence of what the people want, on the assumption that this is what the government of the day ought to supply. If citizens want democratic governance, then governors should supply it. However, in a political system that is only partly democratic, the link between what people want and what government does is problematic, for governors cannot effectively be held to account by voters or institutions of civil society. However, if the populace is much more or much less democratic in outlook than governors, this mismatch may be treated as a sign of underlying political instability.

Democratic ideal and Russian reality

When Russians are asked what they think is essential or important to make government democratic, replies show very widespread agreement that democracy has two major dimensions. One dimension is about political values:

Equality of all citizens before the law	97%
A choice of candidates and parties at each election	85%
There is freedom to criticize government	81%
You don't have to do what politicians say if you don't want to	80%

Democracy also symbolizes economic welfare:

The country is economically prosperous	97%
Government guarantees all citizens a minimum income	94%

Viewing democracy in terms of economic as well as political values is widespread throughout post-Communist societies (Simon, 1998).

When Russian people are asked how democratic they would like their government to be, replies show a strong popular demand for democratic rule (fig. 3.6). On a 10-point scale measuring preferences from complete democracy to complete dictatorship, 36 per cent give the strongest possible endorsement to democracy as an ideal. Altogether, 72 per cent show a positive preference for democratic rule and an additional 13 per cent place themselves at the scale's psychological mid-point, 5. Only 15 per cent of Russians are inclined to favour dictatorship.

Figure 3.6 DEMAND FOR AND SUPPLY OF DEMOCRACY.

Q. Here is a scale ranging from 1 to 10, where 1 means complete dictatorship and 10 means complete democracy.

    a. Where would you place our country at the present time?

    b. And where would you personally like our country to be placed?

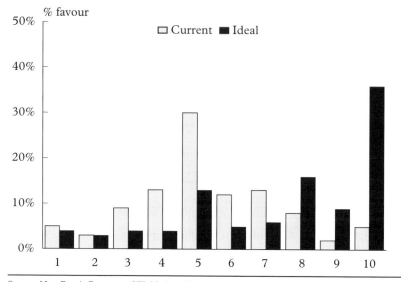

Source: New Russia Barometer VII. Nationwide survey, 6 March–13 April 1998. Number of respondents, 1,904. Mean evaluation of current regime: 5.3; mean preference for democracy as an ideal: 7.4.

The gap between demand and supply is evident when the same scale is used to evaluate the system of government as it actually is. The largest bloc, 30 per cent, place the current regime at the psychological mid-point, 5. A total of 40 per cent describe the regime as more democratic than dictatorial, while 30 per cent see it as closer to dictatorship. There is a gap of more than two points between the mean evaluation for democracy as an ideal and the mean evaluation of the regime as it actually was in Boris Yeltsin's time.

In theory, the gap between how people see their regime and what they would like it to be could cause frustration. However, the electoralist nature of the Russian regime means that it is not completely undemocratic, and the increase in freedoms offers opportunities for citizens to voice demands for improving an incompletely democratic system (cf. Gurr, 1970; Rose, Shin and Munro, 1999). However, Russians have been socialized into a world in which the patient endurance of the powers that be has been a prudential virtue (cf. Rose, 1997). Since the creation of the Russian Federation people have not come out into the streets in massive protests against the political and economic shortcomings of the new system. The Churchill hypothesis offers an explanation for why people will tolerate a far-from-satisfactory new regime. Shortly after the end of the Second World War, Winston Churchill (1947) argued that democratic governance, even if it has faults, remains preferable as a lesser evil:

Many forms of government have been tried and will be tried in this world of sin and woe. No one pretends that democracy is perfect or all wise. Indeed, it has been said that democracy is the worst form of government except all those other forms that have been tried from time to time.

Where democratic rule has been long established, surveys often ask people to evaluate their regime by asking, *On the whole, are you very satisfied, fairly satisfied, not very satisfied or not at all satisfied with the way democracy works in your country?* Such a question is unsuitable in Russia (and in many other post-Communist countries) because it presupposes that citizens see their new regime as democratic when this is not the case. An international rating of regimes by Freedom House describes Russia as partly democratic (Karatnycky et al., 2001), an assessment consistent with the views of most Russians.

Given the gap between what the regime is and democratic ideals, the New Russia Barometer does not make the mistake of describing the current regime as democratic. It simply points to the present regime and invites Russians to say what they think of what they are experiencing. The use of a scale ranging from minus 100 to plus 100 makes it possible to discriminate between regimes that are bad (minus 25), worse (minus 50) and the worst possible system of government (minus 100). It also allows people to identify regimes as good (plus 25) and better (plus 50). Those who are indifferent or of two minds can register this opinion by placing a regime at the mid-point of the scale, zero.

From its inception, Russians have divided in their views of their new regime (fig. 3.7). Those negative have always outnumbered those positive, but the gap has tended to narrow. When the first NRB survey was conducted at the beginning of the Russian Federation in 1992, only 14 per cent were positive and almost three-quarters were negative, with the third group neutral. In the seventh NRB survey, 36 per cent gave the current system of government a positive rating while 48 per cent were negative. Except for 1992, the median respondent has been neutral about the new regime, placing it at the zero mid-point.

When evaluations of the old and new regimes are combined (cf. figs. 3.1, 3.7), a plurality of respondents in the seventh NRB survey appear

Figure 3.7 LIMITED APPROVAL OF CURRENT REGIME.

Q. Here is a scale for evaluating the political system. The top, plus 100, is the best and the bottom, minus 100, is the worst. Where on this scale would you put our current political system?

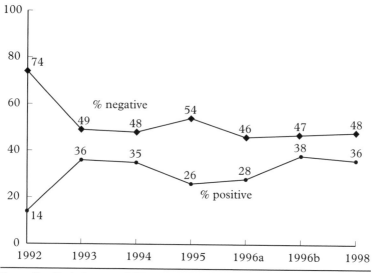

Source: New Russia Barometer I–VII, 1992–8.

nostalgic; 46 per cent are not only positive about the Soviet system that governed before perestroika but also negative about the new Russian Federation. The second largest group appears compliant; a positive view of both past and present regimes was taken by 26 per cent. An additional 18 per cent were doubly dubious, giving a negative assessment to both the old and the new regimes. At that time, only 10 per cent appeared firm supporters of change, giving a positive rating to the new regime and a negative rating to the old.

Undemocratic alternatives

While many Russians are negative about their current system of government, they do not agree about any alternative that would be better. When asked about three historically familiar alternatives – a return to a Communist regime, having the army rule or turning to a dictator – none was endorsed by a majority (fig. 3.8). Two in five said it would be better to restore the Communist regime, but this was barely half the proportion positive about the country's pre-perestroika regime. In any event, a return

Figure 3.8 EVALUATION OF UNDEMOCRATIC ALTERNATIVES.

Q. There are different opinions about the nature of the state. To what extent would you agree with the following statements:
   a. It would be better to restore the Communist system
   b. The army should govern the country
   c. We should restore the tsar
   d. A tough dictatorship is the only way out of the current situation

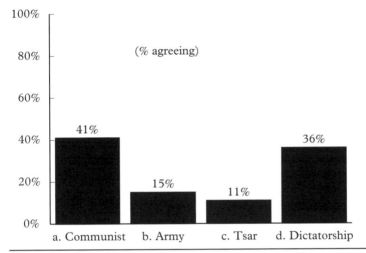

Source: New Russia Barometer VII. Nationwide survey, 6 March–13 April 1998. Number of respondents, 1,904.

to the status quo ante is not possible, for the Communist system was brought into being by the First World War and a civil war, and secured by purges and by terror. The Communist Party of the Russian Federation lacks the ideological will to carry out such measures (cf. Rose, 1996a). Nor is a return to Leninist rule what Russians had in mind when endorsing a golden past. The point is underscored by the fact that when the opportunity to vote Communists back into power is offered, up to three-quarters vote against the candidates of the Communist Party.

When asked about a tough dictatorship, 36 per cent of Russians endorse the prospect. The strongly presidentialist character of the 1993 Yeltsin constitution would require few breaches or amendments for a president to suspend the Duma and cancel elections. However, after the shelling of the White House in October 1993, the Kremlin as well as its critics have avoided pushing disputes to the point of disorder. A second obstacle to dictatorship is that there is neither agreement among political elites about who would be a desirable dictator, nor popular support for a particular strong man. In the years between presidential elections, various personalities have projected a strong-man image, most notably the demagogic nationalist leader Vladimir Zhirinovsky, and a general turned politician, Alexander Lebed. Each has been an also-ran in presidential elections. The individuals drawing support in the VTsIOM monthly popularity polls are almost invariably politicians committed to the electoral process. Vladimir Putin endorses order rather than appealing as a charismatic personality who will turn the system upside down again.

Military dictatorships have been a common form of undemocratic rule in Latin America and in Africa, but not in Russian history. The Soviet tradition of civilian (that is, Communist Party) control of the military has meant that Russian military commanders have concentrated on bureaucratic politics, lobbying for their collective organizational interests, such as salaries, privileges and prestige, rather than plotting to seize government. The pressures to concentrate on organizational interests have increased as morale and integrity have declined with transformation (Reese, 2000; Zisk, 2001). In any event, generals are peculiarly unsuited to deal with problems of economic transformation, as they usually lack both the skills and the money that financial oligarchs command. The seventh NRB survey found that the Russian Army was more trusted, or at least less distrusted, than other major institutions of society: 34 per cent trusted the Army, as against 44 per cent distrusting it; the median Russian was neutral. However, barely one in seven said that they wanted to see the Army take control of government.

The tsar is a familiar figure in Russian history, having ruled the country far longer than the Communist Party of the Soviet Union. Cultural theories of Russian politics have sought to find similarities between the tsar as a father or leader figure and successive Communist Party secretaries or even President Yeltsin. The knowledge that Russians today have of the tsar is drawn from proverbial sayings or from Soviet histories; it is the stuff of myth rather than experience. The myth has little practical relevance. Only a tenth of Russians say that they would like to restore the tsar.

Collectively, Russian attitudes toward regimes have been inconclusive. While more Russians have been negative than positive about the new regime, the same is true of attitudes toward undemocratic alternatives. None of the four undemocratic alternatives reported in figure 3.8 is endorsed by as many as half the people. The current regime's claim to be not too bad or at least a lesser evil is supported by three-fifths to nine-tenths of Russians rejecting alternative forms of rule. Furthermore, the reaction against the Communist-led coup of August 1991 and the president's storming of parliament in October 1993 shows a strong aversion among most of the political elite to introducing a new regime by unconstitutional and potentially bloody means.

There was, however, a mismatch between the government that the Russian people would like to have and the regime that Boris Yeltsin supplied. But a disequilibrium between idealistic demands and unsatisfactory reality need not be a foretoken of collapse. The Republic of Italy shows that a new regime with imperfect commitment to the rule of law can survive for more than half a century, notwithstanding red–black polarization between a Catholic party and a Communist one in the 1950s, violent challenges from the right and left in the 1970s, the collapse of an established party system in the 1990s and high levels of corruption and distrust of politicians throughout.

As Boris Yeltsin's period in office neared its end, Russia's political elite appeared to share the sentiments of the electorate that the current regime, for better and for worse, was the only game in town. The central issue for political elites was no longer how Russia ought to be ruled or how to put the clock back to a one-party state. It was who would hold power in the new regime. Above all, this was the crucial question for those in the Kremlin who had benefited most by supplying Russia with a regime that chose its president by popular election but was not a regime governing by the rule of law.

4 Presidential succession: a Family problem

Transferring control of a new regime from the leader who founded it to a successor is a critical political moment, for it shows whether the regime is personal, ending when its leader leaves the scene, as in Franco Spain, or whether it has continuity independent of its founder, for example the People's Republic of China. As Boris Yeltsin's second term moved toward its close, the critical issue was whether his successor would be the second president of the Russian Federation or the first head of a new regime. Boris Yeltsin's reliance on *vlast* made it uncertain how the transfer of power would occur.

President Yeltsin surrounded himself with a Family of loyal supporters who had as much at stake as he had, for when he left office their access to political power would expire. Its members tended to be people who in an earlier era would have sought to be close to the tsar. A family of close personal advisors is familiar in other countries, for example Tony's cronies in Blair's Downing Street or the Kennedy clan in the White House. However, in modern states personal favouritism is constrained by strong laws and norms missing in the Russian Federation.

Inside the Kremlin, President Yeltsin had a changing set of favourites, some valued for their political or technical expertise, others as companions on the tennis court or in drinking sessions, and some because their loyalty was unquestionable, such as Boris Yeltsin's younger daughter, Tatyana Dyachenko, a campaign consultant in 1996 and appointed to the Kremlin post of media consultant the following year. Members of the Family were linked with the oligarchs who financed Yeltsin's 1996 election campaign and the state itself. While the oligarchs often quarrelled with each other and battled with different members of the Family, they agreed in wanting the best president that money could buy.

As Boris Yeltsin's time in office approached its end, the question of succession was of growing concern to the Yeltsin Family, and to oligarchs too. Once he left the Kremlin, their political influence could plummet, and their wealth too. A new president might deprive oligarchs of their property or even their liberty through criminal prosecutions. In Yeltsin's second term, investigations by the prosecutor general, Yury Skuratov, and by the state auditor had threatened to publicize evidence incriminating the Family and its oligarchic supporters in criminal fraud or worse.

For Boris Yeltsin, the interests of those around him were secondary to looking after his own interests. An upbringing in the rough-and-tumble school of Communist politics made him suspicious of would-be friends as well as of proclaimed enemies. Yeltsin's seemingly erratic behaviour was sometimes a cover for unexpected tactical moves, such as sacking those who he judged were trying to use their position at his expense. In the midst of the 1996 election campaign, he even sacked Alexander Korzhakov, director of the Kremlin security services and a drinking companion with whom Yeltsin had twice sworn oaths of blood brotherhood.

The charismatic qualities that Boris Yeltsin displayed in breaking up the Soviet Union were not suited to institutionalizing power by transferring it from a heroic founder to someone whose claim to authority is impersonal. To achieve this requires not only the proclamation of a constitution, but also respect for the rules and routines it specifies and acceptance that constitutional powers of office are greater than the power of personality. If this does not happen, the passing of the founding leader will produce a power struggle that concludes with the replacement of one personalistic regime by another. Such power struggles have made a messy end of the regimes of many once powerful rulers.

A feeble state: Yeltsin's second term

Soon after Boris Yeltsin appeared as a radical challenger of Mikhail Gorbachev, his popularity overtook that of the Soviet leader. In a VTsIOM poll in July 1990, Yeltsin achieved a mean rating of 8.0 on a 10-point scale, compared to 5.0 for Gorbachev. In the following year the public opinion ratings of both leaders fell, but Yeltsin's consistently remained better. The failure of the August 1991 coup benefited both, but Yeltsin gained more. By the end of December 1991, Boris Yeltsin's rating averaged 5.0, while that of Gorbachev was at its lowest ever, 3.4 (cf. White, Rose and McAllister, 1997: fig. 8.1).

In winning election as president of the Russian Republic in 1991, Boris Yeltsin gained a larger share of the popular vote than in a normal American presidential election. But becoming president of an independent Russia placed Yeltsin in the political hot seat, for no longer could he blame the country's troubles on the failings of Gorbachev and his associates. During Yeltsin's first term as president of the Russian Federation, his ratings consistently averaged below the mid-point.[1] His first-term high point was 4.9 in March 1992 and the lowest point of that term, reached in March 1995, was 2.7, lower than that of the Duma and of his prime minister.

As the June 1996 presidential election drew near, the Kremlin was uncertain about whether it should be held, as the constitution specified, or postponed on the grounds of economic turmoil, military action in Chechnya or any other excuse that could be made up. Korzhakov, the commander of the Moscow Military District, and a number of bankers and industrialists argued for postponing the election and forming an emergency coalition government including Communist leader Gennady Zyuganov. Others in the Family, led by Anatoly Chubais, argued against this strategy. In his memoirs, Yeltsin (2000: 24ff.) states that in March 1996 he told his staff to prepare decrees to dissolve the Duma, postpone the presidential election and ban the Communist Party. Yeltsin's advisors disagreed about whether such action would be effective or desirable, and no action was taken. In a last-minute attempt to discredit the team arguing against postponing the election, Korzhakov's security police arrested two of Chubais's aides carrying $500,000 with them late at night within the Kremlin grounds. Yeltsin backed Chubais and sacked Korzhakov (see McFaul, 2001: 300ff.). In retaliation, Korzhakov (1997) published a lurid account of life with Yeltsin, entitled 'from dawn to dusk', detailing how the Yeltsin Family accumulated and spent substantial wealth.

To the surprise of many critics and supporters, Boris Yeltsin came off the floor to campaign vigorously for the presidency. In the first-round ballot when many names were on the list, Yeltsin won a third of the popular vote, just enough to place him first. In the second round, when the voters' choice was reduced to Yeltsin or the Communist leader, Zyuganov, he won 53.8 per cent of the vote. However, the average rating of Yeltsin in July 1996 was only 3.9; his victory owed much to being the lesser evil compared to the alternative, a Communist (cf. Rose and Tikhomirov, 1996).

The televised broadcast of Boris Yeltsin's inauguration as president in August 1996 confirmed many rumours, for it showed that the 65-year-old president was physically incapable of delivering a proper speech, as he stumbled verbally when articulating the 33-word presidential oath. Most Russians knew people who indulged in binge drinking and could excuse a president who occasionally let himself go. However, a president chronically incapable of meeting the physical demands of the office was another matter.

---

[1] This statement is true whether the mid-point is defined as 5.5, the arithmetic mean and also the median, or as 5.0, which respondents may view as the psychological mid-point.

During President Yeltsin's second term of office, his public appearances were demoralizing, for he was rarely the figure that had won popular backing earlier in the decade. When he appeared unsteady or unwell in public, opponents attacked him as a drunkard or a 'painted mummy'. When Yeltsin avoided public appearances, it encouraged rumours that he was too ill to perform official duties. From time to time, Yeltsin showed that such rumours were exaggerated, appearing healthy on television to announce decrees or unexpectedly sacking his prime minister or other advisors. But the bad days and the bad polls outnumbered the good (fig. 4.1). By March 1997 Yeltsin's mean rating was more than a point lower than at the election, and there was worse to come. By July 1998 Yeltsin's rating averaged only 2.4 and in November, following the collapse of the ruble, it was down to 1.8. For the remainder of his term, Yeltsin remained near the limit of negativism. An absolute majority of Russians gave the president the worst possible rating and for every Russian who gave Yeltsin a minimally positive rating there were at least six placing him at the very bottom of the scale.[2]

Since Boris Yeltsin was most responsible for the creation of the new Russian regime, there were concerns that his unpopularity threatened a massive withdrawal of support for the new system. Yeltsin's entourage pressed this argument in Washington, claiming that if President Clinton and the IMF did not financially support the Russian Federation, they risked the rise to power of an old-style Communist bureaucrat or, even worse, a nationalist brandishing nuclear weapons. In fact, the threat was greatly overstated. Negative views of Boris Yeltsin were held by democrats and economic reformers as well as by Communists and by nationalists. The New Russia Barometer found that those negative about Yeltsin included a majority of Russians positive about the new regime as well as a majority negative about it. Like citizens in an established democracy, Russians discriminated between evaluating an individual incumbent and the political system as a whole.

Appointing and dismissing prime ministers

The appointment of the prime minister was doubly important to Yeltsin and to the Family. Day-to-day responsibility for governing was in the hands of the prime minister, lightening Yeltsin's burdens and providing a convenient scapegoat when things went wrong. The prime minister would

[2] The same point is made by another VTsIOM question asking people to give a pro or con judgment of the president. By September 1998, only 5 per cent approved Yeltsin's performance and 95 per cent disapproved and more than nine-tenths of Russians continued to disapprove of President Yeltsin for the rest of his term in office.

Figure 4.1 PRESIDENT YELTSIN'S SECOND-TERM UNPOPULARITY.

Q. *What marks on a scale of 1 (lowest) to 10 (highest) do you give to the performance of Boris Yeltsin?*

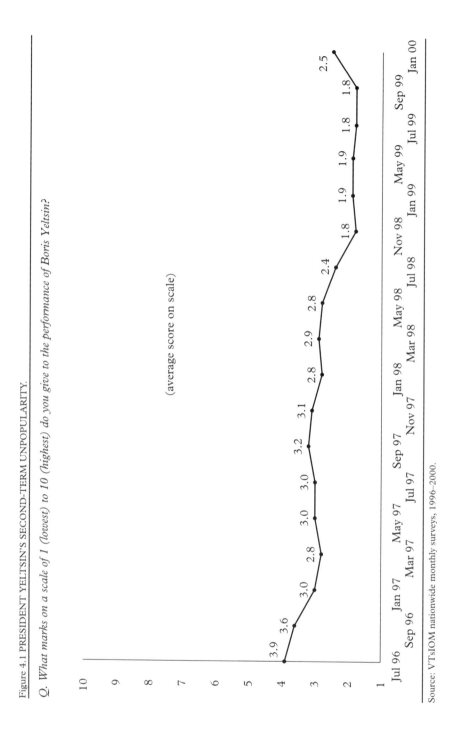

(average score on scale)

Source: VTsIOM nationwide monthly surveys, 1996–2000.

also assume the president's role in the event that Yeltsin died in office or was declared physically incapable. Given the state of Boris Yeltsin's health, it was realistic to describe the prime minister as only one heartbeat away from becoming president.

Notwithstanding health problems, throughout his second term Yeltsin retained the political energy to take unexpected measures that caught critics and associates off guard. He demonstrated this repeatedly by firing and appointing prime ministers (fig. 4.2). The only prime minister who lasted more than a year in office, Viktor Chernomyrdin (1992–8), had been head of the gas monopoly in the last years of the Soviet Union and was able to bridge conflicting old and new political interests. As Yeltsin's second term progressed, the journalist Lilia Shevtsova wrote (1999: 237): 'Everyone took Chernomyrdin for Yeltsin's official successor.'[3]

On the old Roman principle of lopping the ears of corn before they become too tall, Yeltsin unexpectedly fired Chernomyrdin in March 1998. In his place, he named as prime minister a 35-year-old technocrat, Sergei Kirienko. Kirienko's lack of a political base was a plus factor to Yeltsin; it made him totally dependent on the president. But it was a handicap in the Duma, where a diverse coalition twice voted against confirming Kirienko's appointment; but Yeltsin was persistent. He publicly announced that he had told Pavel Borodin, who dispensed patronage to Duma members, to take care of the needs of deputies who showed a constructive approach to Kirienko's nomination after the Duma debated it. He also had the constitutional power to dissolve the Duma and force all its members to stand for re-election if they rejected Kirienko three times. After twice rejecting the Kremlin's candidate, Duma members approved him on the third ballot. In the words of a Moscow newspaper, they were not voting for a head of the executive but to 'save their apartments and their cars' (Reddaway and Glinski, 2001: 596).

When the economic crisis of August 1998 threatened to put the Kremlin into free fall, Yeltsin made a scapegoat of Kirienko, firing him and nominating Chernomyrdin as his replacement. The action was described as 'like changing parachutes in the middle of a jump' (Shevtsova, 1999: 254). Yeltsin's political weakness led the Duma to reject Chernomyrdin twice; the nomination was then withdrawn. Yevgeny Primakov, the foreign minister, was named as a compromise candidate and endorsed by a big majority in the first Duma ballot. Primakov became popular in

---

[3] The remark illustrates the misperception of public opinion from within the Moscow Ring Road. VTsIOM was reporting less than 5 per cent of their nationwide sample of electors saying that they would vote for Chernomyrdin in a presidential election (see fig. 4.3).

Figure 4.2 SHORT SHELF LIFE OF YELTSIN'S PRIME MINISTERS.

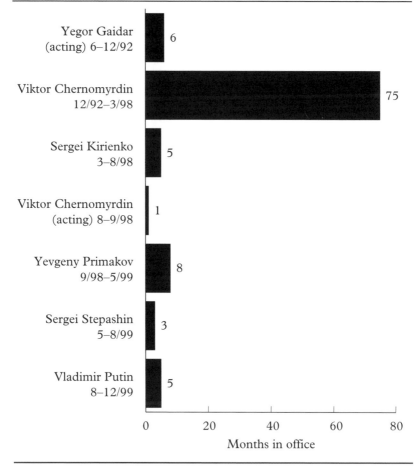

trial-heat polls for the presidency, and in May 1999 Yeltsin sacked him. Sergei Stepashin, a former minister of internal affairs, was named as his successor. The Duma promptly confirmed Stepashin in the post; Stepashin lasted three months.

Boris Yeltsin demonstrated his political clout by sacking and selecting five prime ministers in less than 18 months. But this did not do his personal standing any good, for the Duma judged each firing as another sign of Yeltsin losing his grip on affairs, and sought to enhance its own influence. Nor did it do Yeltsin's public appeal any good; his opinion poll ratings stayed in the basement. Least of all did it do the Yeltsin Family any good, for while prime ministers were shuffling in and out, time was passing without anyone having been found who looked able to protect their interests by succeeding Boris Yeltsin in the Kremlin.

The options

From the start of President Yeltsin's second term of office there were reasons to worry that the president might not live out its duration. The average Russian male born in 1931, the same year as Yeltsin, was already dead and those still alive had a life expectancy of only a few years. Yeltsin's punishing lifestyle and political responsibilities made him a worse-than-average risk for life insurance.

The office of vice president existed when the Russian Federation was created. Alexander Rutskoi held the post, having been vice president to Yeltsin in the Russian Republic. After Rutskoi was named acting president by the Russian Parliament during its confrontation with President Yeltsin in October 1993, the new constitution abolished the office of vice president. In the event of the president's death, the constitution stipulates that a new election should be held within 90 days and that the prime minister temporarily assumes the powers of the president. A bigger problem would arise if the president appeared unable to perform his duties because of physical or mental difficulties, since the constitution does not detail the process by which the president's incapacity is determined.

When Boris Yeltsin gave every indication that he would live out his term of office, the Family faced the prospect of an unfriendly candidate winning the presidential election scheduled for June 2000. It had four alternative courses of action.

1. To accept the loss of power when the president's second term expired. Doing this would contribute to the successful institutionalization of the regime. However, it would not assure the president a peaceful retirement, for if the 'wrong' candidate was elected, then Yeltsin could be subject to investigation or prosecution for real or alleged crimes committed while in office, and risk disgrace, imprisonment or exile. The risks to the Family were far greater.

2. An alternative was to stretch the constitution to allow Yeltsin to run again. Its language appeared to debar Yeltsin from running for re-election in the year 2000, for Article 81.3 declared, 'One and the same person cannot hold the office of president of the Russian Federation for more than two consecutive terms.' With Clintonesque ingenuity, there was talk around the Kremlin that Yeltsin could be interpreted as having been elected president of the Federation for only one term, since first he was elected president of the Russian Republic when it was still part of the Soviet Union (Shevtsova, 1999: 220, 267). When Yeltsin and

Alexander Lukashenko, president of Belarus, declared the creation of an ill-defined union-state in December 1998, this prompted fresh speculation that Yeltsin might try to create a new union-state of which he could become president, just as Slobodan Milosevic had retained power by becoming president of Yugoslavia after his term as president of Serbia expired. In November 1999 the Constitutional Court ruled that Yeltsin's election as president of the RSFSR, the basis of his claim to be president of the Russian Federation at its inauguration in 1992, counted as his first term of office and he was thus ineligible to be a candidate again.

By the time the court ruled against another Yeltsin candidacy, the argument against him seeking re-election was not so much legal as practical: opinion polls consistently showed very few Russians would support Yeltsin. Following the August 1998 economic crisis less than 1 per cent of Russians questioned by VTsIOM said they would vote for him. When VTsIOM asked which politician people would *not* wish to see as leader, Yeltsin led the field. By the end of July 1999 only 7 per cent of Russians approved of Yeltsin as president, and his popularity rating was at its lowest ever.

3. Preventing the presidential election being held on the pretext of an emergency was another option, a tactic that had been considered before the 1996 ballot. A VTsIOM survey in December 1998 found that 71 per cent did not think it permissible to cancel elections to restore order. Given Yeltsin's unpopularity, there was a risk that a presidential decree suspending the election would be challenged by the Duma and the security forces would not back an unpopular president in the ensuing struggle. There was also the medical risk: the very effort of making emergency powers effective could give the president a final heart attack, and have fatal consequences for the Family too.

4. The ideal solution was to create a friendly winning candidate. For Yeltsin a friendly successor promised that his historic achievements would not be besmirched by controversy. Members of the Family would expect a friendly new leader to offer jobs to some and protection to all from investigations by the procurator general. Rich oligarchs would expect a new president backed by their money to protect their previous gains from the state and offer opportunities for future gains.

The practical problems facing the Yeltsin Family concerned mechanics: who could win the 2000 presidential election and how could victory be achieved? Given the unpopularity of Boris Yeltsin, a candidate closely identified with Boris Yeltsin, such as Viktor Chernomyrdin, risked the fate of Mikhail Gorbachev in the 1996 presidential race, that is, being a hopeless also-ran. The nightmare prospect was that the two candidates in the second-round run-off ballot would both be opponents of Boris Yeltsin and his Family.

Searching for a third alternative

A triangle offers a simple way to visualize the race for the Kremlin in the year 2000. At one corner were voters still loyal to the Communist Party, an ageing but substantial bloc that had given its candidate 32.0 per cent of the vote in the first round of the 1996 election. In the second corner were voters who favoured Yeltsin in 1996 and were still willing to back a candidate who had served his government. Neither group could attract enough votes to win the run-off ballot, and a candidate too close to Yeltsin might even fail to qualify for the second round. In 1996, 32.7 per cent cast first-round ballots for neither Yeltsin nor Zyuganov; this third group would again be decisive. It was also heterogeneous, including Communist traditionalists who favoured a hardline candidate; supporters of the demagogic Vladimir Zhirinovsky; liberals who regarded Yeltsin as not having gone far enough in economic and political reform; and Russians who would actively vote against all candidates.

How third-way hopefuls might distance themselves from the Communists and Yeltsin was a matter of tactics and belief. Logically, there was space for a pro-market party that was anti-Yeltsin, and even for a social democratic party that supported welfare policies but attacked the undemocratic Communist record. There were openings for anti-democrats to offer a less or more credible nationalist policy. And there was also an opportunity for a candidate to appeal on personality and avoid commitment on issues.

Early front runners

The Communist Party was the only organized opposition party and Gennady Zyuganov was also distant from Yeltsin. The party's established supporters virtually guaranteed Zyuganov enough votes to qualify for the second-round ballot. However, he also faced a red ceiling, an upper limit on the number who would vote Communist, and Zyuganov's apparatchik personality discouraged floating voters. One scenario was that an anti-Yeltsin candidate finishing second to Zyuganov in the first round of the presidential ballot would win a majority in the second round by being neither a Communist nor a Yeltsin supporter.

In the first round of the 1996 presidential race, General Alexander Lebed took third place with 14.5 per cent of the vote. Lebed ran as an anti-establishment candidate, having fallen out with the military while serving in a mainly Russophone part of Moldova. The programme he offered was in the tradition of interwar East European military dictators, and Lebed showed public admiration for General Pinochet's regime in Chile. At the start of Boris Yeltsin's second term, Lebed was made responsible for negotiating an end to fighting in Chechnya. Lebed accused Russian authorities of incompetence in prosecuting the war and negotiated a truce. The rising popularity of Lebed unsettled the Family. At a press conference on 16 October 1996, Interior Minister Anatoly Kulikov accused Lebed of preparing an armed coup and Prime Minister Viktor Chernomyrdin said that 'home grown Bonapartism is clearly much too evident in the country' (Shevtsova, 1999: 313). The next day Yeltsin announced Lebed's dismissal as a disruptive force in government. The Russian public's rejection of unconstitutional military rule appeared to place a ceiling on General Lebed's support. In polls it never rose above the level of his 1996 electoral support (fig. 4.3).

Figure 4.3 LEADING PRESIDENTIAL CANDIDATES BEFORE PUTIN.

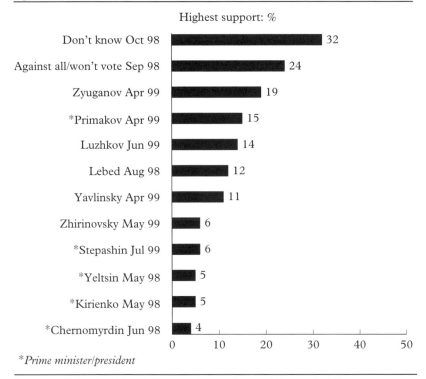

*Prime minister/president

Source: VTsIOM nationwide monthly surveys between January 1998 and July 1999.

Popularly elected governors in the 89 regions of the Russian Federation offered a base for a presidential candidate emerging without responsibility for what had been happening in national politics. Yury Luzhkov, who entered Moscow city politics when Boris Yeltsin was party secretary there, sought to create such a base. Luzhkov had become Moscow's mayor in 1992 and controlled planning permission for real estate highly valued by wealthy Russian and foreign firms. Within six months of Yeltsin's second term starting, Luzhkov was being mentioned as a possible presidential candidate. His candidacy was not supported by the Family. Recognizing the need to expand his support, Luzhkov cultivated good relations with governors of regions distant from Moscow. By the beginning of 1998, Luzhkov had become one of the four leading candidates in the VTsIOM presidential polls. After the collapse of the ruble in August 1998, Luzhkov began to run second to Zyuganov in the opinion polls. In collaboration with prominent regional governors, Luzhkov founded the Fatherland Party in December 1998 to fight the forthcoming Duma election and advance his presidential ambitions.

The surprise appointment of Yevgeny Primakov as prime minister gave national prominence to a potential candidate straddling several camps. In Soviet days Primakov had been chief of foreign intelligence and one of the few Politburo members to oppose the August 1991 putsch against Gorbachev. Becoming prime minister guaranteed Primakov visibility but not necessarily popular appeal, as his predecessors had learned. However, Primakov steered between IMF demands for major cuts in government spending and domestic resistance, and he cultivated good relations with politicians in the Duma. By December 1998, he was one of the three leaders in VTsIOM trial-heat presidential polls. When the Duma tried to impeach a very unpopular president and Yeltsin fought back, Primakov sought to act as a mediator. By March 1999, Primakov was ahead of Luzhkov as the principal challenger to Zyuganov. This encouraged Yeltsin to sack him in May. By pushing Primakov out of the Kremlin, Yeltsin made him appear an anti-government candidate, even though Primakov had served the Yeltsin government since it was formed. Subsequently, Primakov joined Yury Luzhkov in the Fatherland Party.

When Boris Yeltsin appointed Sergei Stepashin as prime minister in May 1999, he simultaneously requested his chief of staff, Alexander Voloshin, to unite healthy (that is, pro-Yeltsin) political groups into a party that would fight the Duma election and then campaign for the presidency. Voloshin proposed that a group called Voice of Russia, led by Samara provincial governor Konstantin Titov, should lead the Kremlin's campaign, and Yeltsin endorsed this. But bad personal relations between

Stepashin and Voloshin prevented their cooperation on a mission that required extraordinary efforts and teamwork.

Trial-heat presidential polls showed that, together, electors who were against all candidates, don't knows or unlikely to vote usually outnumbered supporters of any one candidate. Well in advance of election day, Gennady Zyuganov was the front runner, while one or another anti-Yeltsin candidate came second. All candidates not identified with the Yeltsin camp received more support than Kremlin favourites. In July 1999, VTsIOM found Sergei Stepashin trailing badly behind Zyuganov, Primakov, Luzhkov and Yavlinsky. In aggregate, the three prime ministers identified with the president – Stepashin, Kirienko and Chernomyrdin – were supported by only 10 per cent of those polled. The pro-Yeltsin vote thus trailed the combined support for Luzhkov and Primakov as well as that for Zyuganov. While the name of the candidate most likely to stop Zyuganov varied from month to month, the sure loser was a candidate representing what Boris Yeltsin had stood for during his time in office.

No one in the Kremlin wanted to tell the president that all was not well. When an aide tried to send the president a memo in July reporting these unpleasant facts, Voloshin stopped it from reaching Yeltsin on the grounds that it was ill advised. Three days later the deputy chief of staff, Sergei Zverev, did get word to the president that all was not well. He was fired for his efforts, but the message hit home. On 3 August Viktor Chernomyrdin confirmed the bleak outlook in a private meeting with Yeltsin.

Bombshells – metaphorical and otherwise

At the end of the summer, metaphorical and real bombshells were thrown in quick succession. President Yeltsin sacked Sergei Stepashin and appointed the hitherto unknown Vladimir Putin as prime minister; Chechen rebels sent armed forces into the Russian region of Dagestan; and two Moscow apartment buildings were destroyed by bombs.

Vladimir Putin: a controlled explosion

By contrast with Boris Yeltsin, Vladimir Putin had been a political bureaucrat throughout his professional life. The commitment was consistent with his Soviet patriotism, patience and sense of order. Putin took a degree in Soviet law at Leningrad State University, and in 1975 entered the cloistered life of KGB service. As a KGB employee, Putin was not allowed to go to restaurants for fear of exposure to corrupting influences, his daily work routine was subject to weekly monitoring by superiors and, as he learned to his distaste, 'they were always checking up on you' (Putin,

2000: 231; cf. Knight, 2000a). A decade after he left the security service, Putin remained proud of what he had done there. When challenged about his background at a press conference in Slovenia in 2001, Putin defended his KGB experience by drawing parallels with the background of Henry Kissinger and President George Bush:

When Kissinger and I were talking and I told him where I worked, he had a think and said, 'All respectable people began in the intelligence service. So did I.' So I cannot really understand what makes you so particularly interested. Especially as I believe the 41st President of the United States did not work in a laundry but headed the CIA (Putin, 2001b).

In the KGB Putin was a desk officer concerned with sifting and interpreting intelligence reports rather than participating in cloak-and-dagger operations. His field was counterintelligence, monitoring the behaviour of Soviet citizens to ensure that they were not doing things harmful to the interests of the Soviet state. Putin's knowledge of German gained him an assignment there in 1985, but it was not to a major post. Instead of being sent to Bonn, where he could have spied on the Federal Republic's government, or to East Berlin, a centre of spying in a divided city, Putin was assigned to a backwater, Dresden. The contrast in living standards between life in East Germany and Russia was very striking to him and his wife. As Putin (2000: 70) later recalled, 'We had come from a Russia where there were lines and shortages, and in the GDR [East Germany] there was always plenty of everything. I gained about 25 pounds.' When the Berlin Wall fell, Putin burned so many KGB records on the political loyalties of East Germans that the furnace in his office burst. In January 1990 Putin went back as a KGB active reservist to work in what was, for the moment, still called Leningrad.

Once back home, Putin began looking for another job, although he did not resign from the KGB until after the failure of the August 1991 coup. At Leningrad State University he became an assistant to the pro-rector for international affairs. He then became a staff official of Anatoly Sobchak, one of his former law professors, chair of the City Council, and soon to be elected mayor of what was once again called St Petersburg. Putin dealt with the city's relations with foreigners, including economic development. In the 1995 Duma election he organized the city campaign for Our Home Is Russia, and the following year acted as co-chair of Sobchak's campaign for re-election. When Sobchak was defeated, Putin was out of work.

In search of a job, Putin found that he had more chance of employment in the Kremlin, with which he had dealt while working for Sobchak, than in the new St Petersburg administration. After several false starts, Putin was offered a post by Chief of Staff Pavel Borodin, initially looking after property in the General Affairs Department of the presidential administration. Putin's administrative efficiency and ingratiating low-key manner rapidly won him patrons and promotion. Putin became deputy head of the presidential administration in 1998, a post responsible for contacts with the regions and their governors. Soon afterwards, against his wishes, he was named head of the FSB, the state security agency that was the successor of the KGB. Putin's reliability brought him additional tasks in the field of internal security.

When Boris Yeltsin decided to sack Stepashin as prime minister, he needed someone to fill the gap thus created. Putin was a familiar face to the Family. He was acceptable to the security services as one of them, and to reform-minded economists who hoped that Putin might call on his FSB network to enforce market discipline in the manner of Chile's General Pinochet (cf. Reddaway, 2001: 25). According to Yeltsin's memoirs (2000: 356), when he offered Putin the post, the latter was surprised and hesitant, explaining, 'I don't like election campaigns at all.' When Yeltsin again offered him the post, Putin replied, 'I don't think I'm ready for it.' When Yeltsin insisted that Putin was the man he wanted, Putin dutifully accepted, saying 'I'll work wherever you appoint me.' When Yeltsin announced on television that he was making Vladimir Putin prime minister, he added the hope that Putin might succeed him in the presidency. The Duma promptly confirmed Putin with 233 deputies voting for, 84 against and 17 abstaining. By his own account, Vladimir Putin entered office with no expectation of lasting any longer than his short-lived predecessors.

Another challenge from Chechnya

Two days before Vladimir Putin was named prime minister, Russian media reported Chechen incursions into villages in neighbouring Dagestan. Chechens and Moscow had been in conflict since tsarist forces occupied the region in the 1850s as part of the empire's expansion in the Caucasus. In Soviet times a Chechen–Ingush Autonomous Soviet Socialist Republic was created with a population of one million. Russians migrated there, bringing the Slav population up to one-quarter of the largely Muslim republic. The break-up of the Soviet Union gave independence to most of the Muslim parts of the former Soviet Union, but the Chechen–Ingush Republic remained nominally within the Russian Federation. It was of strategic importance, for pipelines carrying oil from the east to hard currency countries passed through Chechnya. Through their connections in the criminal underworld, Chechen gangs were able to forge links with get-rich-quick entrepreneurs in Moscow.

The first Chechen war of 1994–6 had shown Moscow's military incompetence and the ability of Chechen forces. However, after agreeing a truce Chechens failed to establish a stable dictatorship. Following the 1997 election, Aslan Maskhadov became president and the losing candidate, former field commander Shamil Basayev, returned to leading an armed group. Paramilitary forces turned to banditry and kidnapping Westerners as well as Russians. Islamic militants threatened to carry out a *jihad* against Russia from beyond Chechnya's borders (see Lieven, 1998).

The Chechen incursion in August 1999 into overwhelmingly Muslim Dagestan, an administrative republic of the Russian Federation, was trebly worrying to Moscow. It signalled a breakdown in the truce negotiated in 1996; an expansion of armed ethnic-based conflict within the Federation; and the threat of neighbouring Muslim states becoming involved in armed conflict within Russia. Putin described all this as threatening 'the Yugoslavization of Russia', with independence for Muslim areas being followed by ethnic minorities in other regions that contained valuable natural resources trying to break away:

My historical mission – and this will sound lofty, but it's true – consisted of resolving the situation in the Northern Caucasus. At that time, nobody knew how it would all end. I said to myself, 'Never mind, I have a little time – two, three, maybe four months – to bang the hell out of those bandits. Then they can get rid of me . . .'
If we don't put an immediate end to this, Russia will cease to exist. It was a question of preventing the collapse of the country. I realized I could only do this at the cost of my political career. It was a minimal cost, and I was prepared to pay up. So when Yeltsin declared me his successor and everyone said that it was the beginning of the end for me, I felt completely calm. The hell with them. I calculated that I had several months to consolidate the armed forces, the Interior Ministry and the FSB, and to rally public support. Would there be enough time? That's all I worried about (Putin, 2000: 139f.).

On 8 September 1999 a massive bomb exploded in a Moscow apartment building, and five days later another apartment house was bombed. Further explosions followed in southern Russia. More than 200 Russians were killed. On 23 September the Russian military launched a well-prepared series of air strikes against Chechnya and a week later Russian tanks moved into action there. The measures used were not those of an armed police action intended to maintain or restore civil order, such as Britain has used in Northern Ireland or Spain in the Basque country. Moscow's methods were the means of war. In a statement on the Second Chechen War on 24 September. Vladimir Putin pledged, 'We'll continue striking wherever the terrorists might be', and underscored his point by invoking criminal argot, 'If we find them sitting on the toilet, we'll blow them away right there [*zamochit v sortire*].'

When the Soviet state controlled information, Russians and many Western experts often made judgments about events in the absence of evidence by asking the Marxist question: 'In whose interests is it?' Since the Chechens did not claim responsibility for explosions in Moscow, suspicious critics speculated that the bombs were planted by those close to the government in order to create a national emergency that would justify attacking the Chechens. Speculation was encouraged by evidence that the FSB had planted explosives in an apartment house in a provincial city. The official explanation was that they were dummy bombs intended to test the capacity of emergency services to respond to Chechen terrorists (cf. *Economist*, 9 October 1999). When asked about allegations of government complicity in the Moscow bombs, Putin (2000: 143) denounced this as 'utter nonsense! It's totally insane.' He added without a sense of irony, 'No one in the Russian special services would be capable of such a crime against his own people.'

The eruption of troubles in the Caucasus was not a surprise to the Russian public. In spring 1998, the New Russia Barometer had asked about potential threats to peace and security. Ethnic minorities within Russia were ranked second to the United States as a threat to peace and security; 31 per cent thought ethnic minorities presented a big or some threat and an additional 29 per cent thought they were at least a small threat. Ethnic minorities were deemed a bigger threat than immigrants from other societies or than Germany.

In a society in which ethnic slurs are common, criminal activities by Chechen groups in Moscow and other major cities led many Russians to identify all Chechens as gangsters. There is virtually no pro-Chechen sentiment in Russia. When VTsIOM asked Russians about the war in Chechnya in early November 1999, there was substantial popular support. Offered the alternative of continuing military operations or entering negotiations, 54 per cent favoured continuing military operations as against 29 favouring talk, with the remainder don't knows. By the time of the Duma election in December, those favouring military operations had risen to 71 per cent. Only 7 per cent thought military measures had been too severe; the chief difference of opinion was between the 29 per cent wanting harsher military measures and the 48 per cent who considered them severe enough. Ordinary Russians shared with Putin uncertainty about the outcome of the Second Chechen War. In December 1999, 43 per cent thought that all or part of Chechnya would be returned to Russian hands, while 23 per cent feared that protracted fighting would spread to other parts of the Caucasus, 12 per cent thought there would be a stalemate as in 1996, 5 per cent expected the partition of Chechnya and the remainder were don't knows (*www.RussiaVotes.org*).

Putin's popularity takes off

When Vladimir Putin became prime minister, he moved from being a political unknown to occupying the second most prominent job in Russian government. But political prominence is a double-edged sword. If things go wrong, it can make national leaders unpopular. As prime minister Putin was a potential presidential candidate and his name was immediately added to the list of contenders in VTsIOM's monthly poll. In the first presidential trial-heat poll immediately after Putin became prime minister, only 2 per cent favoured him (fig. 4.4). In the September poll, taken at the same time as Russian air strikes against Chechnya began, 5 per cent said they would vote for Putin and, at the same time, a majority

Figure 4.4 RAPID RISE OF VLADIMIR PUTIN'S POPULARITY.

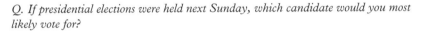

Q. If presidential elections were held next Sunday, which candidate would you most likely vote for?

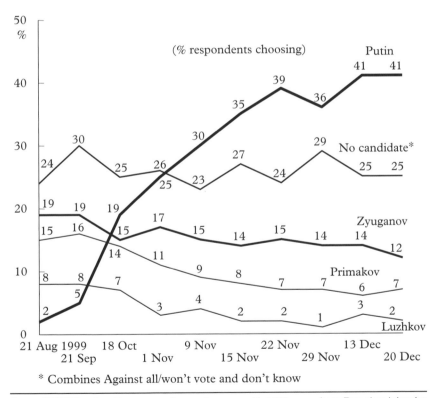

* Combines Against all/won't vote and don't know

Source: VTsIOM nationwide representative sample surveys with 1,600 respondents. Date given is last day of fieldwork, which normally lasts four days.

of Russians said they approved of his performance. By mid-October, when air strikes in Chechnya were showing an effect, Putin's support among electors was up to 19 per cent and Zyuganov was in second place. In a series of polls in November, Putin's support rose to unprecedented heights. In the final VTsIOM poll before the Duma election, Putin was favoured for the presidency by 40 per cent of all respondents, and by 52 per cent of likely voters stating a preference for a candidate.

In less than four months after being presented to the public as Russia's prime minister and three months after launching a war to destroy separatist opponents in Chechnya, Vladimir Putin had achieved greater support in opinion polls than Boris Yeltsin had ever attained as president of the Russian Federation. Putin was now the odds-on favourite to be elected president the following summer. But before that could happen, a Duma election would give the Russian people an opportunity to register their views for and against the nation's political elites.

5   Parties without accountability

Political parties are necessary so that citizens can collectively hold the government of the day accountable. One hundred million Russian electors can give direction to government only if political parties offer them a choice of policies and candidates to vote for. Since the preferences of voters differ and the ways in which people combine attitudes differ even more, a free election must be competitive, with two or more parties nominating candidates. Electoral accountability does not require politicians to be democrats by conviction. Accountability can be achieved if politicians want to win re-election and fear that, if they do not do what their supporters want, then they will be ejected from office when held to account at the next election (Schumpeter, 1952).

Elections create democratic government only if their outcome decides collective control of decisionmaking in government. Political parties combine the ambitions of many individual politicians into a collective team seeking office. The first requirement for elections to hold government accountable is that political elites organize parties to fight elections rather than appeal for votes as personalities independent of parties. Second, parties must nominate candidates nationwide rather than being local groups that differ from one city to another. Only if parties fight elections nationwide will all voters have the same choice of who controls national government. Third, national party candidates rather than independent candidates, local parties or separatist regional parties should win the great majority of votes and seats. If this does not happen, then government decisions are likely to be made by ad hoc and unaccountable coalitions of personalities, and local interests or regional parties may press for independence. A fourth requirement – parties nominate candidates for all elected national offices – is most readily met in a British-style parliamentary system of government, where a single ballot decides which party has a majority and therefore names the prime minister. Fifth and finally, for voters to hold governors to account for their behaviour in office, parties should persist from one election to another. Only in this way can voters reward or punish those they elected for what they have done in office.

The Soviet legacy made the initial organization of political parties difficult. The Soviet Union was a one-party state lacking independent institutions of civil society that could organize dissent. Thus, the initial competitive elections could not offer a clear-cut choice, as in Poland, between Solidarity and official Communist candidates. The Communist Party of the Soviet Union did not split into two well-organized opposing factions competing for votes. The August 1991 failed coup showed that Gorbachev's strongest opponents did not think of repudiating his actions by winning elections. Radical reformers and hardline Communist critics of Gorbachev spoke in the name of the people, but only the Communists had an organization to support their views. Politicians who left the Communist Party had no organization to back their ambitions. The elections that decided the president and first Parliament of the Russian Federation were held in the last days of the Soviet Union, when parties had not had time to organize. In the first two years of the Federation political elites spent much of their time quarrelling with each other and jockeying for position, rather than organizing parties (cf. Reich, 2001). Political elites had the choice of running as independents, and the electoral system offered many incentives to do so.

The constitutional structure of the Russian Federation complicates accountability. As in the United States and France, control of national government is divided between a separately elected president and legislature. As in Germany, the parliament is elected in two halves, one using a proportional representation list ballot and the other election in single-member districts. The federal system can add additional complications, creating a two-chamber national assembly with members elected in different ways. This is the case in the United States and Australia. Russia does not have a directly elected upper chamber; each of the 89 regions of Russia elects their governor or president and a regional assembly according to procedures that it decides.

While a complicated constitutional structure creates difficulties in establishing party accountability, a look at other countries with complex elections shows that it is not sufficient to frustrate accountability. In France, candidates for the presidency run with the backing of a coalition of parties, and it is up to the French electorate to decide whether it wants both the presidency and the assembly in the hands of the same party or coalition of parties, or whether it wants a divided government in which one branch can hold the other accountable on a continuing basis. In the United States there are three different ballots for federal offices, yet the Democratic and Republican parties have dominated the election of presidents, senators and members of the House of Representatives for a century, and elections for state governors and legislatures are organized along the same party lines. The Federal Republic of Germany has two different ballots to elect the Bundestag, and elections at the *Land* level are held independently of federal elections. Yet German parties contest elections on all ballots, with the unique exception of the East German party of ex-Communists.

In the first decade of the Russian Federation, of necessity Russian politicians faced a situation described by Steven Fish as 'democracy from scratch' (Fish, 1995; Kullberg, 2001). There was an instant demand for new political parties. Political elites have shown the capacity to create dozens of parties, but they have also been expert in making parties disappear. And many politicians, starting with Presidents Yeltsin and Putin, have preferred to run as independents rather than party leaders. The result is the creation of four systems of parties, in which there are elections but not accountability.

Four systems of parties

The choice of voters on election day is supply-side determined, for the parties on the ballot depend on the actions of political elites. The decisions elites take about forming parties are influenced by the incentives and disincentives of the electoral system. Its rules determine not only who can vote – in Russia virtually every citizen of the Federation – but also the procedures for nominating candidates and how votes are converted into seats in parliament. For example, a proportional representation system encourages the creation of more parties than does the Anglo-American first-past-the-post system of awarding seats. There is a vast literature on the effects of election laws in established democracies. Most of the experts concerned with writing laws governing Duma elections were unconcerned with the principles of electoral systems, and political circumstances when this was done were so uncertain that any predictions made, whether in the name of science or self-interest, had a limited likelihood of foretelling what would happen (McFaul, 2001: 217ff.; Moser, 2001). Political elites have had to experiment, by trial and error, as to how to win office.

Party competition in Russia takes place in four different arenas, each producing a different form of party competition. In consequence, it is misleading to describe the country as having a multi-party system. In fact, it has *four systems* of parties, each with its own rules and incentives. The president is not required to be a party nominee and the requirement of winning an absolute majority of the votes led both Boris Yeltsin and Vladimir Putin to organize a winning coalition by running as independents. Half the Duma is elected in single-member districts

(SMDs), which in practice have favoured independent candidates, and half is elected by a proportional representation (PR) ballot requiring candidates to run on a party list. The organization of parties during sessions of the Duma follows different rules again.

1. *Independent candidates far outnumber party standard-bearers.* The first decision facing politicians is whether to stand as an independent or as the nominee of a political party. In established democracies independent candidates can contest elections, but few do so because it is an almost certain route to defeat. This is not the case in Russia.

To be elected *president* a candidate must win more than half the total vote, and if no candidate achieves this goal on the first ballot, the two leading candidates meet each other in a second-round run-off. Among the multiplicity of Russian parties, none can claim the support of more than one-quarter of voters and most parties have far less. Thus, running as the candidate of a party does not promise a candidate enough votes to win election. Furthermore, running on a party label can repel as well as attract support; Gennady Zyuganov has demonstrated the polarizing effect of being the Communist candidate in his two unsuccessful campaigns for the presidency. Given weak or nil party attachment among most Russian voters, an independent candidate is best positioned to create a winning coalition from a broad spectrum of voters. In the 1996 presidential election, five of the eleven candidates were independents; and in 2000 six of eleven candidates were independents.

In the *single-member districts* that fill half the seats in the Duma, independent candidates may be nominated by a group of individuals or may nominate themselves.[1] In single-member districts independents are the most numerous category of candidates. There were 873 independent candidates in 1993, and in the second Duma election 1,055. Independents do not constitute a political party; they are a category in which many different types of politicians can be found. The quantity of independent candidates is complemented by the unwillingness or inability of parties nominating candidates for the national PR ballot to contest districts nationwide. In 1993 no party contested as many as half the 225 single-member districts. The Communist Party named candidates in 98 districts, and Russia's Choice, the party of ex-prime minister Yegor Gaidar, nominated only 88 candidates. In 1995 the Communist Party nominated 130 candidates, and Our

---

[1] Candidates in single-member districts are here classified according to the label given on their nomination papers. In some cases, this differs from the party with which a nominee is associated in the district. All election statistics cited in this book are as reported in Munro and Rose, 2001.

Home Is Russia, the party of the then prime minister, nominated 103 SMD candidates.

The *proportional representation list ballot* manufactures a party system, because PR allocates seats according to the votes received by each party. To qualify for a place on the PR ballot, politicians are compelled to organize a party and put forward a list of candidates.[2] A party can conduct a centralized nationwide campaign on behalf of its list through the media without the regional activity required to nominate and elect candidates in single-member districts. Russian electoral law does not offer voters an opportunity to express preferences for individual candidates on a party's list. The Russian list system compels people to vote for a party, to vote against all parties or to abstain from voting.

2. *Independents win most votes and seats.* In an accountable party system, independents can contest elections but nearly all the votes and seats are won by party candidates. However, in each Russian election, independents have been successful as well as numerous. For example, in the initial round of the 1996 presidential election, independents collectively won a majority of the popular vote, and the importance of being a non-party candidate was confirmed when independent Boris Yeltsin beat the Communist candidate in the second round.

In single-member districts, independent candidates have been the most popular party (*sic*), winning almost half the vote. In 1993, a presidential decree forbade placing party labels on the ballot for fear that this would help candidates of the Communist Party, the only party with name recognition. Independents won 45.2 per cent of the vote, and since 14.8 per cent voted against all parties and 7.4 per cent of ballots were invalid, only one-third of the vote was available for division among party candidates. Before the 1995 election, the law was changed to allow party names to appear on the ballot. Notwithstanding this change, 31.0 per cent of the vote still went to independents, and an additional 9.6 per cent was cast against all. Communist candidates polled the largest number of partisan votes in single-member districts, but this was only 12.5 per cent of all the votes cast.

Even though the total independent vote in a single district is usually divided among four or five independent candidates, one of them is most likely to win the seat. In 1993 candidates fighting as

---

[2] The electoral law of the Federation defines a party as a nationwide political organization (*obshchefederalnoe politicheskoe obedinenie*), or bloc of two or more such organizations. The Russian term for party (*partiya*) has a narrower meaning; the Communist Party of the Russian Federation is a party (*partiya*), while at the time of the 1999 election Unity was a movement (*dvizhenie*). The term party here refers to single organizations or blocs grouped together to contest list seats. For a full list of parties, movements and groupings, with Russian as well as English names, see Munro and Rose, 2001, tab. 1.5.

independents took an absolute majority of single-member seats, 146.
In 1995 independents were the largest party (*sic*), winning 77 SMD
seats. Since no party fights all districts, the seats that independents do
not win are dispersed among a great variety of parties, most of which
do not contest or win seats on the list ballot. In 1993 a dozen parties
won single-member seats, and in 1995 there were 23 nominal parties
winning SMD seats.

In the proportional representation contest, dozens of parties compete, but the rules condemn the vast majority to total defeat. To qualify
for PR seats, a party must win at least 5.0 per cent of the list vote. By
the standards of European PR systems, the 5 per cent threshold is high.
In the Netherlands a party can qualify to win a parliamentary seat with
less than 1.0 per cent of the vote. In the Federal Republic of Germany,
which also has a 5 per cent threshold, political elites have organized
parties with a broad enough base of support to clear this barrier. But
this has not happened in Russia. The 1995 Russian election produced
one of the most disproportional results in the history of proportional
representation. The four parties sharing 100 per cent of the seats together claimed only 50.5 per cent of the total vote. Thus, for every
1 per cent of the vote won, each party gained 2 per cent of the seats.
The 39 parties that collectively won almost half the vote gained no
seats because they failed to clear the 5 per cent threshold.

3. *A big disjunction between electoral parties and Duma parties.* A necessary condition of accountability is that representatives belong to the
same party in parliament as the party in whose name they stood when
seeking election. In an established party system, this is invariably the
case; changes in party affiliation during the life of a parliament are
few and idiosyncratic. But this is not the case in Russia. Victorious
candidates often change their party immediately after entering the
Duma, and can change parties again during the four-year life of the
Duma.

The definition of a party in the Duma differs fundamentally from
the ballot definition. Duma parties, officially known as fractions, are
groups that have at least 35 Duma members, 7.8 per cent of the assembly's total. As in established democracies, Duma rules give greater
facilities to members who belong to a recognized party; independent
individuals tend to be isolated. Furthermore, members of Duma parties are better able to influence its activities and government policies
because they can cast a bloc of votes. In response to such incentives,
Duma members elected as independents usually join a Duma fraction.
Some join a group that has nominated and elected list candidates and
some join a fraction opportunistically formed by independents wanting
Duma facilities.

Figure 5.1 DUMA MEMBERS AS QUICK-CHANGE ARTISTS.

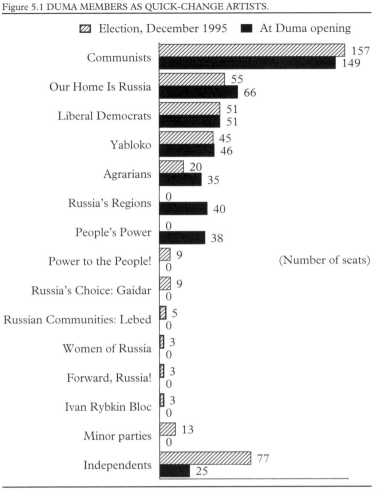

Source: Central Electoral Commission, *Vybory deputatov Gosudarstvennoy dumy 1995*, Moscow: Ves' Mir, 1996, 199–205.

Duma members demonstrate formidable skills as quick-change artists (fig. 5.1). Between the election of December 1995 and the swearing in of the new Duma the following month, 105 deputies switched parties. To qualify as a Duma fraction, the Agrarian Party recruited some independents and acquired additional members from the Communist Party. Two fractions were created in the Duma – Russia's Regions (40 seats) and Power to the People! (38 seats); they were non-ballot parties because they did not offer the electorate the chance to vote for or against them by appearing on the list ballot.

Eighteen parties recorded as winning single-member districts, including the parties of former prime minister Yegor Gaidar and presidential candidate Alexander Lebed, became invisible within a month of the Duma's first meeting. By the time the Duma drew to a close in autumn 1999, accountability was further reduced as some members switched to an exit party different from their entry party. Altogether, more than a quarter of Duma members changed their party label between 1995 and 1999 and at the time of dissolution 90 deputies represented parties that did not exist when they were elected.

4. *A failure to persist.* Voters can hold parties accountable, confirming or withdrawing their support, only if parties appear on the ballot at successive elections. However, most Russian parties are ephemeral. Of the 13 parties that contested list seats in 1993, 5 disappeared from the 1995 ballot and only 4 were still there in 1999. In 1995 there were 35 new party names on the ballot; however, four-fifths had dropped out of the running four years later.

Parties successful in winning seats have more reason to stand for re-election than parties that win few votes and fail to qualify for PR seats. One would therefore expect that persisting parties would take the lion's share of votes and seats, while ephemeral parties come and go because of weak support at their first and last election. However, this is not the case in Russia. More than 12 per cent of the vote in the 1993 list vote went to parties that did not go on to contest the 1995 election, and in addition 28 per cent went to parties that dropped out after the 1995 ballot. In the 1995 list ballot, 41 per cent of the vote went to parties that were not on the ballot two years previously, and 31 per cent to parties that did not go on to contest the 1999 election. In every Duma election voters have had the opportunity to mark their ballot 'against all parties', a vote that is formally directed against a different menu of parties at each election but, more broadly, expresses a rejection of a continuing political elite.

Instead of having a four-party system, Russia has four systems of parties, for Russian political elites respond differently when they face different rules about contesting elections. In the presidential race, about half the candidates run as independents and win the largest share of the vote. In single-member districts of the Duma, the great majority of candidates are independents and independents win the most seats too. In the Duma, the readiness of election winners to drop one label and take up another creates an inside-the-Ring-Road party system different from that in the constituencies. A list system of proportional representation requires politicians to seek seats under a party label, but the unwillingness of many list parties to fight successive elections makes it impossible for voters to hold them accountable.

The federal character of the Russian political system adds more systems of party competition.[3] Elections for the governorship and the legislature in the 89 regions of Russia are held according to rules laid down within the region. Even where the rules are the same as for federal elections, the pattern of competition is not. In 72 regional legislative elections in the period from October 1995 to March 1997, independents won 83 per cent of the seats, while national list parties won 11 per cent and local parties the remainder. In the 73 gubernatorial races that took place in this period, more than two-thirds of the winners ran as independents. In some cases, both the pro-government and Communist blocs claimed that the winner was 'one of ours', but subsequent behaviour demonstrated that even nominally partisan governors prefer tactical alliances to the constraints of a party (Stoner-Weiss, 2001a).

The existence of four systems is primarily due to the leaders of Russian parties refusing to be consistent in contesting elections. To interpret this as showing the failure of party elites is to impose alien standards. The same evidence can equally be interpreted as showing the success of Russian elites in insulating themselves from accountability to the mass electorate. The party system emerging in Russia is not based on an Anglo-American model of party accountability. Instead, it resembles the late nineteenth-century Italian system of *trasformismo*, in which patronage-led political coalitions are formed without regard to accountability to the electorate. In a *trasformismo* system, the labels that politicians use to describe themselves are taken up or abandoned as opportunities arise for enrichment and access to power (Pallotta, 1976: 297).

Why Duma elections matter

The shelling of the White House headquarters of Parliament in October 1993 showed that when push came to shove, the president had more brute force at his command than did the assembly. But the starkness of the event also produced a political reaction: none involved wanted to use guns to resolve differences in the future. Subsequently, the constitution has given the Duma a modicum of powers, while confirming the president's claim to be the central figure in Russian government. The constitution also authorizes a schedule for Duma elections that can be violated only at the price of forfeiting the claim to be an electoralist regime.

---

[3] The upper chamber of parliament, the Council of the Russian Federation, has a sixth method of choosing members. At the time of the 1999 Duma election, the Federal Council consisted ex officio of governors of regions and speakers of regional parliaments. Since then, the law has been amended so that the regional parliament and the governors each nominate a full-time delegate to the Federation Council, and the delegate is subject to recall.

The Constitution of the Russian Federation creates institutions that separate powers. The distribution of powers between the two institutions is unequal. The president and the executive he appoints are very much the active force in Russian government, and the president has decree powers to authorize actions without Duma legislation. The ephemeral and fragmented system of parties in the Duma greatly handicaps initiatives by its members. Furthermore, President Yeltsin was ready to ignore the Supreme Court when it challenged his exercise of *vlast*.

While weak, the Duma is not powerless. It has the right to reject the president's nominee for prime minister, and in 1998 it forced the withdrawal of Viktor Chernomyrdin's nomination for a new term as prime minister. The Duma also has the power to confirm or reject spending and tax proposals in the budget, and it has shown independence in altering the budget. The Duma can and does amend or reject legislative initiatives of the president. If the president vetoes a bill, the Duma and the Federation Council jointly have the right to override the veto, provided that they can muster a two-thirds majority of their total membership. The powers of the Duma are thus greater than those of the British House of Commons, but much less than those of the United States Congress.

Since Russia is not a parliamentary democracy, the president does not need the support of a majority of members in the Duma. But because the Duma has some powers, the Kremlin prefers an assembly that will cooperate with its lead or, at least, not actively obstruct it. Prior to the 1995 election, the Kremlin promoted two Duma parties to support President Yeltsin: Our Home Is Russia, led by the then prime minister, Viktor Chernomyrdin, and a social democratic coalition led by the chair of the Duma, Ivan Rybkin. A two-party strategy offered two chances of gaining list votes, and in single-member districts the Kremlin was free to back agreeable candidates with a chance of victory. However, the initiative was a failure. In the list competition, Our Home Is Russia came third with 10.1 per cent and Rybkin's group failed to win any seats, taking only 1.1 per cent of the vote. In the single-member districts, the two parties did even worse. Together, the parties favoured by the Kremlin gained only 58 of the 450 Duma seats. Reflecting on the failure of the top-down initiative, Chernomyrdin said, 'Our biggest mistake was that we started to build our house from the roof (*krysha*) down'[4] (quoted in Oversloot and Verheul, 2000: 139).

---

[4] The comment reflected the fact that the logo of Our Home Is Russia had fingers of two hands pointing upwards and linked, thus looking like the roof of a house. Critics noted that in Russian politics a roof is also a source of protection for the network of public officials, elected politicians, businessmen and even *mafiya* leaders that gather under it.

The Kremlin can play on the weak party loyalties and strong self-interest of Duma members to gain their support for government measures on the basis of ambition, avarice, constituency interests or shared political values. Offering Duma members material benefits or threatening to withdraw patronage shows a grudging respect for the need for Duma votes, while taking advantage of the desire that many Duma members have for favours such as a flat in Moscow. Up to a point, the government also has the patronage of public expenditure for politically visible building projects and factories that could not survive without state subsidies. But list-system Duma members usually have their base within the Moscow Ring Road rather than in a geographical constituency, and only in very close Duma votes is the support of individual SMD members important. Pork-barrel spending in a specific region is more an asset to gain the support of a particular governor than to win Duma votes. Most central government money allocated to the regions is fixed by formulas for the finance of education, health and other public policies for which population, rather than votes, determines how much is spent (cf. Treisman, 1999; Hanson and Bradshaw, 2000: ch. 5).

Scrambling to form parties

For individual Duma deputies the critical question was whether they should stand in the name of the party they belonged to at the 1995 election or after the Duma was organized, or whether to stand under a different party label, or as an independent. For political elites, the big question was: what party can we supply that has the best chance of winning seats and advancing our particular interests in the Duma and in the subsequent presidential election? Political elites, and especially business enterprise groups, had the option of backing more than one political party or waiting until Duma members were elected and then participating in the formation of non-ballot Duma fractions. Presidential hopefuls required a good showing in the Duma vote in order to demonstrate that they had a credible chance of winning votes in the presidential ballot.

In search of a winning combination

As ambitious Duma members considered their positions in the months before nominations closed, the evidence of opinion polls was unclear. Up to a third or more of electors had no party preference, were unlikely to vote or would vote against all parties. An additional tenth of voters indicated a preference for a group so small that pollsters categorized it as 'other'. The three-fifths of the electorate choosing a party that might

Table 5.1 *Duma voting intentions in pre-nomination polls*

Q. For which of the following parties or movements would you be most likely to vote if there were elections to the State Duma next Sunday?

	1999					
	Mar	Apr	May	Jun	Jul	Aug
	(% all respondents)					
Communist Party	22	26	24	21	24	23
Yabloko	12	12	10	10	10	9
Fatherland	12	13	10	11	14	14
Liberal Democrats	3	6	6	5	5	7
Our Home Is Russia	3	3	5	3	2	4
Union of Right Forces*	1	3	3	1	2	6
All other	14	10	8	12	9	16
Against all/wouldn't vote	17	11	18	21	17	1
Don't know	16	16	16	16	17	20

* Refers to Right Forces from August 1999. Figures for March-July 1999 refer to New Force (Kirienko); in August 1999 New Force merged with Right Cause (Gaidar) and Young Russia (Nemtsov) to form Right Forces.
Source: VTsIOM. Nationwide surveys. Number of respondents for each survey approximately 1,600.

hope to win list seats divided among more than half a dozen parties, some contesting the previous general election and some embryonic (tab. 5.1).

In pre-campaign polls, only two political parties with representatives in the Duma – the Communist Party and Yabloko – attracted the support of at least 10 per cent of respondents. The Fatherland Party created by Moscow mayor Yury Luzhkov also reached this level of support. After excluding from calculations electors who said they would not vote or did not have a party preference, the Liberal Democrats of Vladimir Zhirinovsky and the newly formed Union of Right Forces showed enough support to clear the 5 per cent list threshold. But the statistical margin of error in sampling public opinion is such that 6 per cent support in the polls should be understood as an estimate of between 3.5 and 8.5 per cent of support – assuming no substantial change occurred between the date of the poll and election day. The fragmentation of support among many parties and none was an incentive to what Italians call *combinazione*, forming alliances with other political associations in order to nominate a joint list.

Yury Luzhkov was a power in Russia's biggest city, and up to a point this was a good base for entering the national political arena. It gave Luzhkov money, contacts with oligarchs wanting things done in the capital and media prominence. In 1996 Luzhkov had backed Yeltsin's presidential bid, but subsequently the two had fallen out. The celebration of Moscow's 850th anniversary in September 1997 gave Luzhkov a chance to publicize himself and the city. In an appeal to traditional values, he ordered the Church of Christ the Saviour, razed by Stalin, rebuilt near the Kremlin in accord with its original ornate style. Although Moscow is Russia's biggest city, the metropolitan region has only a tenth of the country's electorate, enough to help a list party clear the PR threshold but not enough to guarantee a top position in the Duma election. To become nationally powerful, Luzhkov needed allies. Before the economic crisis of August 1998, former Yeltsin supporters began indicating support for Luzhkov's political ambitions and the Moscow mayor also cultivated alliances with governors in the regions, including Nizhny Novgorod, Novosibirsk and Russia's second city, St Petersburg.

The collapse of the ruble made a candidate from outside the Kremlin circle appear more attractive. In early 1999 VTsIOM polls indicated that Fatherland could run second in the list ballot. Luzhkov used its popularity to solicit additional backing from ambitious politicians, guaranteeing a seat in the Duma by offering a high place on the Fatherland list. In August 1999, Fatherland's coalition expanded on two fronts. Yevgeny Primakov joined the party, endorsing such vague goals as 'marrying democracy and order', 'the state idea' and expressing respect for private property. Concurrently, Luzhkov gained a nationwide network of supporters through an alliance with regional governors grouped in the All Russia movement. The latter joined with Fatherland to create the Fatherland-All Russia Bloc, known by its Russian acronym, OVR. Regional governors had shown their strength in May 1998 by defeating Kremlin-sponsored candidates in governorship elections. Fatherland-All Russia attracted support from Duma members of two parties without electoral organizations, Russia's Regions and the Agrarians.

Kremlin politicians tended to discount the need for party organization, for they already had the chief office of the state in their hands. But in an electoralist regime, the Yeltsin Family could not ignore the need for its friends to win seats in the Duma and prevent their enemies from doing so. The strategy of the prime minister, Sergei Stepashin, was to create a party based on a coalition of regional governors, tentatively named 'the governors' club'. But this initiative was aborted when he was fired in August 1999. Concurrently, a leading oligarch, Boris Berezovsky, promoted a new inter-regional movement to stop the presidential prospects of Primakov and Luzhkov, initially called Muzhiki (literally, 'fellows'; colloquially, a Russian term roughly equivalent to the American phrase 'good ol' boys'). Support was sought from governors who disliked Luzhkov, and who had received or expected favours from the Family. The group included Alexander Rutskoi, who had initially been Yeltsin's vice president and subsequently led the Duma revolt against him in October 1993, the governor of Yeltsin's home city, Sverdlovsk, and two governors who had been on the 1996 presidential ballot, Alexander Lebed and Aman Tuleev, a Communist supporter. Other Communist governors also expressed support for Berezovsky's initiative. Eventually, 39 regional governors gave their support to the pro-Kremlin group (for details, see Colton and McFaul, 2000).

To qualify for the ballot, Kremlin organizers needed to recruit at least one political association already registered to appear there. Seven political associations were happy to be aligned with the Family's interests; these included associations nominally committed to small business, the family, Muslim interests, Afghan war veterans, the interests of independent deputies and Christian democracy. Coalition-building resulted in the party's name becoming much lengthier, the Inter-Regional Movement Unity. The Russian acronym – MEDVED: *MEzhregionalnoe DVizhenie EDinstvo* – was the Russian word for bear, a traditional symbol of strength. In English, the party became known as Unity. Its first conference was not held until 3 October 1999, ten weeks before the Duma election. Prime Minister Vladimir Putin was a guest at the party's launch, but did not join it. Sergei Shoigu, minister for emergency situations and civil defence, led the new party. Shoigu had previously been associated with Our Home Is Russia and then the All Russia Bloc, and had been discussed as a possible prime minister instead of or after Putin.

Four groups that shared a preference for the market, Kremlin appointments under President Yeltsin and a dislike of Luzhkov and Primakov joined together to form SPS (*Soyuz pravykh sil*), a party known in English as the Union of Right Forces. In both Russian and English the word 'right' ambiguously invokes the twin values of freedom and the market. The group included Anatoly Chubais, a Kremlin maker of economic policy and chair of the major partially privatized electricity firm, United Energy Systems; former acting prime minister Yegor Gaidar; Boris Nemtsov, former governor of Nizhny Novgorod and a former deputy prime minister; and Irina Khakamada, a Duma member and admirer of Margaret Thatcher. Both Kirienko and Nemtsov had links with oligarch and media owner Vladimir Potanin. Right Forces sought to promote the reformist agenda of the Yeltsin era, but doing so made it electorally unappealing. Moreover, intra-Family jealousies meant that any party associated with Chubais and Potanin would encourage the organization of another Kremlin party. In August 1999, prior to the formation of Unity, a VTsIOM poll showed 6 per cent favouring the Union of Right Forces, enough to qualify for list seats but not enough to make it a major player in the presidential race.

Persistent but not popular parties

Three parties that had fought and won seats in the two previous Duma elections – the Communists, the Liberal Democrats and Yabloko – had good reason to fight the 1999 Duma election, for each was intent on nominating its leader as a candidate in the presidential election due to follow.

The Communist Party of the Russian Federation did not have the problem of starting from scratch, for its brand name had not been repudiated as was the case in Central and Eastern Europe. It was founded in December 1992 on the basis of local organizations of the Communist Party of the Soviet Union, which had had its central institutions declared illegal by Boris Yeltsin after the failure of the August 1991 coup. In the December 1993 Duma election the Communist Party finished third, trailing the parties of Vladimir Zhirinovsky and of Yegor Gaidar. In the 1995 election, it led the field with 22 per cent of the list vote. In subsequent opinion polls it was invariably the front-running party. Since polls included upwards of one-third who would not vote, its poll standing implied that it would do even better in the 1999 Duma list vote (cf. tab. 5.1). However, the Communist Party faced a red ceiling on its support, because identification with the old regime generated resistance as well as support. Moreover, its supporters were disproportionately older, requiring more new adherents to hold the party's vote level from one election to the next.

As an unpredictable demagogue, the leader of the Liberal Democratic Party of Russia, Vladimir Zhirinovsky, gained media attention. In the Duma, Liberal Democratic Party members tended to attack liberal reform proposals but frequently voted with the Yeltsin administration. The trajectory of Zhirinovsky's support was downwards. In 1993 the party came first in the list ballot with 21 per cent of the popular vote, but in 1995 it won barely half that total and pre-campaign polls suggested its vote was falling further, as was support for Zhirinovsky as a presidential candidate.

Yabloko, led by Grigory Yavlinsky, maintained an anti-Yeltsin and anti-Communist line from the first Duma election. When the second Chechen War started, Yavlinsky was one of the few politicians to question Vladimir Putin's methods and goals. Yabloko had two major handicaps. First, there was limited electoral support for liberal ideals and pro-market policies. Second, Yavlinsky's personality was an obstacle to a coalition with other reform politicians. When reformers such as Yegor Gaidar and Irina Khakamada were given the choice between combining with Yavlinsky to campaign for liberal reforms or making alliances with Kremlin associates of Yeltsin, they chose the latter alternative.

Two parties associated with presidential candidates in the previous election – Our Home Is Russia and the Congress of Russian Communities –

were registered to qualify for the Duma ballot in 1999. However, they showed so little support in the VTsIOM poll that they had little to contribute to building a winning coalition – and the fact that each had had a politically prominent leader, former prime minister Viktor Chernomyrdin and former presidential candidate Alexander Lebed, made them even less attractive to politicians who already had more than enough prima donnas in their party.

The intrigues, alliances and manoeuvres of party politicians trying to become part of the 'party of power' were over the heads and beyond the concern of many Russians. Just three months before the Duma election, VTsIOM asked people which party they thought of as the party of power. Nearly half said there was no such party or that if there was they did not know its name (fig. 5.2). The party most frequently cited as the party of power was Fatherland-All Russia, a party very visibly campaigning

Figure 5.2 POPULAR UNAWARENESS OF A PARTY OF POWER.

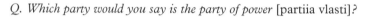

Q. Which party would you say is the party of power [partiia vlasti]*?*

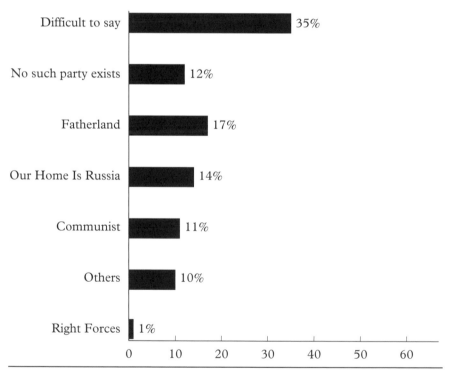

Source: VTsIOM Monitoring Survey, 17–20 September 1999. Number of respondents, 1,545.

against powerholders in the Kremlin. The second group misperceived as the party of power was Our Home Is Russia, whose leader was unable to gain Duma confirmation as prime minister in August 1998. Due to its historical association with the Kremlin, the Communist Party was third among groups mentioned as the party of power. The one pro-government party then in existence, the Union of Right Forces, was seen as powerful by only 1 per cent of the electorate. Unity was not named for it had not yet come into existence. The inability of Russians to identify parties close to power emphasizes the lack of accountability, for people cannot vote to keep the government in or to turn it out if they do not know which party or parties hold power.

6   A floating system of parties

In an accountable party system, the choice of voters may fluctuate between parties from one election to the next but the supply of parties remains constant. By contrast, in a floating party system, the parties competing for popular support change from one election to the next. Some parties disappear from the ballot, new parties appear, others alter their names and much else, and several parties combine in blocs that blur or destroy their previous identities. Accountability is not meaningful when voters can neither reaffirm nor withdraw their support from the party for which they voted at the previous election.

The choice offered Russian voters in 1999 was that of a floating set of parties. The list ballot contained the names of 26 political parties, most of which had been newly formed since the last election. In the average single-member district, there were ten candidates, including several independents, list party and non-list party candidates to choose between. The broadening of local choice was an obstacle to collective national accountability because the choice of candidates differed greatly from one district to another. The unwillingness of political elites to be consistent in supplying parties meant there were two types of election campaign going on simultaneously: a national battle for list votes, and 225 local battles for district seats. Differences in the supply of parties guaranteed that the outcomes would differ. It also meant that the overall result of adding up seats in the two separate contests differed substantially from the results highlighted in the media, the votes and seats that parties won in the list ballot.

The Duma election did not offer a choice of government, as would have happened in a British-style parliamentary system. Nor did the Duma vote offer Russians the opportunity that French voters have to produce a prime minister with different political sympathies than the president. While the Duma can refuse to endorse the appointment of a prime minister, it lacks the power of the French Assembly to install a prime minister of a different party than the president. Because the presidency was not at stake in the December vote, Russians lacked the ability of Americans to split their ticket, voting for a member of Congress of one party while voting for another party to take over the White House.

The lack of accountability of Duma members gave them a tactical electoral advantage. Even though voters could not turn the government out, Duma members could run against the government, denying responsibility for the great difficulties of the previous four years. During the autumn campaign, however, the rapid rise in the popularity of Prime Minister Vladimir Putin introduced a new element, a link between a popular prime minister and Unity, the party that he publicly announced he would vote for. But votes for Unity were not a gauge of Putin's electoral strength, for his name was not on the ballot and the vote of Unity on the list ballot was too low to guarantee a presidential candidate a place in the run-off vote for the presidency.

Getting on the ballot

Parties qualified to place candidates on the *party list* ballot through a complex multi-stage process. The first requirement was to be registered with the Ministry of Justice as a federal political association. To register as an association, a political group had to adopt a constitution authorizing it to participate in federal elections. The deadline for doing so was December 1998, a year before the Duma election. At that time, the prime minister was Yevgeny Primakov. The great majority of parties seeking list seats a year later did not exist or did not exist under the name that they previously registered with the Ministry of Justice. By the time registration closed, 139 groups had registered as political associations, far more than would ever expect to nominate candidates for the Duma.

By registering an association, politicians gained the right to put forward a list of candidates. Of the six parties that subsequently won list seats, only two – the Communist Party and Yabloko – had registered as a political associations in their own right twelve months before election day. The right to nominate a list was a valuable franchise. The law allowed political associations to club together as a bloc, pooling support in hopes of clearing the 5 per cent threshold. For example, if three associations would each expect to get 2 per cent of the vote separately, by pooling their votes they could hope collectively to gain enough votes to win about 15 seats. A politician who headed an association could thus enter negotiations with other associations about forming an alliance for their mutual tactical benefit. An association could offer its franchise to nominate candidates to a more powerful group of politicians who had failed to register an association before the deadline.

Once the election date was officially announced in August, a registered political association or a bloc consisting of several associations had to submit to the Central Electoral Commission a list of candidates for certification. At that time each candidate was assigned a position on the list, ranging from the top place, guaranteeing a Duma seat if the party cleared the 5 per cent threshold, to a lower position that gave no hope of entering the Duma. Next, the association had to collect 200,000 nomination signatures, with no more than 7 per cent from any one region, or pay a cash deposit of 2,087,250 rubles (approximately $84,000), a very substantial sum, and returnable only if the party won at least 3 per cent of the total list vote. Each candidate was required to give a biography, with information about citizenship, income and property, and any record of criminal convictions. The list of candidates had to be approved by the commission.

In all, 31 associations or alliances of associations filed nomination papers by the deadline of 24 October. Four groups were rejected, including a Muslim party, Nur, which was deemed to have made mistakes in filling out forms; the extremist National Salvation Front, which was ruled out because of many invalid nomination signatures; and the Liberal Democratic Party of Vladimir Zhirinovsky and the Russian Conservative Party of Entrepreneurs, both of which were found to have discrepancies in the income and property declarations of leading candidates. Prudently, Zhirinovsky had registered additional political associations, which then banded together to create a Zhirinovsky Bloc guaranteeing his candidates a place on the list ballot. An environmentalist party, Cedar, was automatically disqualified after two of its three leading list candidates withdrew their names from the party's list. Of the 26 valid nominations of party lists, 10 secured a ballot place by collecting 200,000 signatures. In addition, 16 paid the cash deposit in order to qualify; only the Zhirinovsky Bloc received back its deposit by winning at least 3.0 per cent of the vote.

All the parties formed when the Duma opened in January 1996 were still there when the Duma dissolved.[1] However, when it came time to contest the 1999 election three parties holding in total 125 seats did not give voters a chance to hold them accountable by appearing on the list ballot. The Agrarian Party avoided the list contest from weakness; its list vote had fallen below the 5 per cent threshold in 1995. People's Power, a Duma fraction led by Nikolai Ryzhkov, also avoided the list ballot after a part of their membership failed to win seats by that route in 1995.

---

[1] In relation to seats reported in figure 5.1, the following changes occurred in party strength: Communists, down 22 members, Our Home Is Russia, down 5; Liberal Democrats, down 3; Yabloko and Agrarians, no change. Two Duma-only parties gained seats: People's Power, up 8, and Russia's Regions, up 4; independents were up 7, and there were 11 vacant seats.

Russia's Regions, a convenience party of independent deputies, had not fought the 1995 election on the list ballot and did not do so in 1999. The absence of these Duma parties from the 1999 election did not mean that they were leaving politics, but rather that their members preferred to wait until after the next election was held before showing their partisan colours publicly (see below, fig. 8.1).

The floating nature of the parties is evident, for 18 of the 26 parties on the list ballot were new parties. They varied in character from Unity, associated with Prime Minister Vladimir Putin, to parties for pensioners and For Citizens' Dignity, to the Stalinist Bloc for the USSR. Four groups which won a total of two-thirds of the list seats in December were formed by alliances of associations registered under other names. The Unity party was an amalgam of seven associations; Fatherland-All Russia combined five different associations; the Union of Right Forces brought together four associations; and the Zhirinovsky Bloc two associations.

There was no shortage of candidates in the *225 single-member districts*. An aspiring candidate had to be at least 21 years of age and a citizen of the Russian Federation. There were 3,882 would-be candidates certified as eligible. To appear on the ballot, those certified as eligible to become candidates then had to present valid nomination papers with signatures from 1 per cent of the district's electorate, about 4,750 signatures in an average district. In 1999 an alternative – a cash deposit of 83,490 rubles (approximately $3,000), equal to 1,000 times the monthly minimum wage – was accepted. The deposit was returnable if the candidate won 5 per cent of the district vote.

When nominations closed, 2,758 candidates had been nominated, of which 1,957 did so by presenting signatures. In the event, 381 nominees were disqualified and 144 withdrew. There were 1,084 candidates nominated by a party that was either local or else on the national list; and 1,149 independents. Of the candidates whose nominations were accepted, 721 paid a deposit rather than collect signatures in order to secure a place on the ballot. The total of 2,233 candidates averaged almost 10 per district, double the number that would contest a typical British parliamentary constituency and more than double that of an American Congressional district.

The choice of candidates supplied by local, regional and national political elites floated from one single-member district to the next (fig. 6.1). Paradoxically, the only category of candidates appearing on the ballot in all the districts were the independent candidates. But in no sense did the 1,149 independent candidates constitute a movement or a political association, let alone a party. This was shown by the fact that in the average single-member district there were five independents fighting each other. Only two parties – the Communist Party and Yabloko – contested more

Figure 6.1 PARTIES CONTESTING SINGLE-MEMBER DISTRICTS.

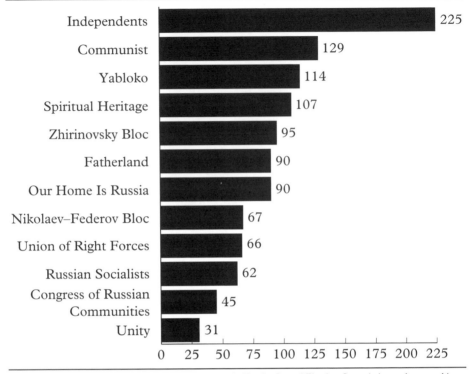

Source: Compiled from district nomination papers recorded by the Central Election Commission and reported in Neil Munro and Richard Rose, *Elections in the Russian Federation*, Glasgow: University of Strathclyde Studies in Public Policy No. 344, 2001, table 2.5. Data include eight districts in which high votes against all candidates required follow-up elections in March 2000, plus Chechnya, which held a ballot in August 2000.

than half the single-member districts. Spiritual Heritage, a nationalist party led by Aleksei Podberezkin, elected as a Communist deputy in 1995, contested almost half the seats. The normal party of power, Unity, nominated fewer candidates than ten other parties. Many incumbents fought in their district under a different label than that of their Duma party.

The extent to which party choice reflected supply-side decisions by political elites rather than demand-side pressures from voters was inadvertently demonstrated by an American political scientist, Arthur Miller. In a sample survey in Russia in May 1998, he asked respondents about their attachment to 14 parties that appeared at that time to be the emerging Russian party system. However, before the article could be published in an academic journal, nine of the parties had floated away, failing to nominate candidates for the 1999 Duma election. A majority of Russians voted for parties that did not exist when the 1998 survey was undertaken (Miller and Klobucar, 2000).

Competing to fill a vacuum

On the eve of the election campaign in mid-September, the largest group of electors had no party preference. VTsIOM found that 20 per cent said they would not bother to vote or they would mark their ballot 'against all' if they did so, and an additional 14 per cent were don't knows. Furthermore, 13 per cent endorsed other parties, groups which were uncertain to be on the ballot or which, if they did appear, were almost certain not to win any list seats. Altogether, 47 per cent of the electorate had no inclination toward a party with a chance of winning list seats in the Duma.

The floating party system created a partial vacuum, because many electors could not vote for the party for which they had voted at the previous election, since it was not on the ballot. At the start of the campaign, parties that had fought the 1995 election were endorsed by only a third of the electorate, and newly formed parties were supported by a fifth of the electorate. The relatively largest bloc of electors, 20 per cent, were inclined to the Communist Party, and 16 per cent favoured Fatherland-All Russia. The party in third place, Yabloko, was named by 9 per cent of respondents, the Zhirinovsky Bloc by 3 per cent and Women of Russia by 2 per cent. Unity had yet to be formed and was therefore not included in the September poll. With so much of the electorate without any party preference, new parties did not need to woo voters with an established party identification. Their goal was to attract support from undecided electors or those not inclined to vote.

In campaigning for Duma votes, all politicians faced a big obstacle: widespread distrust of parties and of the Duma. In NRB surveys, political parties are consistently the most distrusted of all institutions in society, and the Duma comes a close second. In the survey immediately after the Duma election, only 9 per cent expressed trust in political parties, compared to 75 per cent actively distrusting parties, and the remaining sixth neutral. Only 12 per cent expressed trust in the Duma, while 71 per cent were actively distrustful.

Media attack

The first aim of the Family was to attack its most feared opponents, Fatherland-All Russia and its presidential hopefuls, Yevgeny Primakov and Yury Luzhkov. Attack campaigning is appealing to campaigners who are unpopular, as was Boris Yeltsin's Kremlin, and to politicians who do not have (or do not want to talk about) a political agenda, a group including Vladimir Putin.

The Family attacked through an air war, that is, centrally controlled television reports from Moscow likely to reach the four-fifths of the electorate that regularly viewed television. This type of campaign avoided becoming bogged down in a ground war in the regions and single-member districts. The main television networks were state-owned and had no tradition of political impartiality. Nor were privately owned television stations independent of government, for the Kremlin controlled television franchises. In the 1996 presidential election, all the television networks aggressively promoted Yeltsin's candidacy, fearing that a Communist victory would mean the end of independent media. As Boris Berezovsky, an oligarch and part-owner of ORT, the major state television channel, explained to a Western journalist, 'Our media are something different from yours. It wasn't possible just to go on the air and calmly explain things. This was a huge war of interests, a dangerous war' (Remnick, 2000: 41).

The means of attack was *kompromat* (literally, compromising material). A foretaste had been given in March 1999, when the prosecutor general, Yury Skuratov, began probing the financial affairs of Family members and companies owned by oligarchs, including Berezovsky. To dispose of Skuratov by humiliation and ridicule, agents of the state security forces set him up with two prostitutes and he was filmed in a semi-successful attempt to have sexual intercourse. The film was then given to two Family-controlled television networks. It was re-run during the campaign in the main ORT weekend news magazine, with comments spliced into it from Yury Luzhkov and other backers of the prosecutor. Opponents of the Family charged that the film was fraudulent, featuring an actor made up to look like Skuratov. Yevgeny Primakov, who was fit enough to be prime minister in 1998–9, was attacked on television as physically unfit to hold office. Allegations were also televised that Primakov was sympathetic to the Chechens and had been involved in an attempted assassination of the former Soviet foreign minister and president of Georgia, Eduard Shevardnadze. Luzhkov too came in for vitriolic attacks. An analysis by the European Institute for the Media (2000: 2, 43) found that ORT television devoted 28 per cent of its coverage to Unity, and 14 per cent to Fatherland-All Russia. Coverage of Unity was positive while that of Fatherland-All Russia was overwhelmingly negative.

The impact of election television depends not only on what is broadcast but also on whether voters take any interest in political programmes or believe what is beamed at them. Living in the Soviet Union was an education in learning not to believe everything the media said. Before the Duma election campaign, a majority of Russians distrusted both television and newspapers. Only 23 per cent in the seventh NRB survey thought

Figure 6.2 VOTERS TRUST OWN EXPERIENCE MORE THAN MEDIA.

Q. How useful were the following in helping you decide what to do in the Duma election? (Can choose more than one alternative.)

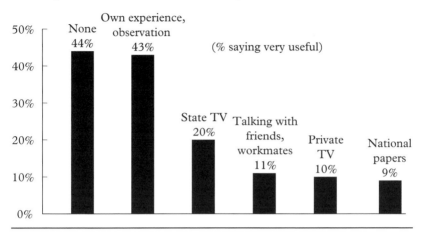

Source: New Russia Barometer VIII. Nationwide survey, 13–29 January 2000. Number of respondents, 1,940.

television stations were looking after the interests of ordinary people, and only 22 per cent trusted newspapers. These views were shared by many media magnates, who saw themselves as looking after their own interests. The Family paid close attention to political television, but most Russians do not. Political news is a minority taste. The eighth NRB survey found that 17 per cent paid no attention at all to media reporting of the Duma election, and 35 per cent paid a little attention. Only 13 per cent spent a lot of time watching the election campaign on television and 35 per cent paid some attention.

When Russians were asked how useful five different sources of political information were in deciding how to vote, the most common reply given was 'None of them' (fig. 6.2). Among those identifying a source, the most frequently named was that most impervious to the national media: my own experience and observations. By contrast, only a fifth described state television stations, the medium most subject to influence by the Family, as very helpful, and this group voted by a margin of four to three for anti-Family parties (Communist, Fatherland-All Russia, Yabloko or the Zhirinovsky Bloc) rather than for Unity or the Union of Right Forces. More detailed statistical analysis[2] shows that there are three groups of

---

[2] A factor analysis of the five questions reported in figure 6.2 shows that the three national media load highly on a single factor (state television .83; private television .79; and national newspapers .79) that explains 50 per cent of the total variance in a three-factor solution.

media users in the Russian electorate. The two largest groups rely on their own experience or did not have any good source of information about the campaign. The smallest group relies on a combination of state and private television and national newspapers. Because avid consumers of political news use a variety of media, they are most likely to be exposed to multiple points of view and therefore better able to discount blatantly biased or untrue reports.

Party tactics

To win Duma seats, Unity first had to become visible as a political party. There was no time to recruit members, for the party held its founding meeting only ten weeks before election day. With good reason, the leaders of the Unity campaign treated their newness as an electoral asset, distancing the party from the record of President Yeltsin. Unity's federal list was headed by Sergei Shoigu, visibly an ethnic Tuvan and minister for emergency situations. The second and third names were well known but newcomers to politics, Alexander Karelin, aged 32, an Olympic medallist in wrestling, and Alexander Gurov, a Ministry of the Interior official nationally known as an opponent of organized crime.

Unity campaigned with simple appeals that verged on the anodyne. Its election manifesto claimed that it was in favour of 'political stability' and against 'stagnation'. Shoigu told interviewers that Unity's philosophy was 'the absence of an ideology'. The party was in favour of a 'normal society with a normal mixed economy and guaranteed rights and freedoms', and that it did not matter what a society was called if its people lived well and peacefully. It sought nationalist support by attacking Mikhail Gorbachev for the collapse of the Soviet Union. Unity's carefully chosen acronym, MEDVED (bear), enabled it to use as its logo an animal that Russians traditionally associate with strength. A campaign poster showed the Unity bear disposing of a snarling wolf wearing a purple jacket and gold chain, dress habits associated with new rich Russians.

Unity paraded its support for the war in Chechnya, but it was only one of many parties pledging support for Vladimir Putin's military effort there. Less than a month before polling day, when Unity showed it was catching up with Fatherland-All Russia in popular appeal (tab. 6.1), Vladimir Putin announced that, although he could show no partiality between parties because he was prime minister, 'as a citizen, I will vote for Unity' (Korsunsky, 1999).

The leaders of Yabloko and of the Union of Right Forces were liberal advocates of the market. The founders of Right Forces, such as Yegor Gaidar, had tried to work within the Yeltsin government, whereas Yabloko leader Grigory Yavlinsky has been a permanent outsider. The Union of

Right Forces manifesto proclaimed a commitment to the 'values of a free society' and to 'European capitalism', both terms more contentious in Russia than in Europe. Yabloko's manifesto added an explicitly anti-government twist, stating it would 'clear corrupt elements out of the state apparatus', and bring in 'honest professionals'. Both parties faced the same problem: there was a limited number of Russian voters favouring market reforms. Having fought two elections previously, Yabloko's first priority was to retain enough of its previous support to clear the 5 per cent threshold for list seats.

The Union of Right Forces had to create awareness of its existence. During the campaign a series of private discussions occurred between its leaders and former colleagues in the Kremlin. The upshot was that on 13 December Putin and Kirienko appeared together on an ORT news programme to discuss economic policies of the Union of Right Forces. Later in the programme Kirienko told viewers that the discussion showed that Putin endorsed his party's views, and four days later Kirienko announced that his party would back Putin for the presidency. The motives of the Kremlin in reaching out to Right Forces were variously interpreted. Optimistic liberals saw this as a sign that Putin would promote market reforms. A realistic calculation was that the Family believed an increase in the vote for Right Forces would come at the expense of its opponents, Fatherland-All Russia and Yabloko.

The Fatherland manifesto had a social democratic tinge, calling for a 'socially oriented market economy', and emphasizing the need to improve industry (the real economy) as against the new wealth created by financial oligarchs. It detailed 100 laws that it would introduce as soon as it won enough votes to do so. The manifesto of its partner, All Russia, said that the party was 'neither on the right nor on the left' and rejected both 'pseudoliberal reforms' and 'a return to the totalitarian past'.

When the election campaign opened, the Communist Party was the party most certain to clear the 5 per cent barrier. With the oldest tradition, biggest organization and most candidates in single-member districts, the Communist Party had a manifesto that sought to mobilize traditional supporters, including poorer Russians and those who had lost most from transformation. It sought to distance the party from the Soviet past by calling for a 'renewed socialist system'. The concentration of the Kremlin's attack on Fatherland-All Russia meant that the Kremlin did not regard the Communist vote as a threat in the Duma or presidential races. There was no anti-Communist scare campaign like that run by the Family in the 1996 presidential election. The best outcome it could hope for was one it could not influence: a repeat of the 1995 Duma result in which many parties fell just below the list threshold, thereby boosting the number of seats awarded the parties that did clear the barrier.

Table 6.1 *Change in party support during the 1999 Duma campaign*

Q. For which of the following parties or movements would you be most likely to vote if there were elections to the State Duma next Sunday?

	Sep 17–21	Oct 15–18	29 Oct –1 Nov	Nov 5–9	Nov 12–15	Nov 19–22	Nov 26–29	Dec 3–6	Dec 10–13	Dec 17–20	Change during campaign
					(% all respondents)						
Won't vote/Against all	20	19	18	17	19	19	19	13	17	4	–16
Don't know	14	18	23	21	20	19	18	19	13	8	–6
Communist	20	18	21	20	21	21	19	20	19	25	+5
Fatherland-All Russia	16	17	11	11	9	11	8	8	10	10	–6
Other	13	10	7	8	7	5	5	6	6	9	–4
Yabloko	9	7	8	7	7	6	7	9	7	4	–5
Liberal Democrats/Zhirinovsky Bloc	3	3	4	3	5	4	3	4	4	4	1
Union of Right Forces	3	3	3	4	5	5	5	5	6	10	+7
Unity	—	3	3	6	6	8	14	13	16	24	24
Women of Russia	2	2	2	3	2	2	2	3	2	2	0

Source: VTsIOM. Nationwide surveys, 1999. Final poll held over weekend with election on 19 December.

What the polls showed

The most predictable effect of the election campaign was the fall in the proportion of electors who were without any party preference (tab. 6.1). However, the decline was only 4 per cent in don't knows, wouldn't vote or voting against all. The failure of many political associations to nominate candidates in their own name and the campaign focus on a limited number of parties led to a decline of 7 per cent in those ready to vote for other parties. Concurrently, there was an increase of 11 percentage points in those preferring one of the major contenders for list seats.

Because Unity did not come into existence until the election campaign was about to start, its vote could only go up, and it rose sharply. At the end of October only 3 per cent endorsed Unity, one percentage point less than those in favour of the Zhirinovsky Bloc. By the middle of November Unity's support was above the level necessary to qualify for list seats. After Vladimir Putin expressed his intention to vote for Unity, the party moved into second place in the opinion polls, ahead of Fatherland-All Russia. In the final VTsIOM pre-election poll, Unity was in second place, only three percentage points behind the Communist Party; its poll over the election weekend showed the gap virtually closed. The Union of Right Forces gained sufficient support during the campaign to rise above the PR threshold too. Together, support for the two pro-Kremlin parties rose from 3 per cent of the electorate in September and 6 per cent in mid-October to 22 per cent in the final week pre-election poll. After discounting those not intending to vote, a week before the election the two pro-Kremlin parties were together favoured by significantly more voters than the Communist Party.

A big rise in support for one party must come at the expense of competitors. As the Kremlin intended, the creation of Unity depressed support for Fatherland-All Russia. When Unity was launched, Fatherland was running neck and neck with the Communist Party for the lead in popular support. After Putin endorsed Unity, its support fell below 10 per cent of the electorate. Although Fatherland was still in third place in the final pre-election VTsIOM poll, during the campaign it lost two-fifths of its quondam supporters.

During the campaign, support for the Communist Party held steady, fluctuating between 18 and 21 per cent of the electorate. However, a somewhat different picture emerges when the period is extended back to July 1999, before Vladimir Putin, the Chechen war and Unity all appeared on the political landscape. At that time, the Communist Party was endorsed by 24 per cent of the electorate and by more than two-fifths naming a major party preference, a substantially higher figure than its 1995 Duma vote. By the final pre-election poll, Communist support was down by more than a fifth from its July peak. The decline in Communist vote included the drift of some Russians to Unity, an indication of the success of the latter's big-tent (or, its critics said, fuzzy-focus) appeal to Russians with a hankering for what life was like in Soviet times, as well as from voters wanting a fresh party label and political faces.

Throughout the campaign Unity's leaders, with the support of the Kremlin, sought to make it appear as a party of, or at least close to, power – and to marginalize its opponents as irrelevant. However, it did not succeed in its goal. It only added to the electorate's confusion about which party was *the* party of power. At the end of the Duma campaign VTsIOM again asked voters which party they thought was the party of power, and uncertainty had actually increased. Whereas in September 47 per cent could not identify any party as the party of power, by December the proportion had risen to 56 per cent. Moreover, 11 per cent identified the anti-Kremlin party, Fatherland-All Russia, as the party of power, the same proportion as identified Unity as powerful.

Multiple outcomes

In a floating party system, the campaign is bound to be important, inasmuch as the supply of political parties is not fixed until after the deadline has passed for parties to hand in nomination papers. In 1999, the abrupt emergence of Vladimir Putin, of Unity and of Right Forces added to the complications of decision. Only a third of voters had made up their mind before the campaign warmed up, and they were mostly Communist voters. The median voter said that she or he did not decide how to vote until some time in October or November. One-quarter made up their minds in the last week of the campaign or on election day (tab. 6.2).

Table 6.2 *When voters made up their minds*

	When decide	Cumulative
	(%)	
Before the campaign	34	34
September or summer	13	47
October or November	14	61
Early December	14	75
In the last week	16	91
On election day, at the polling station	9	100

Source: VTsIOM. Nationwide survey, 17–20 December 1999. Number of voters interviewed, 1,143.

Election turnout is the starting point for evaluating the Duma election of 19 December 1999. The grotesquely inflated turnout of virtually 100.0 per cent in Soviet elections is a reminder that turnout can be too high. Notwithstanding demoralizing political developments since the previous Duma election, more than 61 per cent of the registered electorate cast a list vote and a vote in their single-member district. Thus, the turnout was higher by more than 2 per cent than in the British general election of 2001; it was 10 per cent higher than in the American presidential election in 2000.

Most non-voters were not trying to make a political protest. When the post-election NRB survey asked non-voters to explain their behaviour, less than a third gave anti-political reasons, such as distrust of politicians. The majority gave non-political reasons for their absence from the poll, such as being ill, travelling on election day or exercising their new-found right not to be interested in politics. The ballot encouraged voters to register a protest by offering the option of voting against all parties. In the list ballot, the percentage voting against all list parties was low, 3.3 per cent, only 0.5 per cent higher than in the previous election. In single-member districts, 11.6 per cent voted against all parties, an increase of 2.0 per cent from 1995.

The extent of fraud in election administration is critical in societies in transformation. To evaluate this, the New Russia Barometer did not ask people whether they thought elections were conducted honestly, a question inviting responses that media reports can bias. Instead, the nationwide sample was asked about its own experience: *On election day, did you or any member of your family experience any irregularities, such as ballots refused at the polling station or seeing ballots marked by polling officials instead of voters?* A big majority, 75 per cent, had no knowledge of irregularities. Only 1 per cent reported seeing electoral irregularities, and 7 per cent said they had heard about irregularities from friends or neighbours.[3] Nor did Russians feel themselves subject to undue influence before election day. When the New Russia Barometer asked *Did anyone pressure you to vote in a certain way in the Duma election, for example, by offering gifts, giving you instructions, threatening you or other measures?*, 97 per cent said there were no pressures; the remaining 3 per cent said that pressures were applied, but that it made no difference in how they voted.

Fairness is a higher standard than fraud for evaluating an election. A substantial minority of Russians did have reservations about the way in which the Duma election was conducted. When the NRB asked whether

---

[3] More than twice as many, that is 17 per cent, said they had heard accusations of election irregularities on television or in the press.

Table 6.3 *1999 Duma election results*

	List			SMD			Total	
	N votes	% vote	N seats	N votes	N candidates	N seats	N seats	% seats
Communist Party	16,196,024	24.3	67	8,893,547	129	46	113	25.1
Independents	—	—	—	27,661,392	1,149	114	114	25.3
Unity	15,549,182	23.3	64	1,408,801	31	9	73	16.2
Fatherland-All Russia	8,886,753	13.3	37	5,670,169	90	31	68	15.1
Union of Right Forces	5,677,247	8.5	24	2,016,294	66	5	29	6.4
Yabloko	3,955,611	5.9	16	3,289,760	114	4	20	4.4
Liberal Democrats/Zhirinovsky Bloc	3,990,038	6.0	17	1,026,690	95	0	17	3.8
Our Home Is Russia	790,983	1.2	0	1,733,257	90	7	7	1.6
Movement in Support of the Army	384,404	0.6	0	466,176	19	2	2	0.4
Russian People's Union	245,266	0.4	0	700,976	27	2	2	0.4
Communist Workers for the USSR	1,481,890	2.2	0	439,770	20	0	0	0
Women of Russia	1,359,042	2.0	0	326,884	11	0	0	0
Congress of Russian Communities	405,298	0.6	0	461,069	45	1	1	0.2
Party of Pensioners	1,298,971	1.9	0	480,087	28	1	1	0.2
Nikolayev-Fedorov Bloc	371,938	0.6	0	676,437	67	1	1	0.2
Russian Socialist Party	156,709	0.2	0	662,030	62	1	1	0.2
Spiritual Heritage	67,417	0.1	0	609,344	107	1	1	0.2
Against all	2,198,702	3.3	—	7,695,171	—	—	—	—
Others	2,355,215	3.5	0	648,068	83	0	0	0
Invalid ballots	1,296,992	1.9	—	1,429,779	—	—	—	—
Total	66,667,682	100	225	66,295,701	2,233	225	450	100
Electorate	108,073,956			107,633,708				
	61.7			61.6				

Source: Compiled by the authors from Russian sources; for details see Neil Munro and Richard Rose, *Elections in the Russian Federation*, Glasgow: University of Strathclyde Studies in Public Policy No. 344, 2001.

television reporting of the Duma campaign was fair, 40 per cent said it was not very or not at all fair; the same percentage took this view of the campaign in their single-member district. When asked whether electoral administration and the counting of votes was fair, 29 per cent described it as unfair. Since few voters saw any evidence of fraud, the unfairness alluded to could refer to the unusual or even arbitrary way in which votes are sometimes converted into seats in the Russian two-ballot electoral system. Advocates of proportional representation in Britain would be just as ready to describe the British first-past-the-post system as unfair.

Six parties sweep the list

Among the 26 list parties on the ballot, 6 passed the 5 per cent threshold qualifying them for a share of 225 Duma seats. The Communist Party, Unity, Fatherland-All Russia and the Union of Right Forces cleared the barrier comfortably. The Zhirinovsky Bloc and Yabloko did so by no more than 1 per cent (tab. 6.3). There were no near miss parties falling just short of the threshold. Seventh place was taken by the 3.3 per cent who voted against all parties. In eighth place was the party of Communist Workers for the USSR with only 2.2 per cent of the vote.

Fluctuations in the number of parties just over or just under the 5 per cent threshold cause big disparities in the degree of proportionality or disproportionality in the Duma list ballot. In 1995 six parties fell just short of the threshold, each taking between 3.8 and 4.6 per cent of the vote, and only half the total vote went to parties that cleared the threshold for receiving list seats. In accordance with the law, parties that did clear the threshold received bonus seats from parties that did not. This happened in 1999, but there were many fewer bonus seats, for the parties clearing the threshold altogether took 86 per cent of the list vote. Thus only 14 per cent of the seats could not be allocated to parties below the PR threshold; the result in 1999 was therefore far more proportional. For example, the Communist Party won just under 30 per cent of the list seats with 24 per cent of the list vote, whereas in 1995 it won 44 per cent of the list seats with 22 per cent of the vote.

Unlike previous Duma elections, when the party finishing first was deemed the winner, in 1999 the party coming second in the list vote, Unity, was hailed as the winner by political commentators. Starting from scratch, albeit with very strong backers, Unity took 23 per cent of the list vote, just 1 per cent less than the Communist Party. The Union of Right Forces also scored some success, polling 8 per cent of the vote. But the idea of winning is relative to expectations: together Unity and the Union of Right Forces won only 31.8 per cent of the list vote.

Fatherland-All Russia and the Communists were regarded as losers because they did not do as well as their earlier showing had promised. At the end of the summer, Fatherland-All Russia was running neck and neck with the Communists in VTsIOM polls, but when Unity began to rise the political vultures began to circle around it. Fatherland-All Russia won 13.3 per cent of the vote, enough to have earned it second place in the 1995 election but, because of high expectations earlier, its result was regarded as a defeat. The Communist Party's vote went up two percentage points, but this was a small gain compared to the enormous opportunity offered by the unpopularity of the government of Boris Yeltsin. In most Central and East European countries, rebranded parties of former Communists have used the unpopularity of government to return to power. The result showed that the Communist Party of the Russian Federation is not rebranded like its Polish or Hungarian counterparts – and old-brand Communists still appeal to some Russian voters.

The vote for both the Zhirinovsky Bloc and Yabloko was down from 1995, but each won list seats, so their showing had no impact on the overall result. Each had been dismissed on the basis of poor results in the previous presidential race and in subsequent opinion polls. Our Home Is Russia, no longer the party of the prime minister, was expected to do badly in the Duma election and it met these expectations; it took 1.2 per cent of the list vote. The Social Democratic Party backed by Mikhail Gorbachev received 0.08 per cent of the vote, a fall of almost half from its vote in 1995.

Independents dominate the districts

Competition in single-member districts was very different. In two-thirds of the districts, independent candidates of many hues and stripes were of primary importance. In 21 per cent of the districts, both the winner and the runner-up were independents; in 12 per cent of districts the contest was between an independent and a candidate of an unsuccessful list party; and in 33 per cent of contests an independent defeated a runner-up who was a candidate of a party winning list seats. Parties unsuccessful in the list ballot also did well. In 19 per cent of SMD contests a party that failed to clear the list threshold was first or second in competition with the candidate of a successful list party, and in 3 per cent two unsuccessful list or local parties came first and second. In only 12 per cent of districts were both the winner and runner-up candidates representatives of successful list parties.

Collectively, independent candidates won the most SMD votes, 42 per cent. Communist Party candidates came second, with 13 per cent, and votes against all were third, almost 12 per cent of the SMD total. Fatherland-All Russia came fourth with 8 per cent of the district vote and it was followed by Yabloko with 5.0 per cent. Unity candidates took 2.1 per cent of the SMD vote less than Our Home Is Russia. When a party's share of the vote is restricted to the seats it contested, Communists took an average of 22 per cent in these districts; Fatherland-All Russia averaged 19 per cent where they fought; and Unity took 16 per cent in the limited number of districts it fought.

In the first-past-the-post electoral system, the number of votes a party needs to win a seat depends on the number of candidates and the dispersion of the vote among its opponents. If there are only two candidates, then victory requires 50.1 per cent of the vote. As the number of candidates increases beyond two, the minimum share of the vote required by a winner drops. In a district with three candidates, winning half the vote need not be necessary and a candidate has a chance of victory with just over a third of the vote. However, votes are not spread evenly between candidates; in the SMD districts 308 candidates received less than 1 per cent of the vote, less than the number of signatures required to lodge nomination papers. Unevenness in the distribution of votes means there is no fixed threshold of votes that a candidate needs to win a particular district. The winner's total fluctuates with the candidate's local appeal and with the division of the vote among opponents.

In more than five-sixths of the Duma districts the winner did not take half the vote. There were ten districts in which the winning candidate had less than 20 per cent of the vote and six in which the winner had only 16 per cent of the vote or less. The median winning candidate took just over 30 per cent of the district vote. There were only 26 districts in which the winning candidate took more than half the vote. The great majority of Duma members from single-member districts cannot claim to speak for the whole of their district, since at least two-thirds of the district's voters supported their opponents.

Altogether, independent candidates won 114 of the 225 single-member district seats in the Duma. The Communist Party came second with 46 seats, and Fatherland-All Russia third with 31 seats. In eight districts the most votes were cast against all parties; in the follow-up elections held later, independent candidates were the winners. Nominating lots of candidates was no guarantee of a party winning seats. Yabloko contested more than half the districts but won only four seats, and Spiritual Heritage's 107 candidates took only one seat. The Zhirinovsky Bloc did worst; it fought 95 districts and failed to win a single seat. Although Our Home Is

Russia failed to qualify for list seats, it won seven single-member districts. Unity showed a great discrepancy between the two ballots: it won only nine SMD seats while taking 64 list seats. To excuse the poor showing of Unity in the districts as due to a lack of candidates raises the question: why did Unity have far fewer candidates than other successful list parties?

Single-member districts offered potential scope for individuals to influence results. The extreme case was Aginsky Buryatsky, a predominantly non-Russian district, where independent Joseph Kobzon, a former popular singer with business interests which had caused him to be denied an American visa, polled 91.2 per cent against two other candidates. Two oligarchs, Boris Berezovsky and Roman Abramovich, each won a district seat by a wide margin, thereby gaining immunity from prosecution as Duma members. In St Petersburg, Vladimir Putin's former professor and patron, Anatoly Sobchak, was defeated.

The federal structure of Russian government creates incentives for the 89 regional governors to create political machines to secure their own election and that of a compliant legislature. Moscow-based political elites courted governors in hopes that they could deliver Duma votes in the single-member districts in the region, as well as for the list ballot. The Fatherland-All Russia Bloc had the public backing of 11 governors. As the favoured party of the Kremlin, Unity had 40 governors sign a statement of support in September 1999. Two governors showed their opportunism by endorsing both Fatherland-All Russia and Unity. Forty governors put local concerns first and did not endorse either party.

At a minimum, one would expect a party enjoying the backing of the governor to nominate candidates in all the single-member districts in that region. Although Unity was endorsed by governors in regions with 86 single-member districts, the party failed to nominate candidates in 72 of these districts. Although Fatherland-All Russia was endorsed by governors covering 55 districts, it nominated candidates in only 33 of them. Most of their candidates, 57 in the case of Fatherland-All Russia and 17 of Unity, contested districts in which the governor had not endorsed their party.

If the governor did endorse a party *and if* the party did nominate a candidate within the region, its vote was well above its average for the country as a whole (tab. 6.4). In single-member districts in which the governor backed Fatherland-All Russia, the party's candidate averaged 27.2 per cent of the vote, almost 12 percentage points higher than where its candidate ran without the governor's support. Where Unity ran SMD candidates supported by the governor, its vote was almost 10 percentage points higher. In the list vote, gubernatorial support was even more important to Fatherland-All Russia. In regions in which the governor supported the party, it averaged 26.5 per cent of the vote; where it lacked

Table 6.4 *Electoral value of endorsement by a governor*

	Unity	Fatherland-All Russia
	% share of vote	
SMD vote for candidates		
Governor supports party	21.8	27.2
No support by governor	12.2	15.4
Difference	9.6	11.8
List vote in region		
Governor supports party	27.8	26.5
No support by governor	21.2	8.6
Difference	6.6	17.9

Source: Calculated by the authors from Central Electoral Commission reports.

this backing, its vote was two-thirds lower. With generous nationwide media publicity, Unity benefited less from the backing of governors; in these districts its vote was only 6.6 per cent higher than in regions where it had no gubernatorial support.

Aggregation without accountability

The only way in which a Russian elector can be sure of voting consistently is to vote 'against all', the one choice that appears on both ballots nationwide. The failure of list parties to nominate SMD candidates in most districts forces voters to split their support between different parties or between a party and an independent candidate, and 68 per cent report doing so. Among the group most likely to have a long-term partisan attachment, Communist list voters, two-fifths said they voted differently in their district. Among those who voted for Unity on the list ballot, four-fifths voted differently in their district.

In a Duma election there can be no winner in the American or British sense, that is, a single party that takes a majority of seats or votes. Nor can the government be described as the winner or the loser, since it is not accountable to the Duma. Nonetheless, the media is under great pressure to declare a winner on election night. It does so by concentrating on the votes and seats cast for half the seats in the Duma, the proportional list seats, for these results can be summarized in a few lines. Except for the marginal party teetering on the PR threshold, votes and seats can be reported with a high degree of accuracy well before all the results are in. By contrast, the outcome cannot be known quickly in 225 single-member districts scattered across eight time zones. Moreover, each result reflects local

Figure 6.3 SHARING OUT DUMA SEATS.

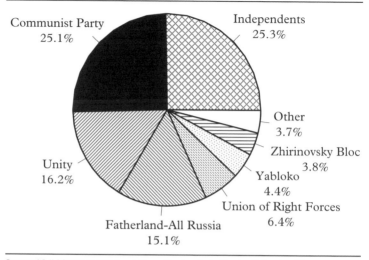

Communist Party
25.1%

Independents
25.3%

Other
3.7%

Zhirinovsky Bloc
3.8%

Unity
16.2%

Yabloko
4.4%

Union of Right Forces
6.4%

Fatherland-All Russia
15.1%

Source: Neil Munro and Richard Rose, *Elections in the Russian Federation*, Glasgow:
University of Strathclyde Studies in Public Policy No. 344, 2001.

patterns of competition so that, even after information is centrally compiled in Moscow, complexity makes the results difficult to present on television.

The lopsided (and different) pattern of success for parties in the two ballots produced a very different *total* result than the headline result flashed by the media on the basis of list votes. Ironically, the parties with the most consistent results to report were those that ran candidates on both the list and district ballots and did badly on both, such as the Russian Socialist Party or Spiritual Heritage. In aggregate, the Communist Party of the Russian Federation and independent candidates were the most successful, each winning one-quarter of the total seats (fig. 6.3). Although Unity won almost as many list votes as the Communist Party, it gained a third fewer seats in the Duma because it nominated so few candidates in the districts. Even though it was 10 percentage points behind Unity in the list vote, Fatherland-All Russia came close to Unity in total seats won, because it contested and won far more single-member seats. The remaining fifth of the seats were scattered among three successful list parties, plus eight parties that took one or more district seats but did not contest or did not win list seats.

Accountability is frustrated because citizens are so often denied the opportunity to vote for or against the same party on both ballots. If the whole of the Duma were elected by list PR, this would increase accountability by offering a uniform choice nationwide. If the whole of the Duma

Figure 6.4 FLOATING PARTIES IN 1999 DUMA LIST VOTE.

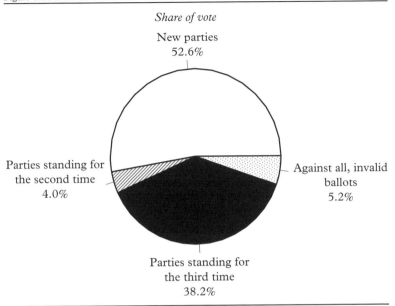

Source: Neil Munro and Richard Rose, *Elections in the Russian Federation*, Glasgow: University of Strathclyde Studies in Public Policy No. 344, 2001.

were elected by the first-past-the-post system in single-member districts, then according to the 'law' propounded by Maurice Duverger (1954), this would produce a two-party system with a pro- and an anti-government party between which voters could choose. However, Russian political elites have shown that they are no more inclined to obey political science laws than to respect anti-corruption laws. An election held solely under first-past-the-post rules in single-member districts could produce a Duma with even more parties than the Duma now has (cf. Moser, 2001).

The 1999 Duma election results confirm the floating character of the party system. Of the 65 parties that have contested list seats, only four have fought all three Duma elections, and two of these, the Communist Party of the Russian Federation and Vladimir Zhirinovsky's party, are far from being conventional advocates of democratic accountability.

Comparing party competition in the 1999 Duma election with earlier contests confirms that Russia has a floating system of parties.[4] There

----

[4] Since the 1999 election two developments have produced further changes in the floating system of party competition. First, Unity and Fatherland merged in December 2001. Second, a new law on the registration and finance of political parties is intended to reduce the total number of parties and encourage mergers between parties, thus promoting further discontinuities in the list ballot at the next Duma election.

was an enormous turnover of parties between 1995 and 1999. Only nine parties on the 1995 list ballot survived four years later. The four parties that could most readily be held accountable on the basis of their record, those fighting all three Duma elections in the 1990s, took only 38 per cent of the list vote in 1999. An additional 4 per cent went to parties that had contested list seats in both 1995 and 1999. New parties that had not presented themselves to the electorate before took 52 per cent of the list vote. The biggest portion of that vote went to Unity, a party of first impressions, for it was only formed weeks before polling day. Offered the choice between what they knew and disliked and what they didn't know, most Russians chose the unknown or the untried rather than known party alternatives.

In a society in transformation, the big questions facing voters are much bigger than in an established democratic system, and this is especially true in Russia. Ideology and interests make transformation divisive. Those who were accustomed to or benefited from the old regime will be unhappy, while those who could not wait to be free of it will prefer the present and look forward to the future. Many people are of two minds about transformation, for example, liking newly gained personal freedoms while being disturbed by economic insecurity. Therefore, parties can compete by being for or against transformation – or they can blur their positions to attract the support of voters confused or uncertain in the face of change.

In an established democratic system, parties do not compete by offering voters a choice between democratic and undemocratic regimes, and economic differences are about how a market economy ought to be managed rather than about whether markets should be introduced or avoided. In an established party system, competition is in equilibrium, for the same parties are on the ballot from one decade or one generation to the next, and most voters have a stable party identification. A system in equilibrium is adaptable rather than static, for parties change leaders and policies in pursuit of votes (Downs, 1957). In the short run, economic cycles can affect voting for the governing party and the opposition. In the long run, changes in the class or educational structure of society can cumulatively alter the distribution of support of parties. However, adaptation simply involves marginal changes of a few percentage points in a party's vote and marginal changes in how the country is governed. An occasional shock such as war or the 1930s depression can lead to the re-alignment of parties, but the net effect is to leave the regime intact.

By default, voting in a system in equilibrium is analysed in terms of stable party loyalties and marginal changes in party preferences, for the nature of the political regime has not been challenged for generations. But to confine analysis solely to equilibrium measures in a system in transformation is a fundamental mistake. It projects a Western perspective where it is inappropriate and fails to take into account the point of view of people who have grown up in a Communist regime. In the 1999 Duma election every voter was a child of the Soviet Union; it will not be until the year 2030 that the median Russian elector will be a child of the Russian Federation. Of course, before then many Russians may have put behind them the Soviet past and begun to make judgments based solely on experiences in a transformed society. For example, Germans who had been compulsorily mobilized into the Hitler *Jugend* in their youth became good democrats in the Federal Republic of Germany. The sooner voters evaluate parties solely on the basis of the current regime, the more elections are about competition in equilibrium rather than a judgment on transformation. However, in the American Deep South it took almost a century after the Civil War before people no longer voted along cleavages established by that war.

The 1999 Duma election was the third in less than a decade. No party winning seats argued for overthrowing the constitution, returning to the command economy or recreating the Soviet Union. While there is a floating system of parties, all parties accept the constitutional rules as the rules of 'the only game in town'. On the basis of this, one can hypothesize that Russians decide about voting by the same criteria as in an established democratic system – identification with a party, the personality of party leaders, the condition of the economy or one-off events. Alternatively, one can hypothesize that for people socialized in the Soviet era the impact of transformation on themselves and on the country remains the chief influence on party choice.

To determine how Russians decided which party to vote for, we analyse the eighth New Russia Barometer survey, which collected copious data about transformation and equilibrium influences in a survey that went in the field in January 2000, three weeks after the 19 December 1999 Duma election. For the sake of clarity and statistical reliability, we concentrate on voting for the six parties that won list seats: the Communist Party, Unity, Fatherland-All Russia, the Union of Right Forces, the Zhirinovsky Bloc and Yabloko. The next section looks at the influence of transformation. Since voters have not been able to develop a long-term identification with floating parties, the second section looks at the presence or absence of identification with a political ideology, whether Communist, pro-market or other. Marginal influences important in political systems in equilibrium, including short-term economic fluctuations and social structure characteristics such as class and education, are examined in the third section. While a variety of influences correlate to some degree with voting for one or more parties, none by itself accounts for choices among successful list parties. The concluding section uses multivariate analysis to identify the most important combination of influences. It shows that Russian voters are most influenced by their views of transformation.

Transformation influences

The first requirement for transformation having an influence is that voters must have opinions about the issues it raises. Given the pervasive impact of the upheavals of a decade ago, few Russians are likely to be indifferent to what happened. Second, the public must be divided in its opinion. When there is a high level of agreement, for example, about the achievement of personal freedom, a consensus cannot account for the division of votes among half a dozen parties. Third, voters should be able to identify a party with a position close to their own views. If this does not happen, then a person may not vote or may vote against all. In a floating system of parties, it is especially difficult for electors to identify where many parties stand on important issues.

Because no party secured more than a quarter of the list vote, none can be the sole representative of the interests of the majority. Nor do voters divide into a single group supporting a pro-transformation party, and another supporting a single anti-transformation party. Voters favouring transformation can choose between several parties favouring it, or at least agree in shunning the chief opponent of transformation, the Communist Party. Small parties can draw most of their vote from a particular social group, yet not win a majority of that group. For example, most supporters of Women of Russia are female, but 96 per cent of women do not support that party. Therefore, the most we can expect is that correlations between influences and party preferences affect voting for some parties but not others. Since the six major Duma parties cannot be ordered along a single dimension, whether left/right or pro-/anti-transformation, and some independent variables are also nominal, an appropriate statistic to measure the relationship between hypothesized influences and party choice is eta. Its association can range between 0.00 and 1.00; the great majority of correlations reported here are low.[1]

Competing parties and competing regimes

When asked to evaluate the Soviet regime before perestroika (cf. fig. 3.1), almost three-quarters of voters for the list parties gave it a positive rating in the eighth New Russia Barometer survey.[2] Because there

---

[1] For the sake of clarity, tables 7.1, 7.2 and 7.3 report the primary positive characteristic of each independent variable. All eta correlations are calculated on the basis of crosstabulating all values of a variable against voting for six parties, except for scales rating of past, present and future political regimes and economic systems, which are divided into three categories: for, neutral and against. For details of the independent variables, see the appendix and discussions elsewhere in the book.

[2] In the tabular analysis in this chapter, percentages are based on voters for the six successful list parties, and therefore tend to differ marginally from figures reported elsewhere in the book for the electorate as a whole.

Table 7.1 *Transformation influences on party choice*

	Right Forces	Yabloko	Unity	Zhir'y Bloc	Fatherland	Communists	Eta
			(% major party list vote)				
	10	**7**	**31**	**8**	**14**	**30**	
Total, %							
POLITICAL TRANSFORMATION							
73 Pro pre-perestroika system	8	5	29	8	13	36	.10
38 Pro current political regime	13	9	34	8	16	21	.09
65 Pro regime in five years	12	7	33	8	16	24	.07
53 Feel freer on four counts	12	8	35	7	15	23	.11
32 Dictatorship only way out	7	4	30	5	13	41	.08
5.3 m System now democratic	5.0	4.9	5.5	5.7	5.5	5.2	.17
7.5 m Democratic ideal	8.3	8.0	7.8	7.4	7.5	7.2	.09
3.0 m Pro-Yeltsin	3.9	3.0	3.4	3.0	3.1	2.2	.14
ECONOMIC TRANSFORMATION							
47 Communist regime blamed	16	9	38	7	16	14	.17
45 Prefers market, high prices to low prices, shortages	15	10	37	8	16	14	.17
74 Prefers state ownership	7	7	29	7	14	36	.08
84 Pro pre-perestroika economy	9	6	31	7	14	33	.05
29 Pro current economic system	15	8	33	8	16	20	.03
61 System better in five years	12	8	32	8	16	24	.05
56 Past better for household	8	8	27	7	14	36	.08
32 Household better in five years	13	9	35	10	15	18	.11

m=mean score on 1–10 scale.

Source: New Russia Barometer VIII. Nationwide survey, 13–29 January 2000. Number of respondents, 1,940.

is a broad consensus about the old regime, the correlation with party choice is limited (tab. 7.1). Most voters positive about the old regime do not vote for the Communist Party. There is more variation in attitudes toward the current regime. However, no party benefited to a noteworthy extent from those positive about the regime, although the Communists did lose support among this group. When asked about the regime in the future, almost two-thirds are positive. Optimists are less likely to vote Communist but they also divide their support among a variety of parties. There is a consensus too that the new regime gives freedom from the state on four counts: speech, religion, association and the right to participate or not in politics (cf. tab. 3.1). Those most appreciating all the freedoms gained through Russia's transformation tend to be more inclined toward Right Forces and Unity, and less inclined to vote Communist.

The reality of Russian government is a long way from the democratic ideal, and Russians are realists. When asked whether the current regime is closer to a complete dictatorship or a complete democracy, Russians gave the same mean rating after the Duma election as in the NRB survey two years earlier (cf. fig. 3.5). The association with voting is statistically the strongest of all the influences of political transformation (eta: .17). Those voting for the Zhirinovsky Bloc, Unity or Fatherland-All Russia are more likely to regard the current regime as democratic, Communists are almost average and those least likely to see Russia as democratic are the most liberal, pro-market parties, Right Forces or Yabloko. When asked how democratic the regime ought to be, the replies given are almost as positive as in the seventh NRB survey, and this reduces the association with party preferences. Those most positive about democracy as an ideal are more inclined to favour Right Forces and Yabloko, and those not quite so enthusiastic are most inclined to the Communist Party.

For a decade Boris Yeltsin personalized transformation. While against the Communist Party, Yeltsin was not positively identified with a party. Since he was extremely unpopular and heading for retirement at the time of the 1999 election, no party campaigned as the party of Boris Yeltsin. When the NRB survey asked people to rate Yeltsin on a 10-point scale just after he had resigned from the presidency, the mean was low, 3.0, but not so low as in his darkest time. Those less negative in evaluating Yeltsin were more inclined to vote for Right Forces or Unity, and those rejecting what he stood for were more likely to vote Communist.

In Russia endorsement of dictatorship reflects ideology more than personality. Those favouring dictatorship are more likely to vote Communist, a party favouring the dictatorship of the proletariat, than for parties with strong personalities as their leader. Although Vladimir Zhirinovsky behaved in a demagogic manner, this did not gain him support among the 32 per cent who favoured a dictatorship. In fact, those favouring a dictator are less likely than average to vote for the Zhirinovsky Bloc, and voters for two other parties associated with major personalities, Unity (Vladimir Putin) and Yabloko (Grigory Yavlinsky), are no more inclined to favour dictatorship.

Competing economic systems too

In Soviet times, the economy was pre-eminently a political economy; decisions of the party-state commanded what happened in the economy. The transformation of the Soviet Union into the Russian Federation was a political act too. The once-for-all impact of moving from a non-market to a market economy is of a different order of magnitude than annual changes in a market economy of a percentage point or two in the growth rate or a few percentage points in the rate of inflation or unemployment.

When asked to assess the past, the current and the future economic systems, Russians tend toward consensus. A big majority is positive about the pre-perestroika economy, and a big majority is also negative about the current economy. Three-fifths are positive about what they believe the system will become in five years, that is, beyond the life of the Duma for which they are voting. Associations with party preferences are therefore weak (tab. 7.1).

Russians share with Western voters a readiness to hold the government accountable for the economy. At the 1999 Duma election, as at previous elections, enormous majorities blamed government officials and President Yeltsin for what had happened to the economy. Because Vladimir Putin was a new arrival on the political stage, only 12 per cent blamed him for the state of the economy. By being consistently in opposition, the Communist Party was not responsible for economic transformation, but the former Communist regime could be blamed for its economic legacy, and 47 per cent did so. Those giving the Communists a share of the blame for current economic difficulties are more likely to vote for the Union of Right Forces and Unity.

Economic transformation has an impact on individuals both as workers and as consumers. To replace state monopolies, the Yeltsin government promoted the privatization of enterprises. However, the implementation of privatization was very unpopular. Workers faced the prospect of losing their jobs as inefficient enterprises adapted to market conditions and oligarchs close to the Yeltsin Family got valuable assets at prices far below their market value. When asked in the post-election NRB survey whether state or private ownership is best for running an enterprise, almost three-quarters of voters favoured state ownership, and consensus meant that this issue had limited influence on party choice.

Russian consumers have known two types of economies: a command economy in which state planning kept official prices low but generated chronic shortages, and a market economy in which there are lots of goods in shop windows but high prices restrict what people can buy. Voters divide almost equally between those who prefer window-shopping for goods they cannot afford and those preferring low prices for goods that are often unavailable. People who prefer to be consumers in a market economy are more likely to vote Right Forces, Unity or Yabloko, while those preferring low prices for goods in short supply are more likely to vote Communist. The correlation between consumer preferences and voting (eta: .17) is double that for attitudes toward state or private ownership (eta: .08).

National economic conditions differ in their impact on households, as some families benefit while others see their household conditions worsen. In a stable society, questions about changing economic conditions usually refer to the previous year or next year. In a society in transformation, the appropriate comparison is with household conditions before and after transformation and expectations of long-term consequences. Those whose household economic conditions were better before transformation are more inclined to vote Communist, while those who are optimistic about the future are more inclined to endorse the pro-market parties – and optimism has more of an impact on voting than does a household losing from transformation.

Ideologies and party choice

In a political system in equilibrium, a voter does not need to spend a lot of time thinking about how to vote, because parties supply the same choices at one election after another. Theories of political socialization postulate that voters inherit a party identification from parents or that, after participating in several elections, most voters develop a lifetime loyalty to a party and at each election simply vote the same as before (Butler and Stokes, 1974; Rose and McAllister, 1990). However, in a political system in transformation, there has not been time for voters to develop lifetime loyalties, except to the Communist Party. This strengthens the likelihood that the answers that individuals give to questions about party identification are tautological, just another way of naming the party they prefer.

Because there is a floating supply of parties from one Russian election to the next, links between voters and parties tend to be ad hoc rather than based on long-term commitments, as theories of political socialization predict. After a Duma campaign that could have boosted identification with parties, the eighth New Russia Barometer asked whether there was any party that electors felt close to. A total of 51 per cent said there was no party they were close to. Of those who said they felt close to a party, less than half said they felt strongly attached to a party. Those who did not feel close to any political party were disproportionately likely to vote for the Unity list or Fatherland-All Russia and least likely to vote Communist (eta: .15). The ad hoc or tautological nature of party identification is shown by 55 per cent of those naming a party referring to one that did not exist four years earlier or even a few months before the Duma election. Only a sixth of Russians, those feeling close to the Communist Party, fit the model of party identification developed in party systems in equilibrium. In Russia, party identification is simply another way of describing the party a person has voted for – but may not vote for four years hence, even if it is still on the ballot.[3]

The distance between parties in a political system in transformation can be great, and voters find it as easy or easier to identify a party they would never vote for as to name a party that is their momentary choice (cf. Rose and Mishler, 1998). Russians are more likely to identify a party they are against than a party that they are for. When VTsIOM asked a month before the Duma vote whether there were any parties they would *not* want to see represented in the Duma, 65 per cent named a party that they were strongly against. The party most frequently rejected was the Liberal Democratic Bloc of Vladimir Zhirinovsky: 44 per cent did not want it in the Duma. The Communist Party came second, with 18 per cent rejecting it. In a two-party system in equilibrium, being against one party is sufficient reason to cast a vote for the alternative. However, with 26 parties on the list ballot, being against one or two parties is insufficient to give a positive direction when marking a ballot.

Transformation choices are different in kind from marginal changes of a party system in equilibrium. Choices tend to the extremes and can involve multiple dimensions. Transformation confronts citizens with broad ideological choices between dictatorship and freedom, a market or a non-market economy, and nationalism. All these choices arose in consequence of the collapse of the Soviet party-state.

The inability or unwillingness of political elites to organize stable parties does not prevent individual Russians from having a political ideology. When the eighth New Russia Barometer asked people whether they were inclined to one of a variety of political outlooks, 65 per cent of the

[3] Changes in Russian law on parties approved by the Duma in 2001 are intended to reduce the supply of list parties at the Duma election in December 2003. Fewer and larger parties will reduce wasted votes but increase the floating character of parties.

Table 7.2 *Political ideologies and party choice*

Q. What broad political outlook are you most inclined to favour?

		Right Forces	Yabloko	Unity	Zhirinovsky Bloc	Fatherland	Communists
		(% major party list vote)					
		10	7	31	8	14	30
Total, %	Outlook						
31	Communist	0	0	6	2	6	86
25	Pro-market	34	11	40	5	9	1
19	No ideology	5	9	45	11	23	7
10	Social democrat	5	15	38	17	21	4
6	Great power patriot	2	7	45	8	32	6
3	Green, environment	3	13	43	10	23	7
6	Other	2	9	43	21	23	2
				(eta: .51)			

Source: New Russia Barometer VIII. Nationwide survey, 13–29 January 2000. Number of respondents, 1,940.

electorate and 81 per cent of those voting for one of the six major parties were able to name an ideology (tab. 7.2). The most frequently cited, Communist, was named by just under a third and a pro-market view by one-quarter of major party voters. Although Russia has yet to establish a social democratic party that wins votes and seats, one in ten voters endorsed this outlook. Six per cent associated themselves with the traditional tsarist idea of great power patriotism, and 3 per cent with a new political movement, environmentalism.

Communist outlooks reflect commitments formed by political socialization in the Soviet era. Among those 60 or older, 43 per cent called themselves Communist, but only 7 per cent of the under-30s did so. Altogether, nine out of ten voters for the Communist list saw themselves as having a Communist outlook and five-sixths who thought of themselves as Communist voted for that party, a fit between ideology and party vote that was not matched by any other party. There was, however, a big difference between having been a member of the Communist Party of the Soviet Union and seeing oneself as a Communist. Because membership in the CPSU was required for holding high-level jobs or securing privileges, many joined the party for opportunistic reasons. The Communist Party's desire to include all people of talent meant that ideological tests of recruits were nominal. Thus, party members reflected the variety of opinions and responsibilities of officials in Soviet society (Rose, 1996a).

In consequence, there is little relationship between having been a member of the CPSU and how one votes today (eta: .06).

Voters committed to the market dispersed their support among three parties. The Union of Right Forces drew four-fifths of its vote from those who saw themselves as pro-market, and it had few voters with other outlooks or none. More pro-market Russians voted for Unity, but they contributed only a third of its much larger vote. Social democrats spread their support widely, giving Unity the largest proportion of their vote, with Fatherland-All Russia coming next. Among the small group who identified themselves as great power patriots, two parties were disproportionately favoured – Unity and Fatherland-All Russia. Environmentalists were few in number and widely dispersed between political parties.

Among the large bloc of the electorate without any ideology, a majority did not bother to vote. Of those who did vote, Unity was the party most favoured, gaining 45 per cent of the group, and Fatherland-All Russia won 23 per cent. The Communist Party was the least favoured, getting only 7 per cent of the vote of those without any ideology. The association between being apolitical and favouring Unity was of limited value, since electors without any commitment to a political outlook were much less likely to vote than supporters of the market or Communism.

Unity's strength was due to its ability to gather votes from people with many different political outlooks: a third of its vote came from adherents of the market; more than a quarter from those with no political ideology; and two-fifths from people who variously described themselves as social democrats, great power patriots, other, Communist or environmentalist. Fatherland-All Russia was even more diverse in drawing support in almost equal numbers from pro-market, social democratic, Communist and great power patriot voters, as well as more than a quarter from voters with no outlook. Two parties had ideologically cohesive blocs of supporters: nine-tenths of Communist voters endorsed the party's nominal ideology and four-fifths of Right Forces voters were pro-market.

Equilibrium influences

In established democratic regimes, voting behaviour is about accounting for persisting party loyalties in terms of current economic conditions, priority issues, political personalities and social structure. In a system in transformation with a floating system of parties, the lack of stable party loyalties gives conventional equilibrium influences the potential to exert a big influence on voting too. However, this appears not to be the case in Russia.

Economics and issues

In an established market economy, income is the conventional measure of household economic wellbeing, but in Russia its significance is problematic, since wages are paid erratically and many households also rely on non-wage resources. Among voters in households in the top quarter of the income distribution, support for the pro-market Union of Right Forces was almost double the national average, and support for Yabloko was higher as well (tab. 7.3). Communist support was disproportionately high for voters in lower income brackets, while it was close to average for the other major parties (eta: .08). The subjective evaluation that people make of their household's economic conditions also correlates with party preferences, but not strongly. Among the fifth of voters who are currently satisfied with their economic situation today, both Unity and Right Forces drew more support, and the Communist Party less (eta: .08).

To avoid the reductionist mistake of assuming that only economic conditions influence voters, the post-Duma NRB survey asked *Government has to deal with many problems – but it cannot solve all of them at once. How much priority do you think the next Russian government ought to give to each of the following problems facing this country?* Ten different issues were enumerated, and respondents were asked to grade each as of the highest priority, important, low priority or unimportant. Russians had a lot of issues on their minds: an absolute majority said each of the following were of the highest priority: rising prices, the war in Chechnya, unemployment, crime, corruption, terrorist attacks in Russian cities and health care. The median respondent described Russia's status as a great power, environmental pollution and the unfair treatment of Russians in other CIS countries as important too.

Because of agreement in identifying many issues as high priority or important, these questions showed very slight correlations with party choice. The biggest correlation (eta: .11) was between the priority given unemployment and party choice. Interestingly, unemployment was least important for Communist Party voters as well as pro-market Right Forces. Communists had less reason to worry about losing their job because more were already retired. Concern with crime showed almost as high correlation with party choice.[4]

The outbreak of war in Chechnya was an event rather than a perennial issue. It catapulted Vladimir Putin into the political spotlight and stilled criticism from parties that did not want to side with an unpopular

---

[4] Other eta correlations between the priority given an issue and party choice were: corruption, .08; health service, .06; environmental pollution, .06; terrorist attacks, .05; Russia's standing as a great power, .05; problems of Russians in other countries in the CIS, .03; Chechnya, .03; rising prices, .02.

Table 7.3 *Marginal influences on the vote*

	Right Forces	Yabloko	Unity	Zhir'y Bloc	Fatherland	Communists	Eta
			(% major party list vote)				
	10	**7**	**31**	**8**	**14**	**30**	
Total, %							
23 Income: top quartile	19	10	31	6	16	18	.08
19 Current household economy okay	15	6	38	8	14	19	.08
67 Priority issue unemployment	7	9	31	9	14	30	.11
72 Crime	8	10	31	8	14	30	.10
5.8 m Pro-Putin	6.1	5.8	7.0	6.2	5.6	5.4	.18
38 Strongly pro-Chechnya action	11	8	36	8	10	27	.11
29 Education limited	7	3	26	10	12	42	.11
31 Age 60+	6	7	26	4	15	42	.08
28 Village resident	6	2	33	9	13	37	.10
30 Self-assessed class low	10	8	24	9	12	37	.07
51 Gender: woman	12	7	30	5	13	32	.06
55 Very proud of Russian citizenship	9	6	33	7	14	31	.05
22 Strongly identify with Europe	9	6	28	11	15	31	.05
25 Very good if CIS one country	6	3	30	8	14	40	.02
23 Attends church	12	7	31	3	17	31	.02

m=mean score on 1–10 scale.

Source: New Russia Barometer VIII. Nationwide survey, 13–29 January 2000. Number of respondents, 1,940.

Figure 7.1 PARTY CHOICE AND SUPPORT FOR WAR IN CHECHNYA.

Q. What is your attitude to the actions of the Russian government in Chechnya?

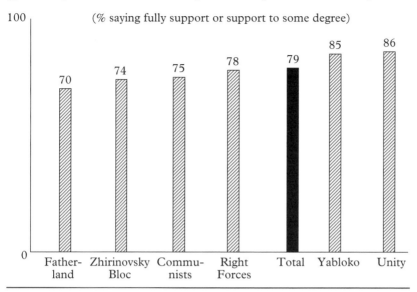

Source: New Russia Barometer VIII. Nationwide survey, 13–29 January 2000. Number of respondents, 1,940.

minority while a war was being fought. The war has been widely supported by the public. In the post-election NRB VIII survey, 31 per cent
fully supported Russian government actions in Chechnya and 41 per cent
gave some support, a fifth voiced substantial criticisms and 8 per cent definitely opposed the war. Because of widespread support for action against
Chechens, it was not a discriminating influence on voters. At least 70 per
cent of those voting for each of the six major Duma parties supported
the Chechen war (fig. 7.1). Among those strongly supporting the war in
Chechnya, Unity's vote was only five percentage points above its overall
share and the Yabloko vote was not significantly affected.

Personalities

Evaluations of political personalities usually reflect party loyalties in an
equilibrium system. Democrats approve the Democratic candidate for
president, and Republicans like the Republican candidate, not because of
their personal attributes but because of their party label. But for personalities to be evaluated as partisans presupposes long-lasting party loyalties

and political personalities who are partisan. Neither condition has yet been met in Russia. Of the six parties that won Duma list seats, three had leaders who were presidential candidates: the Communist Party, Yabloko and the Zhirinovsky Bloc. However, the Communist leader, Gennady Zyuganov, was a party apparatchik rather than a politician with a following independent of party. Vladimir Zhirinovsky was a political personality, but by 1999 his persona had alienated far more voters than it attracted; and the vote for Grigory Yavlinsky and Yabloko was never as high as 10 per cent.

By the time of the Duma ballot, Vladimir Putin had become far more popular than President Yeltsin. His average rating was 5.8 out of 10 in the post-election NRB survey. Although Putin announced he was voting for Unity, his name was not on the ballot nor was he a party member. By avoiding being a party leader, Putin was able to gain approval from supporters of all the major parties; the only difference was in the strength of approval shown. Putin supporters were more inclined to vote Unity and less inclined to vote Communist (tab. 7.3). However, even among Communist voters the average rating of Putin was above the psychological mid-point.

Social structure

Political sociology theories explain differences in party choice in terms of social differences. According to Lipset and Rokkan (1967), when universal suffrage was being introduced in Western Europe, political elites established parties that mobilized support by appealing to those on either side of divisions between church-goers and anti-clericals; peasants and urban dwellers; the working class and the middle class; or dominant and minority ethnic or language groups. Once party loyalties were established, the relative stability of social divisions from one year to the next maintained an equilibrium in voting.

The Soviet party-state claimed to have abolished class differences, and certainly deprived classic Weberian categories of class, status and power of their conventional meaning. Occupationally defined class was often less important than power in the Communist Party. In contemporary Russia a meaningful way to assess class is to ask people to rate their social status. When the New Russia Barometer asks *In our society there are people of high social position and people of low social position. What position do you have now?*, 99 per cent have no problem in assigning themselves to a position on a 10-point scale. In the eighth NRB survey, the mean was 4.0, and 70 per cent placed themselves below the mid-point of the subjective class scale, including 18 per cent at the very bottom. The tendency of most Russians to rate themselves low in status means that the association between subjective class and party voting was limited (eta: .07). Low-status voters tended to be more likely to vote Communist and less frequently to vote Unity (cf. tab. 7.3).

Education can be a more relevant influence than class today, insofar as more educated people differ from the less educated in lifestyles and values as well as occupational status and income. Both pro-market parties – Yabloko and the Union of Right Forces – drew a disproportionate amount of support from those with university education. While the appeal of Right Forces to educated voters reflects recruitment of youthful supporters, Yabloko's appeal is to older, more mature voters (cf. tab. 7.3). The support of the Zhirinovsky Bloc comes from a distinctive marginal group: relatively uneducated, youthful voters, the cadres of a *lumpen* proletariat.

In Russia age differences reflect radical differences in the political experience of generations. The oldest generation has vivid first-hand memories of the Great Patriotic War (Second World War) and of Stalinism, while the youngest generation experienced political socialization under Gorbachev and after (cf. Rose and Carnaghan, 1995). Voters for the Union of Right Forces and the Zhirinovsky Bloc are disproportionately young. However, no medium-term inferences can be drawn from this, since youthful voters are a party asset only if they develop a long-term commitment to a party and the party itself persists. The Union of Right Forces was less than a year old at the time of the Duma election, and the Zhirinovsky Bloc depends on a single person. It is more reasonable to extrapolate the implications of the age profile of Communist support, which comes disproportionately from voters over the age of 60. From one election to the next the Communist Party must try much harder than its competitors to replace supporters who die off.

The development of factory-style collective agriculture in the Soviet era introduced industrial skills in rural areas and free secondary schools raised education levels there. Concurrently, the shortages of food in the command economy turned many urban residents into part-time peasants growing food for their own consumption (Rose and Tikhomirov, 1993). Together, these measures reduced differences between urban and rural areas, and the transformation of the 1990s affected Russians wherever they lived. In 1999 the Agrarian Party split into supporters of the Communist Party and of Fatherland-All Russia. Up to a point, voters in the countryside also split; their only distinctive feature was the avoidance of voting for parties with a more cosmopolitan outlook, Yabloko and the

Union of Right Forces (tab. 7.3). Reciprocally, these two pro-market parties also did relatively well in the biggest cities, although not running as strongly as Fatherland-All Russia, the party of Moscow's mayor.

Gender is a prime example of a social difference without political salience in Russian elections. As part of Soviet egalitarianism, women were mobilized into the labour force. Although the leadership of Communist institutions was almost exclusively male, there was virtually no difference in the number of men and women in paid employment. In post-Soviet Russia women's groups, including feminist activists, are free to organize and Women of Russia has offered candidates at each Duma election. Although needing only one-tenth of the votes cast by women to clear the 5 per cent threshold to qualify for Duma seats, Women of Russia failed to do so in 1995 and 1999. In voting for the six major list parties, women and men divide very similarly.

The Russian Federation continues the Soviet practice of registering the nationality of its citizens, and ethnic Russians are four-fifths of the population. The non-Russian fifth is fragmented into many different nationalities. The New Russia Barometer asked respondents, whatever their nominal ethnicity, *To what extent are you proud to be a citizen of Russia?* A total of 48 per cent were definitely proud and 30 per cent somewhat proud of being Russian citizens, a high figure by comparison with stable European societies. A sixth said they had just a little pride and only 4 per cent said they were not at all proud. Pride in citizenship does not vary substantially between Russians and non-Russians, nor do differences in the degree to which people are proud of their country have much effect on voting.

Historically, national identity has involved clashes between those who have viewed European values as hostile to Russian culture, and Westernizers, who have seen Europe as a model that Russia should emulate, whether in the form of French culture or German Marxism. Pro-market political elites have seen themselves as Westernizers, while the rhetoric of Vladimir Zhirinovsky has evoked nationalist traditions. To differentiate between contrasting outlooks, the NRB asked whether people ever think of themselves as Europeans.[5] In reply, 18 per cent said they often think of themselves as Europeans, while 19 per cent never do so. The rest are divided evenly between those who sometimes think of themselves as European and those who rarely do. However, differences in attitudes toward Europe are unrelated to voting.

---

[5] Identification with 'Europe' is not to be confused with identification with the European Union. When asked to select the chief city of the European Union from a list of five cities, only 31 per cent named Brussels, 9 per cent named either London, Paris, Berlin or Rome, and 60 per cent said they did not know.

The break-up of the Soviet Union was not only a political cause for regret but also disruptive of the economy, for the command economy had been integrated with little regard for boundaries of republics. Its break-up has disrupted economic relations between what are now independent states. It has also reduced fiscal transfers from Moscow to poorer parts of the former Soviet Union. The eighth New Russia Barometer asked if Russian living standards would be better or worse if all the CIS countries were joined together in a single state. A total of 50 per cent said this would make Russian conditions better, 33 per cent anticipated no difference and 17 per cent thought it would make things worse. However, opinions about reuniting former Soviet territories had no significant relation with party choice (eta: .02).

For centuries the Orthodox Church has been a prime voice for traditional and undemocratic Russian values. However, generations of social and economic change, reinforced by aggressive atheist campaigns by the Soviet party-state, have made the majority of Russians indifferent to religion or even hostile. Only 2 per cent of Russians claim to go to religious services once a week, 4 per cent monthly, 17 per cent at least a few times a year, a fifth less often and 57 per cent never go to church. There is no significant relation between church attendance and party preference.

Transformation most important for party choice

The preceding tables show a normal pattern: among a multiplicity of potential influences, some but not all are associated with party choice. But which influences are most important? In addition, which parties are most affected? When half a dozen parties compete, influences salient for two or three parties may not influence voting for other parties. Multiple discriminant function is appropriate for analysing multi-party competition, since it is a multivariate form of statistical analysis that simultaneously assesses the net importance of dozens of influences – transformation, ideology and marginal. Unlike regression analysis, discriminant function analysis does not reduce party competition to a single dimension; it generates a number of functions according to their capacity to account for voting behaviour. Moreover, a party's position can vary between functions; it can be at the extreme on a dimension defining its core support and in the middle on a dimension unimportant to its electoral appeal (Klecka, 1980).

In the initial stage of discriminant function analysis, more than three dozen potential electoral influences reviewed above were included in order to see whether measures showing a weak bivariate correlation gained impact in combination with other measures. A few did, but most did

Table 7.4 *Combining influences on party choice*

	Functions explaining voting	
	Transformation	Apathy
(Variance explained)	(74%)	(13%)
Pro-market	62	−62
Communist regime blamed for economic problems	38	15
Private ownership better	35	−11
Against past political system	33	−10
Against controlled prices, shortages	31	14
Against past economic system	31	−18
Pro-Yeltsin	30	05
Family income last month	25	−12
Current political system	22	14
Against resorting to dictatorship	21	−05
Education	21	02
Future household economic situation better	20	07
Pro-action in Chechnya	09	08
No political outlook, ideology	18	58
Does not feel close to a political party	15	44
Great power patriot	08	35
Pro-Putin	18	30
Village or small town	−20	27
Current system is democratic	02	21
Urgent to solve problem of unemployment	03	18

(Boxed numbers are variables best characterizing each function.)

Source: New Russia Barometer VIII. Nationwide survey, 13–29 January 2000. Number of respondents, 1,940.

not and were therefore discarded. For clarity, the second stage of analysis is reduced to variables that loaded at .20 or higher on one function or more, plus attitudes toward Chechnya and unemployment, which are included to show that, although often thought to be important, they had little influence on Duma voting.[6] Each potential influence is combined statistically into functions that classify how individuals have voted. The analysis successfully classifies 53 per cent of voters for the six major list parties, more than three times what would be expected if voters were assigned randomly. Two functions together account for seven-eighths of the variance in party preferences, thus making it unnecessary to calculate additional very weak functions. For emphasis, the 12 strongest influences, loading above .25, are boxed in table 7.4.

[6] For details of a full discriminant function analysis with more than 30 influences, see Rose, Munro and White (2001).

Competition in two dimensions

Duma voting is most influenced by the way in which people have reacted to the transformation of the polity and the economy. The first function identifies seven attitudes toward transformation that substantially influence party choice. The function discriminates between voters who do or do not have a pro-market outlook, who blame the Communist legacy for current economic problems, who favour private ownership over the old state enterprise system, who reject the shortages and controlled prices of the command economy and who reject the Communist political regime and economic system. Attitudes toward Boris Yeltsin, the personal embodiment of transformation, are also significant in this dimension. While most indicators constituting this function nominally refer to economic conditions, they do not characterize an economic system in equilibrium; they reflect a political economy in transformation.

The chief transformation influences do not apply in a political system in equilibrium. By definition, voters in an established regime have no basis for comparison with government in another regime or of living in a non-market as well as a market economy. In Russia, the debate about the economy is not about how much or how little a government should tax and spend but whether there should be a market or whether the government should command the whole of the economy, as in the Soviet era.

The transformation outlook of each party's voters can be plotted on a single dimension measuring the distance between the party whose voters are most in favour of transformation and the party with voters most against.[7] At one extreme is the Union of Right Forces, which drew votes from Russians consistently in favour of the transformation of polity and economy under President Yeltsin in the past decade. At the other extreme is the Communist Party, whose voters were almost as consistent and firm in rejecting the break-up of the command economy and the party-state (fig. 7.2). Since Russians against transformation are much more numerous than those in favour, the Communist Party received almost three times the vote of Right Forces. Voters for Yabloko and Unity also favoured transformation, but much less strongly so than supporters of Right Forces. The two parties together polled more votes than Right Forces because they were closer to the centre than to the latter's extreme position.[8] Voters for Fatherland-All Russia and the Zhirinovsky Bloc were the fuzziest in their view of transformation, having group means

---

[7] The group centroid score for a party is the unstandardized canonical discriminant function evaluated at group means.

[8] Because discriminant function analysis relates a function to a combination of attitudes rather than to a single variable, the relative importance of individual indicators in table 7.4 need not be the same as the bivariate eta correlations.

Figure 7.2 PLACING PARTIES BY DIVISIONS BETWEEN VOTERS.

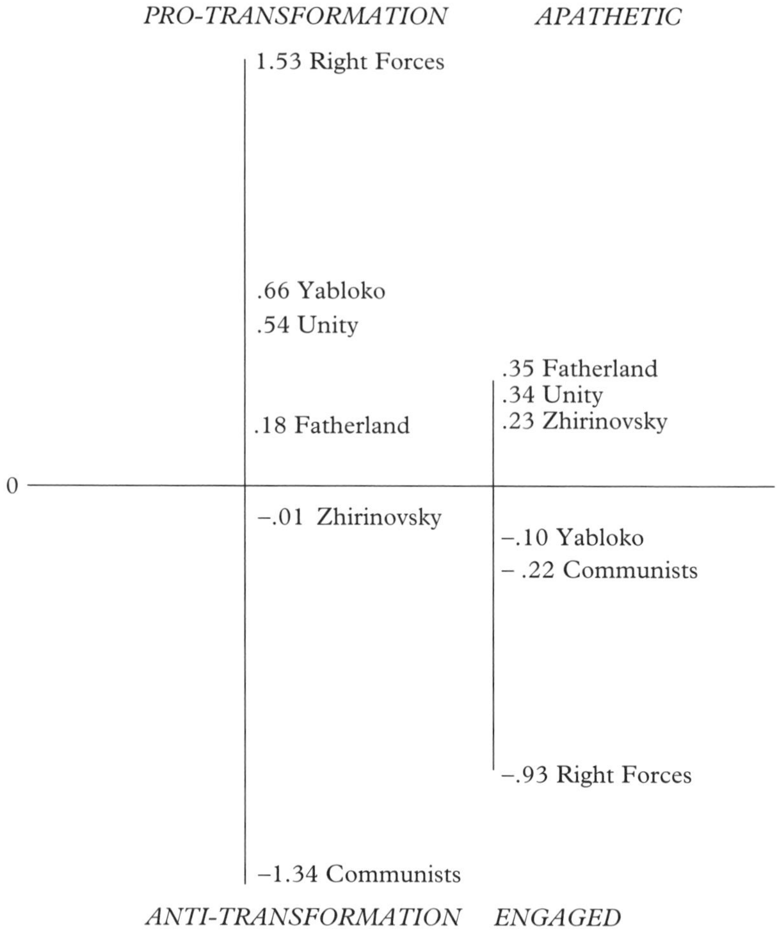

PRO-TRANSFORMATION   APATHETIC

1.53 Right Forces

.66 Yabloko
.54 Unity

.35 Fatherland
.34 Unity
.18 Fatherland   .23 Zhirinovsky

0 ——————————————————————————

−.01 Zhirinovsky
−.10 Yabloko
− .22 Communists

−.93 Right Forces

−1.34 Communists

ANTI-TRANSFORMATION   ENGAGED

(Party locations are group centroids for unstandardized canonical discriminant functions.)

Source: New Russia Barometer VIII. Nationwide survey, 13–29 January 2000. Number of respondents, 1,940.

placing them very close to the centre of the dimension for and against transformation.

The second function discriminates between voters who are apathetic and those who are politically committed. The apathetic do not have any political ideology and do not feel close to a political party, and tend to come from smaller towns or villages. They are pro-Putin and include a small number with a great power patriot ideology. They are also very unlikely to favour the market, for the pro-market ideology loads almost as high on the second function as the first, but its sign is negative. The second function is much less important, accounting for only 13 per cent of the variance.

Parties divide very differently on the second dimension than on the first. Three parties – Unity, Fatherland-All Russia, and the Zhirinovsky Bloc – are close together in appealing to apathetic voters and village residents. Supporters of the Union of Right Forces are at the other extreme. Its voters are very likely to have a clear pro-market outlook, to be sceptical about Putin and to live in big cities. Communist and Yabloko voters are in the middle on this dimension. The lesser importance of the second function is shown by the distance between Fatherland-All Russia and Right Forces, at the extremes of apathy and commitment, being less than half that between Right Forces and the Communists on the first function (fig. 7.2).

Clear-cut and fuzzy-focus parties

Party competition can be mapped in two dimensions, attitudes for and against transformation and apathy or engagement. Doing so shows that a position that might be called moderate in a political system in equilibrium can appear in Russia as avoiding taking a position on major issues about the future of the polity and economy (fig. 7.3).

Two blocs of voters, those supporting the Communist Party and the Union of Right Forces, held committed views about transformation, placing them at opposite poles. The leaders of the Union of Right Forces included ex-prime ministers Yegor Gaidar and Sergei Kirienko and former deputy prime minister Boris Nemtsov, committed technocrats identified with the market. Their voters were extremely in favour of transformation. Unlike Central and Eastern Europe, where Communist parties disbanded and party apparatchiks re-emerged as social democrats in favour of transformation and rejecting the past, in 1999 the Communist Party of the Russian Federation continued to appeal to old values opposed to transformation.

Two parties, Yabloko and Unity, drew support from those inclined to favour transformation but not strongly committed to all that it involved. Yabloko voters were slightly more in favour of the market while Unity voters were more apathetic. Altogether, Unity voters were closer to the fuzzy centre of the electorate than Yabloko; they were also more numerous. The parties with the fuzziest focus were Fatherland-All Russia and the Zhirinovsky Bloc. The flamboyant statements of Vladimir Zhirinovsky

Figure 7.3 COMPETITION FOR DUMA VOTERS IN TWO DIMENSIONS.

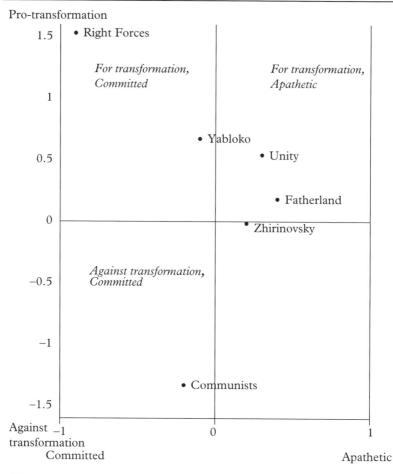

Pro-transformation

1.5   • Right Forces

For transformation,   *For transformation,*
Committed   *Apathetic*

1

• Yabloko
0.5   • Unity

                              • Fatherland

0 ————————————————•—————————————
                        • Zhirinovsky

Against transformation,
−0.5 *Committed*

−1

                • Communists
−1.5

Against −1   0   1
transformation
Committed   Apathetic

(Placement by party's canonical scores on two discriminant functions in table 7.4.)

Source: New Russia Barometer VIII. Nationwide survey, 13–29 January 2000. Number of respondents, 1,940.

have won him international media attention, but his demagogic expressions have appealed most to voters apathetic about politics and neutral about the transformation of Russia. The origin of Fatherland-All Russia as a bloc of regional leaders disengaged from the Kremlin appears to have resulted in its vote depending more on regional and local appeals rather than national concerns, for its voters tended to have no coherent views about transformation and were most apathetic.

The sharply focused appeal of the Communist Party and of Right Forces is confirmed by the discriminant functions correctly identifying 91 per cent of Communist voters and 72 per cent of Right Forces voters. The fuzzy focus of Unity is shown by only three-fifths of its voters being correctly identified. In addition, 22 per cent of Unity voters had attitudes that made them appear like Communist voters, and 20 per cent held views more like Right Forces than core Unity supporters. The fuzzy appeal of Unity is underscored by the largest groups of Fatherland-All Russia, Yabloko and the Zhirinovsky voters appearing similar to Unity voters in their low commitment to transformation.

The contrasting tendencies of voters reflected strategies of political elites, some emphasizing more ideological approaches to transformation while others sought to 'stir up apathy', avoiding contentious positions and stressing personalities or vague slogans. Interviews with party leaders in 17 regions of Russia by Regina Smyth (2001) document the point. Smyth asked leaders in Right Forces, the Communist Party, Fatherland-All Russia and Unity to indicate their party's position on issues similar to those covered here. Consistently, party elites placed their organization in similar positions to voters surveyed by the New Russia Barometer. Communist Party and Right Forces elites were far apart, and Unity and Fatherland-All Russia in the middle. For example, Communist politicians gave their party a mean placement of 9.1 on a 10-point scale in which the end points were state control of the economy or support for the free market while leaders of Right Forces gave their party an average placement of 1.9.

Together, the four fuzzy-focus parties won 60 per cent of the major list party vote. If most voters for unsuccessful list parties were also fuzzy, voters inconsistent or unclear about transformation are an even larger majority of Russians.[9] But the two parties with committed views on transformation did not show equal electoral appeal: the anti-transformation Communist list took almost three times as many votes as the strongly pro-transformation Right Forces. The Duma result was encouraging for Vladimir Putin, because it showed that, while Boris Yeltsin remained a polarizing political figure appealing to a minority, the fuzzy-focus appeal to which Putin was inclined won a majority of votes.

---

[9] Since a big majority of non-voters are almost certainly apathetic and unclear in their views about transformation, the size of the group in the electorate as a whole is even larger, for the list vote for the Communist Party and Right Forces together represented only 18 per cent of the whole of the electorate.

8   From acting to elected president

The Duma election was important in itself and as the prelude to the presidential election. Although Vladimir Putin's name was not on the Duma ballot, the outcome was interpreted as a triumph for him. The two parties backing Putin, Unity and Right Forces, took almost 32 per cent of the vote, while among parties associated with other candidates 24 per cent voted Communist; 12 per cent favoured Fatherland-All Russia, which had two potential presidential candidates; and parties led by Grigory Yavlinsky and Vladimir Zhirinovsky barely cleared the 5 per cent PR barrier. Other would-be candidates were associated with parties that won even fewer votes. The Duma vote implied that Putin would have a generous lead over Zyuganov in the first-round ballot for the presidency and would undoubtedly win the second-round ballot against a Communist candidate.

A VTsIOM poll taken during the weekend of the Duma election confirmed the apparently unassailable lead of Putin. He was endorsed by 41 per cent, compared to 12 per cent backing Gennady Zyuganov, and 7 per cent favouring Yevgeny Primakov. No other would-be candidate was favoured by more than 3 per cent of the electorate. When don't knows, would not votes and against all respondents were excluded, support for Putin stood at 55 per cent of voters, with 16 per cent for Zyuganov and 9 per cent for Primakov. If Putin could maintain such support until election day, he had a good chance of winning the presidency outright in the first-round ballot.

Since opinion polls forecast that the Family's candidate was a winner, there was no need for anyone in the Kremlin to argue for postponing the presidential election, nor was that what the public wanted. When the January 2000 NRB survey asked whether the presidential election should be held as the law stipulated, or postponed because it would only stir up trouble, 92 per cent said it should be held. While Vladimir Putin appeared the certain winner, a week is a long time in politics; the six months between the Duma vote and the scheduled date for the presidential election contained 26 weeks in which the lead of a front runner might be vulnerable to uncontrollable events at home, abroad or both.

164

Laying on of hands

The Russian constitution sets out three different routes by which a new president can take office: popular election; the death, persisting physical infirmity or resignation of the incumbent; or impeachment by the Duma. From the start of Yeltsin's second term, there were substantial medical doubts about whether the president would live to complete his second term. There were also unsettled political questions about the procedures for deciding whether the president was physically unable to fulfill the duties of his office. When the Russian Federation began, succession rested with the vice president, an office filled by Alexander Rutskoi, a protege of Boris Yeltsin. After Rutskoi was named acting president by the Parliament during its confrontation with Yeltsin in October 1993, Yeltsin decided that he could do without a vice president. The Federation Constitution that Yeltsin sponsored in a referendum the following December abolished the office of vice president. It stipulated that, if the presidency became vacant, the office should be filled by the prime minister and a presidential election called within three months.

Yeltsin's last surprise

In retrospect, Boris Yeltsin's surprise resignation appears an obvious move, for there was nothing more that he could accomplish in office. Nor was there anything that he or the Family could gain by waiting, when their candidate, Vladimir Putin, appeared certain to win an election called soon – especially if Yeltsin's resignation moved the event forward by three months and Putin was acting president. In the television announcement of his resignation on 31 December 1999, Boris Yeltsin explained that he was leaving with a sense of accomplishment:

I [have] done the main job of my life. Russia will never return to the past. Russia will now always be moving forward. I must not stand in its way, in the way of the natural progress of history.

Yeltsin also apologized to the Russian people for what he did not achieve:

I ask you to forgive me for not fulfilling some hopes of those people who believed we would be able to jump from the grey, stagnating, totalitarian past into a bright, rich and civilized future in one go. I myself believed in this. But it could not be done at a stroke. In some respects I was too naive. Some of the problems were too complex. We struggled on through mistakes and failures (Yeltsin, 1999).

Immediately after President Yeltsin resigned, VTsIOM asked Russians to evaluate the Yeltsin years. Russians were much more conscious of the costs than of the benefits of transformation (tab. 8.1). A total of

Table 8.1 *Positive and negative evaluations of the Yeltsin years*

Q. What good things and what bad things did the years of Yeltsin's rule bring? (Multiple answers accepted.)

POSITIVE (mean per respondent: 1.0)	%
Political	
Political rights, freedom, democracy	23
Freedom of action for energetic, capable people	12
Ending Communist rule	10
Improved relations with the West	7
Destroying totalitarianism, interference in personal life	7
Hope for the renewal of Russia	5
Removing the threat of a new world war	3
Economic	
Getting rid of shortages, ration cards and queues	16
Restoring private property, can start own business	13
Improved quality of goods and services	4
Nothing positive; don't know	(54%)
NEGATIVE (mean per respondent: 3.7)	
Political	
Chechen war of 1993–6	34
Collapse of the Soviet Union	31
More crime and organized crime penetrating state	28
Looting of state property and the riches of Russia	28
Political instability, conflicts in the leadership	16
Lack of confidence and hope in the future	15
Freedom of action for swindlers and bank robbers	15
Loss of Russia's great power status	11
Dominance of foreigners and Russia dependent on West	7
Economic	
Economic crisis, fall in production	40
Closure of enterprises, mass unemployment	36
Worse living conditions, consumption for masses	34
Inflation wiping out savings	32
Non-payment of wages, pensions	26
Collapse of education, health, social security	19
Nothing negative; don't know	(6%)

Source: VTsIOM. Nationwide survey, 8–10 January 2000. Number of respondents, 1,600.

54 per cent could not think of anything positive that President Yeltsin had achieved, while only 6 per cent could not think of anything negative that Yeltsin had done. Among those identifying positive achievements, political gains outnumbered economic gains by a margin of two to one. Yeltsin's most popular achievements were the introduction of political rights and freedom of action, along with getting rid of the shortages and queues of the old command economy and giving people the right to start their own business. Only one in ten Russians saw Yeltsin's destruction of Communist rule as a positive achievement.

With no limit to the number of comments that could be volunteered, negative comments about the Yeltsin years outnumbered positive by a margin of almost four to one. Criticisms were directed at political failings: the first Chechen war, the collapse of the Soviet Union, the way in which privatization led to illegal riches, and organized crime. Criticism was also directed at economic failings, starting with the decline in industrial production, mass unemployment, lower standards of living, inflation and wages being paid late or not at all.

Given the consistently low standing of Boris Yeltsin's presidency, his departure could only raise his public evaluation – but it did so by very little. In VTsIOM's first poll after Yeltsin left office, the former president's rating was higher than at any time since the ruble collapsed in August 1998, but in absolute terms it was still very low, averaging 2.5 on a 1 to 10 scale (cf. fig. 4.1). When VTsIOM asked *In historical perspective, do you think the Yeltsin epoch brought more good or more bad to Russia?*, 67 per cent said he brought more bad, 18 per cent were uncertain and 15 per cent credited Yeltsin with doing more good.

The verdict of instant history need not be the same as the long view. By making a peaceful and lawful exit from office, Russia's first popularly elected president made sure he was not its last one. By contrast with the purges that had marked transitions in Soviet times, the transition was bloodless, literally and metaphorically. It also brought immediate benefits to the Yeltsin Family. The day after becoming acting president Vladimir Putin signed a decree granting immunity from criminal prosecution, search or interrogation to the ex-president and his immediate family members.[1] The amnesty was in keeping with political practice of the previous decade. In 1994, against the opposition of President Yeltsin, the Duma granted an amnesty to the leaders of the August 1991 coup and of the October 1993 parliamentary stand against the Kremlin.

---

[1] In February 2001 President Putin signed a Duma bill allowing a simple majority in both houses of Parliament to lift the immunity of a former president charged with a serious crime such as murder, rape or large-scale theft.

Table 8.2 *Voters unmoved during presidential campaign*

	1999 Dec 17–20	24–27 Dec	2000 Jan 8–10	14–17 Jan	21–24 Jan	28–31 Jan	4–7 Feb	11–14 Feb	18–21 Feb	25–28 Feb	3–6 Mar	10–13 Mar	17–20 Mar	Change during campaign
						Vote in presidential election: all replies %								
Vladimir Putin	41	42	48	55	49	49	49	53	52	49	49	47	45	4
Gennady Zyuganov	12	14	15	13	12	13	13	14	15	17	18	17	16	4
Yevgeny Primakov	7	6	6	4	6	5	3	—	—	—	—	—	—	−4
Vladimir Zhirinovsky	2	5	3	3	3	3	3	2	—	—	—	4	4	2
Grigory Yavlinsky	3	3	2	2	3	2	3	3	3	4	4	4	5	2
Yury Luzhkov	2	1	1	—	—	—	—	—	—	—	—	—	—	−1
Other	8	8	5	6	3	7	5	5	5	7	6	6	6	−2
Against all/won't vote	11	12	10	5	11	10	14	14	15	11	16	12	14	3
Don't know	14	9	10	12	13	11	10	9	10	12	7	10	10	−4

Source: VTsIOM. Nationwide surveys. Number of respondents in each survey approximately 1,600.

Tying up a winning coalition

Promotion to the acting presidency boosted Vladimir Putin's competitive advantage. In the first VTsIOM poll taken just after Putin assumed office, 48 per cent said they would vote for him, a clear majority of those with a candidate preference (tab. 8.2). By the simple fact of *not* being Boris Yeltsin, Putin gained instant popularity; after two weeks in office 76 per cent declared their approval of his performance in the Kremlin, and before a month had passed 84 per cent voiced approval. Such evidence made Putin appear unbeatable; in January, a VTsIOM survey found that two-thirds thought Putin was sure to win, with 9 per cent naming other candidates and the remainder being uncertain.

Taking charge

In accord with the constitution and the wishes of the new occupant of the Kremlin, the Federation Council set the date of the presidential ballot at 26 March 2000. But before then, Putin had to confirm his position. The first priority of the acting president was to negotiate with would-be rivals for his vacated job and to appoint ministers responsible for administering government departments that faced problems that were far from routine.

The job that Putin left vacant was filled by promoting Mikhail Kasyanov, the first deputy prime minister. Kasyanov, a 42-year-old technocrat, had worked in Soviet planning ministries since the last days of Brezhnev and taken an active part in negotiating the restructuring of Russia's debts to foreign governments and banks. Colleagues described Kasyanov as 'a good negotiator' with no known policy commitments, inexperienced in politics and 'not famous for making decisions' (Jack, 2000). Kasyanov's blandness and lack of a political following was part of his appeal to Putin, who intended to look after major political issues himself. Most Yeltsin appointees continued in office, but some were assigned to new jobs.

The acting president could not be indifferent to what happened in the new Duma, for it had the power to confirm or reject the president's choice of prime minister, to vote the budget and to reject or amend legislative proposals from the Kremlin. Although Unity had won enough list votes to boost Putin's political stock, it had only one-sixth of the total seats in the Duma.

When the Duma held its first meeting on 18 January 2000, Russian politicians once again showed their skill as quick-change artists; 141 members adopted a new party label (fig. 8.1). In order to secure the advantages of belonging to a party, five-sixths of the independent deputies joined Duma-only parties that had not been on the list ballot. A group

Figure 8.1 FAST-MOVING DUMA POLITICIANS.

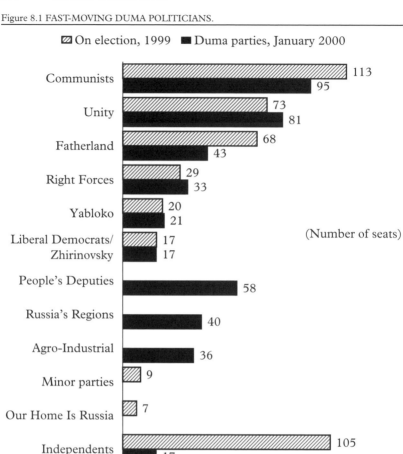

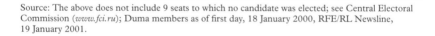

Source: The above does not include 9 seats to which no candidate was elected; see Central Electoral Commission (*www.fci.ru*); Duma members as of first day, 18 January 2000, RFE/RL Newsline, 19 January 2001.

calling itself the People's Deputies was created with 58 members, making it the third-largest party in the Duma. Russia's Regions was formed with 40 members, including 17 recruits from Fatherland-All Russia, which had been launched as an alliance of regional politicians. An Agro-Industrial non-ballot party was formed with 36 members, of which 26 were elected as Communist Party representatives, sufficient to dominate the new bloc, whose agrarian constituents were Soviet-era collective farmers. Deputies elected on the ticket of Our Home Is Russia, once the party favoured by the Kremlin, differed as to where opportunities were best in the new Duma: four joined the People's Deputies group and three joined Unity.

A survey of 200 newly elected Duma deputies organized by Thomas F. Remington (2000) found party groups widely dispersed on a left vs right scale reflecting opinions on five economic issues, such as strengthening the role of private property, selling land in the market and further privatization of state-owned enterprises. The mean views of each party's delegation were close to that of their voters' attitudes toward transformation (cf. fig. 7.2). Deputies of the Union of Right Forces and the Communist Party were at the two extremes, along with the Agro-Industrial allies of the Communist Party. The Union of Right Forces was even further out on the pro-market end of the scale than Communist deputies were on the collectivist end. Yabloko and Unity deputies were pro-market but not extremely so. Fatherland-All Russia, the Zhirinovsky Bloc, People's Deputies and Russia's Regions tended to be in the centre. On the basis of economic views, the strongly collectivist parties had 131 deputies, the more pro-market parties 135 deputies; the balance of power rested with a motley middle group of more than 150 deputies of Fatherland-All Russia, the Zhirinovsky Bloc, Duma-only parties and independents.

When the Duma met, its first order of business was to elect officers and chairs of 27 Duma committees, posts conferring status, financial advantages and a measure of political influence. The Kremlin had several obvious logical options. One choice was to endorse the previous Duma's practice of sharing posts in proportion to party strength. Another was to avoid taking sides in bargaining for Duma posts. The third alternative was to back posts being given to a pro-market coalition of Unity, the Union of Right Forces, People's Deputies and Fatherland-All Russia, opposed by parties more in favour of state direction of the economy.

In the event, Vladimir Putin preferred arithmetic to ideology, backing a Duma coalition of large parties on opposite sides of the left–right divide – the Communists, Unity, and People's Deputies. The logic was simple: together, these three parties held an absolute majority of Duma seats and Putin's opponents in Fatherland-All Russia were left out. The Putin-brokered coalition re-elected a Communist, Gennady Seleznev, as speaker, and prevented Yevgeny Primakov, a leading contender for the presidency, from presiding over the Duma. Communist deputies took 10 posts, Unity received 8 posts and 6 went to the People's Deputies. Together, they had a disproportionate share of major Duma posts. Angered by being offered a disproportionately small share of the remaining leadership positions, Right Forces, Fatherland-All Russia and Yabloko deputies boycotted plenary meetings of the Duma, and Primakov denounced the deal as a total collapse of democracy. (Rutland, 2000:

334ff.; Stephen Smith and Remington, 2001: 148ff.) In April 2002, after the merger of Unity and Fatherland, committee chairs were reassigned to reward pro-Putin parties and greatly reduce the influence of Communist deputies.

Struggles for influence and status in the Duma left voters unmoved. When VTsIOM asked in early 2000 what people made of the alliance between Unity and the Communists, a majority had no opinion, 25 per cent were negative and 20 per cent positive. Similarly, in April 2002, two-thirds had no opinion about the redistribution of posts, 29 per cent were negative and 5 per cent positive.

Co-opting or marginalizing opponents

As acting president, Putin attracted support from those in the Russian political elite who adhered to the traditional belief 'What counts is being close to the king' (Oversloot and Verheul, 2000: 133). A founder of the anti-Yeltsin All Russia party, President Mintimer Shaimiev of the Tatar Republic, announced his endorsement of Putin before the new Duma met. By March 2000, Vladimir Putin had received the support of 49 governors of Russian regions. Among Putin's supporters at the governorship level, 21 had supported Unity in the Duma election, 12 Fatherland-All Russia and 9 had been identified with Our Home Is Russia, the Kremlin party until Viktor Chernomyrdin was dismissed as prime minister. The second-largest group of governors did not commit themselves to any presidential candidate. Only two governors went on record as opposed to Putin (TACIS, 2000; polit.ru, 1999).

As the Putin bandwagon gained momentum, many politicians who had appeared serious contenders for the presidency dropped out of the race. In July 1999, Primakov, Luzhkov, Stepashin, Lebed, Kirienko and Chernomyrdin had together accounted for 51 per cent of the preferences of likely voters. However, by December, together they had the support of only 15 per cent. Given this sea change, the six would-be candidates did not seek nomination for the presidency and Primakov, Luzhkov and Kirienko endorsed Putin.

While a competitive election gives the mass of people the right to choose a president, political elites choose the candidates. To qualify as a presidential candidate, a politician needs to be a Russian citizen who has lived continuously in the Russian Federation for the previous ten years and is at least 35 years of age; these criteria are met by tens of millions of Russians. An additional requirement, that a candidate must be nominated by a party conference or by a registered citizen group with a minimum of 100 members, was not onerous. The final criterion was difficult: to collect 1,000,000 valid signatures on nomination papers, of which no more than 7 per cent can be from any one of the 89 regions of the Federation. The great majority of candidates paid canvassers to produce signatures. In addition, information was required about the candidate's property, debts and personal income in the two years preceding the election, and information about the income, property and liabilities of the candidate's spouse and children too.

When nominations closed on 13 February 2000, 15 candidates presented nomination papers. One candidate was rejected for having too many invalid signatures, one for not having enough signatures and two subsequently withdrew, leaving a field of 11 candidates. Vladimir Zhirinovsky had to go to the Supreme Court to prevent objections to his nomination papers leaving him off the ballot. Aman-Geldy Tuleev, an awkward Communist, again came forward as an independent candidate, allegedly with the encouragement of Putin's staff to draw votes away from Gennady Zyuganov. Of the four nominees who had been on the ballot in the 1996 election, only Zyuganov had previously won a substantial share of the vote; Yavlinsky and Zhirinovsky were also-rans.

The seven new names on the ballot were led by Vladimir Putin, standing as an independent. Konstantin Titov, governor of the Samara region and chair of the Union of Right Forces, sought to stand as the party's candidate. However, Right Forces endorsed Putin, and Titov ended up standing as an independent. Umar Dzhabrailov, an ethnic Chechen and a Moscow-based associate of Yury Luzhkov, stood as an independent candidate campaigning for a diplomatic solution to the Chechen war. Following the withdrawal of Primakov from the race, a prominent member of the Fatherland Party, Stanislav Govorukhin, was nominated as a nominal independent. Ella Pamfilova, the only woman on the ballot, was known as a campaigner for democratic rights; in the Duma election her party, For Citizens' Dignity, took only 0.6 per cent of the list vote. Spiritual Heritage, a nationalist party that had won only 0.1 per cent of the list vote in the Duma election, nominated an ex-Communist, Aleksei Podberezkin. Yury Skuratov, the prosecutor-general blackmailed from office while investigating corruption by members of the Yeltsin Family, ran as an independent anti-corruption candidate.

Confirmation without campaigning

As acting president, Vladimir Putin could campaign as a national leader above the party fray. Putin's strategy was described as an 'anti-campaign campaign', because it stressed his role as head of government and distance from parties, which were distrusted by a big majority of Russian voters (Boxer and Hale, 2000). At a pre-election party conference in

Moscow in late February, the leader of Unity criticized Boris Yeltsin for not developing a Gaullist-style presidential party. He appealed to Putin – 'Vladimir Vladimirovich! We should not miss this opportunity. The head of the state should rely on the party of power.' The acting president rejected Unity's overture, 'Our parties of power have always turned into parties of bureaucrats. That is a mistake' (Oversloot and Verheul, 2000: 140).

In an effort to find out whether voters saw Putin as close to any political party, several or none, VTsIOM asked Russians in January 2000 to say how he was seen in relation to each of the parties winning list seats. In response, one-quarter on average were don't knows. A majority of those with opinions thought Putin very close to Unity, somewhat close to Right Forces and neither close to nor distant from Fatherland-All Russia and Yabloko. A majority also saw Putin as distant from two list parties, the Communists and the Zhirinovsky Bloc.

Manifestations of disorder were a major concern of the electorate. When the post-presidential election ninth New Russia Barometer asked people to select from a menu of eight topics the two most important problems facing government, the war in Chechnya was named by 40 per cent, 39 per cent stressed corruption in government and 17 per cent were concerned about terrorism in Russian cities. Two economic issues were named as important: rising prices, 41 per cent, and unemployment, 36 per cent. Less than 10 per cent thought health and education, crime in the streets or environmental pollution the highest priority issues. The Open Letter to the Russian Voters delivered by Putin on 25 February affirmed the president's concern with these issues. The letter was not only open in being widely publicized, but also wide open in not committing the Kremlin to specific measures to resolve these problems. Putin simply said that he would do his best to deal with the problems in order to restore Russia's greatness. When asked a few weeks before election day what his plans would be for government if he won election, Putin replied, 'I won't say' (quoted in Shevtsova, 2001: 93).

Looking presidential

Like Tony Blair or Bill Clinton, Vladimir Putin's strategy was to appear presidential, treating his role as leader of all the people. This strategy avoided engagement with awkward or divisive political issues, including past policies of the Yeltsin administration. Thus, when VTsIOM asked in a January 2000 survey how people compared Putin's economic policies with those of his predecessors, only 15 per cent linked Putin's position on economic issues with that of President Yeltsin. Half thought Putin was following his own course on economic affairs, while 18 per cent thought he had no definite course and 17 per cent were don't knows.

Presidential candidates in the public eye long before Vladimir Putin appeared on the horizon were more disliked than admired. A month before the presidential ballot, 56 per cent told VTsIOM that they would definitely not want Zhirinovsky as president, almost twenty times the number prepared to vote for him. Similarly, 29 per cent said they would not like to see Zyuganov as president, almost double the proportion saying they would vote for him. By making a fuzzy-focus appeal without a clear-cut statement of principles, Putin avoided leaving himself open to attacks based on policy; only 4 per cent, less than one-tenth those preparing to vote for him, said they would not like to see Putin as president.

Given the virtual certainty of the outcome, most of Putin's competitors refrained from attacking him, fearing that this would stir up the enmity of the Kremlin to their subsequent disadvantage. In television appearances Zhirinovsky, Podberezkin and Tuleev each praised Putin. Zyuganov sought to appeal to voters by promising tax cuts and increasing the minimum monthly pension and the pay of doctors and teachers. Acting President Putin trumped this by increasing pensions and the wages of all state workers by 20 per cent.

In a contest with more than 100 million electors, national television is uniquely suited to reach voters. A content analysis found that Putin received as much television election coverage as the total for Zyuganov, Yavlinsky and Zhirinovsky (European Institute for the Media, 2000: 2). ORT, the major state television channel, in which Boris Berezovsky had a major interest, promoted Putin's candidacy through its news coverage. The war in Chechnya was a continuing news story. Putin's flight to Chechnya in a military fighter shortly before polling day showed the Kremlin ready to milk the war for as much favourable publicity as it could. The gap between Putin and Zyuganov was so great that there was far less negative campaigning against the Communist candidate than in 1996. Zyuganov's public appearances were also low-key; he emphasized policy issues rather than personality. Grigory Yavlinsky had the money to finance a series of television advertisements identifying him with 'reason, will, results', while ORT publicized a bogus press conference of gays for Yavlinsky (Hale, 2000).

Voters relied on television much less than did candidates. The ninth New Russia Barometer found that 92 per cent who voted in the presidential ballot regarded their own experience and observations as very or somewhat helpful in making their choice. By comparison, 59 per cent said state television was helpful and 38 per cent regarded private television as important. Discussions with friends and workmates were cited as helpful by 57 per cent of voters, and newspapers by little more than a quarter of voters.

Official confirmation: the result

While Russians divided their support amongst many parties in the Duma election, they were consistently lopsided in their presidential preferences. During the campaign, Putin was the choice of between 47 and 55 per cent of electors (tab. 8.2); over the same period, support for Gennady Zyuganov rose by four percentage points. The decline in support for other candidates was matched by statistically insignificant gains of 1 or 2 per cent by also-ran candidates. The proportion of respondents saying they were undecided or would not vote for a candidate remained virtually constant at 25 per cent.

The principal uncertainty was whether Putin would win 50 per cent of the vote in the first round, and thus make a run-off ballot unnecessary. The headline opinion poll figures underestimated Putin's support, since they included those who reported they would not vote, the undecided and the unlikely to vote. In the final pre-election poll Putin was endorsed by 60 per cent of Russians naming a candidate preference, and by 59 per cent of those stating a candidate preference and likely to vote.

Although journalists complained that the presidential election campaign was a dull no-contest, the turnout of 68.6 per cent was only 0.5 per cent lower than for the hotly contested 1995 Duma election and much higher than turnout in the 2001 British general election or an American presidential election. Only 1.9 per cent voted against all candidates, two-fifths the proportion in the second round of the 1996 presidential election. Among NRB respondents who did not cast a ballot, 45 per cent said this was because of sickness or absence from home and an additional 8 per cent lacked any interest in the election. Distrust of politicians or of the efficacy of elections were mentioned by less than half the non-voters.

Necessarily, voters had to make up their minds late because Vladimir Putin was not a candidate until six months before the election, and, as an independent candidate, he could not start with support due to party loyalties. When Russians were asked when they made up their mind about how to vote, 4 per cent said they did so on election day and 17 per cent decided in the week before the election. The largest group of voters, 53 per cent, decided how to vote after the Duma election and before the week of the ballot. Only a quarter of the electorate had made up their minds in the autumn or earlier. Among Zyuganov voters, half said they had decided how to vote the previous summer or earlier.

Table 8.3 *Vote for the president, 26 March 2000*

	Votes	%
Electorate	109,372,043	100.0
Valid votes	74,369,754	68.0
Invalid votes	701,016	0.6
Total votes	75,070,770	68.6
Candidates		100.0
Vladimir Putin, Independent	39,740,467	52.9
Gennady Zyuganov, Communist	21,928,468	29.2
Grigory Yavlinsky, Yabloko	4,351,450	5.8
Aman-Geldy Tuleev, Independent	2,217,364	3.0
Vladimir Zhirinovsky, Liberal Democrats	2,026,509	2.7
Konstantin Titov, Independent	1,107,269	1.5
Ella Pamfilova, For Citizens' Dignity	758,967	1.0
Stanislav Govorukhin, Independent	328,723	0.4
Yuri Skuratov, Independent	319,189	0.4
Aleksei Podberezkin, Spiritual Heritage	98,177	0.1
Umar Dzhabrailov, Independent	78,498	0.1
Against all candidates	1,414,673	1.9

Sources: Central Electoral Commission, *Vybory prezidenta Rossiiskoi federatsii 26 marta 2000 goda, www.fci.ru/prez2000/default.htm,* Results of Elections Total Country and by Region and Constituency, 3/10/2000; Central Electoral Commission, *Vybory prezidenta Rossiiskoi federatsii 2000: elektoral' naya statistika,* Moscow: Ves' mir, 2000, 84–6, 191.

When the votes were counted, Vladimir Putin had won an absolute majority with more than two million votes to spare (tab. 8.3). Whereas in the first-round ballot in 1996 Boris Yeltsin had finished only 3.3 percentage points ahead of Gennady Zyuganov, Putin finished 23.7 percentage points ahead of Zyuganov. A substantial portion of those favouring also-ran candidates would have swung to Putin faced with a run-off choice between him and a Communist. The vote of Grigory Yavlinsky dropped by 1.5 percentage points from the 1996 election, and Vladimir Zhirinovsky's vote more than halved, falling to 2.7 per cent. Aman-Geldy Tuleev, the breakaway Communist, took 3.0 per cent of the vote, twice that won by Konstantin Titov. Ella Pamfilova's appeal For Citizens' Dignity gained the vote of only 1 per cent of Russian voters. The most prominent anti-corruption campaigner, Yury Skuratov, gained less than half of 1 per cent of the vote. Had Putin fallen short of an absolute majority and a second-round run-off been held, he would have received a much higher share of the vote than Boris Yeltsin did.

By international standards, Vladimir Putin won an outstanding victory. By comparison with France, where the presidential election similarly requires an absolute majority of votes, Putin's first-round vote was higher than that of General de Gaulle or any of his successors, and more than double the share that President Jacques Chirac gained in 2002. Putin's margin of victory was also greater than that in American landslide victories by Richard Nixon in 1972, Lyndon Johnson in 1964 and Franklin D. Roosevelt in 1936. His percentage share of the vote was greater than that of George W. Bush, Bill Clinton or John F. Kennedy.

The election campaign was observed by more than a thousand election monitors from abroad, plus teams of Russians representing the media, political parties and civic groups. As in the Duma election, foreign observation teams criticized the strong pro-government bias of the media, but endorsed the election as substantially free. Episodic violations of electoral procedures were observed: for example, some election officials campaigned for candidates, campaign leaflets were distributed anonymously in violation of the law and family members or friends gathering at a polling station sometimes marked their ballots openly and together. Given old Soviet habits and the level of corruption in Russian public life, an election without some maladministration or fraud would not have been a normal Russian election (OSCE: 2000: 30; IFES, 2000).

The question is: how much did fraud distort the outcome of the presidential ballot? The Office of Democratic Institutions and Human Rights monitoring team concluded that shortcomings were 'not sufficient to alter the outcome'. The ninth New Russia Barometer asked whether respondents or any member of their family had seen or heard about irregularities on election day, such as presidential ballots being marked by polling officials. Only 1 per cent had first-hand knowledge of irregularities and an additional 5 per cent had heard stories about irregularities from friends and neighbours. In addition, 14 per cent heard accusations of vote fraud on television or in the newspapers. In sum, four-fifths had no knowledge of electoral irregularities at first hand or by hearsay, six percentage points higher than at the Duma election.

The logic of vote fraud is that it should produce a very big vote for the favoured candidate, acting president Vladimir Putin. Reputable nationwide polls forecast that Vladimir Putin would win between 50 and 60 per cent of the total vote. In the event, Putin's official vote tally was four percentage points below VTsIOM's final estimate of 57.6 per cent of likely voters favouring Putin, a strong indication that the official Kremlin candidate did not benefit in aggregate from electoral irregularities.

The party-of-power doctrine also focuses attention on the political influence of governors. As the leading elected politician in a region, a governor is expected to be able to deliver votes wholesale for a presidential candidate or a list party. During his rise within the Kremlin, Vladimir

Putin had at one time been responsible for links between the presidency and governors. The logic of the delivery vote is that each region's presidential vote ought to be lopsided in favour of the governor's candidate. Since Putin won just over half the total vote nationally, this implies that in favoured regions he should have been given 75 per cent or more of the vote, while taking less than 25 per cent in other regions. But this did not happen. In the 49 regions where the governor backed Putin, his average vote was 57.0 per cent, only 5.3 per cent higher than in the districts where the governor was officially neutral. The standard deviation in Putin's vote in the regions, 9.8 per cent, was much lower than for the Labour Party's parliamentary candidates at British general elections or for American members of Congress. It indicates that two-thirds of regions should report a vote for Putin between 64 and 45 per cent and all but four or five regions a vote between 36 and 73 per cent. In fact, there were only four regions where Putin's vote was outside this range, exactly what would be expected statistically (cf. Clem and Craumer, 2000: tab. 3). The impact of opposition by governors was greater; in the two districts where governors opposed Putin, his vote averaged 44.4 per cent.

While the NRB estimate of irregularities was very low, given the massive size of the electorate, it left scope for a million examples of vote manipulation. Six months after the presidential vote, the *Moscow Times* (Anon., 2000) published a detailed series of allegations of irregularities at polling stations, information gathered by a team of reporters at considerable personal risk. It singled out twelve regions as high in voting irregularities. However, in five of the regions – Nizhny Novgorod, Chechnya, Kursk, Primorye and Novosibirsk – Putin's share of the official vote was actually *below* his national average. Only in three selected regions – Dagestan, Kabardino-Balkariya and Tatarstan – was Putin's vote more than one standard deviation above the average. In Dagestan, where Putin received 81.0 per cent of the official vote, an American academic (Ware, 2000) interpreted this as showing that Dagestani politicians delivered support to Moscow in return for economic benefits, a patronage-style vote that wardheelers in every country would understand. The *Moscow Times* conceded that, even if fraud had been on a massive scale, producing the millions of votes that gave Putin an absolute majority in the first round, in the second-round run-off he would have been the certain winner.

Multiple influences on presidential choice

Although close in time, the logic of competition in a presidential election differs fundamentally from that of the Duma contest. The race for the presidency is a winner-take-all contest, with one person entering the

Kremlin. By contrast, in a Duma election many parties win seats and a plurality of outlooks are represented there. In a society in transformation, a winner-take-all contest can involve a choice between political regimes as well as personalities, if candidates offer stark alternatives. The 1996 presidential election was a vote for or against transformation. In spite of his low personal standing, Boris Yeltsin won because the electorate was confronted with a forced choice between maintaining the new regime and risking a turn to another regime by voting for a Communist candidate. A discriminant function analysis shows that Russian voters divided according to where they placed the blame for the travails of transformation: on the Communist legacy or on actions that were the responsibility of Boris Yeltsin (Rose and Tikhomirov, 1996: tabs. 4, 7).

In the 2000 presidential race, Vladimir Putin appealed for votes *as if* transformation was no longer the issue and a stable equilibrium had been achieved. Instead of emphasizing that voters were forced to make a choice between regimes and ways of life, he sought to make his personal character of primary importance and avoid taking sides on divisive issues involving comparisons between what the Soviet regime and what Boris Yeltsin had done. In doing so, Putin appeared like a Russian Tony Blair, dismissing normative debates about the rights and wrongs of the past as pointless, since both the Communist regime and President Yeltsin were gone. Putin sought to make personality, not ideology, the principal theme of his campaign. As acting president, he was immediately responsible for how government dealt with major issues, but his time on the political stage was so brief that voters did not hold him to account for what had happened more than six months before. The one policy with which Putin was identified – the vigorous prosecution of the war in Chechnya – was supported by all parties and by most voters.

Although the Communist Party of the Russian Federation was a different party than the CPSU, its principal source of votes came from Russians who had a positive attitude toward the old regime, and this was even more true of its active members. Thus, Gennady Zyuganov could not repudiate the past. The passage of time diminished the prospect of the clock being turned back to a Communist regime, and Zyuganov avoided suggestions that he would attempt to do so. Zyuganov sought votes by emphasizing what he and many Russians saw as undesirable consequences of transformation, such as inflation, unemployment and inadequate social services. The issues were discussed on the assumption that Zyuganov could deliver better economic and social policies without repudiating the new regime.

To determine how Russians responded to the choice of Putin or Zyuganov, the ninth New Russia Barometer survey went in the field immediately after the presidential election. A nationwide representative

Figure 8.2 PERSONALITY AND POLICY IN PRESIDENTIAL CHOICE.

Q. Some people vote for a candidate because they favour his policies or political
programme. Others do so because they fear the alternative will be worse. In casting
your vote, which most influenced you? (Choose only one.)

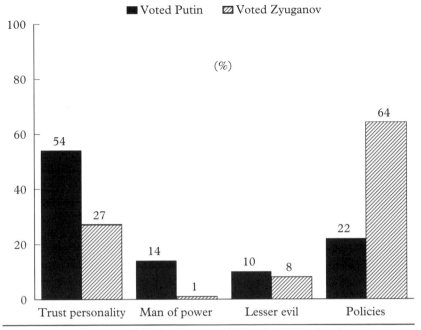

Source: New Russia Barometer IX. Nationwide survey, 14–18 April 2000. Number of respondents, 1,600.

sample of 1,600 was interviewed between 14 and 18 April 2000. Since the questionnaire was prepared after the preliminary analysis of Duma voting reported in chapter 7, it included all the questions that had influenced Duma voting as well as many specific to the presidential competition.

When asked whether personality or policy was more important, the electorate divided. A plurality, 43 per cent, said that trust in the person of the candidate was most important; additionally, 8 per cent believed it best to support a man of power. By contrast, 36 per cent considered agreement with policies most important. In 1996, when the regime appeared at stake, 36 per cent said they voted for the candidate who was the lesser evil; in the 2000 election, only 12 per cent took this position.

The importance of personality as against policy differed greatly according to the choice of candidates (fig. 8.2). Among Vladimir Putin's supporters, 54 per cent emphasized a trustworthy personality, whereas only half that number thought personality was important in voting for his opponent. By contrast, among Zyuganov voters, 64 per cent put policies first, almost three times the number of Putin voters who gave priority to policies. One-seventh of Putin's voters thought it most important to vote for a man of power, while this appeal was of no use to Zyuganov. When a choice of regimes is at stake, electors who dislike both candidates may nonetheless vote to keep the greater evil out. In the 2000 ballot, less than a tenth felt they were voting for a lesser evil, and they were divided almost equally between the two principal candidates.

The ability of Vladimir Putin to distance himself from political ideologies is shown by the absence of any clear view in the electorate about his broad political outlook. While Gennady Zyuganov was ineluctably identified as a Communist, the ninth NRB survey found no agreement among Russians about Putin's political outlook. Just under half saw him as pro-market, one-quarter did not associate him with any ideology and 16 per cent saw him as a great power patriot, with the remaining tenth attributing other outlooks to him.

To identify the most important influences on voting, we again turn to multiple discriminant function analysis. Four candidates – Putin, Zyuganov, Yavlinsky and Zhirinovsky – each had a potentially distinctive appeal, and together accounted for more than nine-tenths of the vote for presidential candidates. In the first stage of analysis, dozens of potential influences, including all those important in Duma voting, were included. As is inevitably the case, many were of no importance and have therefore been omitted in order to concentrate attention on important influences, defined as those loading .25 or higher on a function (for an analysis with more variables, see Rose, Munro and White, 2000: tab. 3). Insofar as the presidential election was again about candidates representing different regimes, then influences pre-eminent in the first function for Duma voting should again be important. Insofar as the presidential election was a move toward choice within a regime in equilibrium, then the most important influences ought to be like those that are found in established democratic regimes, for example, personality, current issues and the social characteristics of voters.

Together, two functions correctly classify 75 per cent of the voting for Putin, Zyuganov, Yavlinsky or Zhirinovsky. This is three times better than the result of randomly assigning respondents to the four candidates in equal numbers. The two leading functions correctly identify 85 per cent of Putin voters, 73 per cent of Zyuganov voters, 21 per cent of Yavlinsky voters and none of Zhirinovsky's few voters (tab. 8.4).

Confirming the contrast between a personality, Vladimir Putin, and a policy candidate, Gennady Zyuganov, the eight indicators combined in the first function are a combination of transformation and equilibrium

Table 8.4 *Combining influences on presidential choice*

Functions explaining choice of Putin, Zyuganov, Yavlinsky or Zhirinovsky

	Personality/ policy	Old Soviet/ liberal
(Variance explained)	(79%)	(18%)
Blame for economic problems: Communist regime	.48	−.45
State TV useful in deciding vote	.45	.16
Pro-market ideology	.43	−.18
Voted for personality	.34	.31
View of current political system	.30	−.03
Pro-Yeltsin	.29	−.05
View of current economic system	.29	−.09
Voted for man of power	.29	.26
Low household income	−.11	.48
Village, small town	−.06	.45
Low education	−.09	.45
View of past economic system	−.38	.44
View of past political system	−.35	.41
Supports action in Chechnya	.10	.40
Age	−.26	.38
Believes tough dictatorship only way out	−.12	.26

(Boxed numbers are variables best characterizing each function.)

Source: New Russia Barometer IX. Nationwide survey, 14–18 April 2000. Number of respondents, 1,600.

influences. Putin voters blamed the former Communist regime and were pro-Boris Yeltsin. Views of the current political and economic systems can influence voters in established democratic states as well as in transformation systems, but in the latter context the choices and judgments are much broader, being informed by contrasts with the past. Although Putin did not campaign on a pro-market platform, the anti-market ideology of Zyuganov drove voters committed to the market toward Putin. As in an established system in equilibrium, Vladimir Putin gained support from voters who said they voted on personality and from the small number who voted for a man of power. Television, another influence important in equilibrium systems, also delivered votes to Putin, if people relied for political information on the state television network that the Kremlin dominated. Zyuganov did not rely on personality for appeal; transformation considerations, such as endorsement of the old system and rejection of the new, were most important. The distance between Putin and Zyuganov on the first dimension was substantial, but the blurring effect of Putin's appeal resulted in it being more than two-fifths less than the distance in the

Figure 8.3 PRESIDENTIAL COMPETITION ON TWO DIMENSIONS.

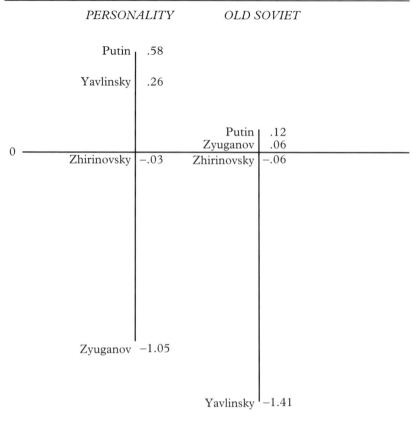

PERSONALITY   *OLD SOVIET*

Putin .58

Yavlinsky .26

Putin .12
Zyuganov .06

0 ————————————————————

Zhirinovsky −.03   Zhirinovsky −.06

Zyuganov −1.05

Yavlinsky −1.41

POLICY   *LIBERAL*

(Candidate locations are group centroids for unstandardized canonical discriminant functions.)

Source: Multiple discriminant function analysis, as reported in table 8.4.

Duma election between the most ideological parties, Right Forces and the Communist Party (cf. figs. 7.2 and 8.3).

The second function discriminates between voters with more traditional Soviet outlooks and those with liberal outlooks more congenial to post-Soviet life. Supporters of Grigory Yavlinsky are at one end of the continuum, while those voting for Putin, Zyuganov and Zhirinovsky are bunched together at the other end (fig. 8.3). The tendency of Yavlinsky voters to be more yuppie – that is, to be big city residents, to have higher income, and to be more educated and younger – is consistent with equilibrium competition in party systems as they have evolved in Western democracies in recent years. In addition to the equilibrium socio-economic influences, the vote for Yavlinsky also reflects transformation values, for example rejection of the old political and economic regimes and dictatorship. However, Russian-style yuppies are not very numerous and their political influence is much less than that of a small number of new rich Russian oligarchs who concentrate their support on candidates who are powerful.

Vladimir Putin won an absolute majority in the first-round vote because he was able to draw support from across a broad spectrum of Russian opinion, rather than polarizing support as in an election fought on transformation issues. This is symbolized by the closeness of Putin and Zyuganov voters on the second function, liberal vs traditional Soviet attitudes (fig. 8.3). Moreover, both candidates are near the mid-point of this function, rather than being extremely in favour of old Soviet values. In Zyuganov's case this reflects a movement away from his party's past. In Putin's case, it reflects his readiness to avoid attacking the Soviet regime as Yeltsin had done, and as Yavlinsky and Right Forces have done because of their commitment to liberal, pro-market values.

The failure of more transformation influences to register as important statistically is due to Putin and Zyuganov voters being similar in their attitudes. For example, at least five-sixths in each group endorse the pre-perestroika economic system, three-quarters endorse state ownership of enterprises in preference to privatization and more than two-thirds are positive about the Soviet political system. As for the war in Chechnya, 87 per cent of Putin's voters and 81 per cent of Zyuganov's favour the government's measures there.

Vladimir Putin appealed to voters with many different political ideologies or none. From three-fifths to three-quarters of voters who thought of themselves as pro-market, great power patriots, of other ideologies, or having no ideology voted for Putin. Even among those who saw themselves as Communists, Putin won almost a quarter of their vote. Ironically, the support of those who said they were Communists and voted for Putin turned his plurality of votes into an absolute majority, thus avoiding a second-round run-off ballot. The inclusive character of Vladimir Putin's majority is shown in figure 8.4. His mosaic of support is not dominated by voters with any one political outlook. Neither of the two largest groups in the mosaic – those who say they have no political outlook and those who say they are pro-market – account for as much as two-fifths of his support. Three in eight were pro-market, and three in eight said they had no political outlook. Any pressures applied on Putin from one ideological

Figure 8.4 MOSAIC OF VLADIMIR PUTIN'S SUPPORT.

Q. What broad political outlook are you most inclined to favour?

(Broad political outlooks of Putin voters)

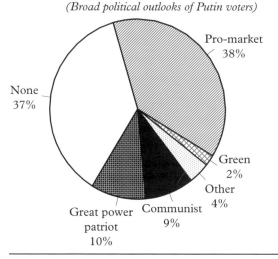

Source: New Russia Barometer IX. Nationwide survey, 14–18 April 2000. Number of respondents, 1,600.

tendency can be more than offset by pressures from others in the diverse mosaic of his support.

After a decade of turbulent transformation, the endorsement of Vladimir Putin by the electorate marked a big step toward confirming that, even though Russia does not have a modern state, elections are now the final arbiter of who governs. More than that, Putin has avoided raking the ashes of transformation and thereby polarizing the electorate. Instead, he distanced himself from debates about the past. In an address to the Russian people on 3 April 2001, Vladimir Putin spoke proudly about the relative calmness of his first year in office by contrast with the revolutionary turbulence of the preceding decade. He pledged:

Revolution is usually followed by counter-revolution, reforms by counter-reforms and then by the search for those guilty of revolutionary misdeeds and by punishment, all the more so since Russia's own historical experience is rich in such examples. But I think it is time to say firmly that this cycle has ended. There will be no revolution or counter-revolution (Putin, 2001a).

9   Campaigning and governing

A democratic leader must be popular, for unpopularity raises the prospect of electoral defeat and that undermines a leader's capacity to influence others within government. A US president runs a permanent campaign to boost popularity and to reduce opposition to White House initiatives. In Moscow, Vladimir Putin is doing the same. But governing is about policy as well as popularity: to govern is to choose.

Initially, a president's popular support reflects the breadth of his electoral appeal. By winning an absolute majority in the first-round presidential ballot, Vladimir Putin took office with well above average support, embracing individuals who did not vote for him or did not bother to vote. He has maintained this for the first half of his term in office. When difficulties arise, support also depends on the intensity with which citizens approve or disapprove of a president. Putin's appeal across the political spectrum deprives him of the dedicated commitment and opposition that Margaret Thatcher's political principles attracted, while giving him greater, but less intense support. A president's support must also be durable. Vladimir Putin emerged on the political scene so abruptly that the durability of his popularity was untested before he became president.

After years of paying the costs of transformation, the Russian people initially had very high expectations for the success of Vladimir Putin in promoting the dictatorship of law. On the eve of the presidential election, VTsIOM found that 89 per cent expected him to bring order by enforcing the law, 75 per cent expected him to promote national self-reliance and 63 per cent expected him to strengthen the security services. A very large majority, 82 per cent, also expected Putin to respect freedom of speech while pursuing order.

The shift from campaigning to governing is a shift from votemaking to policymaking. To win votes, Vladimir Putin did not need to spell out in detail what he would do to achieve the popular goals that he enunciated. However, once in office, the president is under pressure to move toward electorally popular goals. In addition, he must respond to the challenges and opportunities of unexpected events. In reacting to events the Kremlin deals not only with other branches of government but also with market forces, foreign governments and transnational and international forces beyond its control.

A decade of incomplete transformation meant that when Vladimir Putin arrived in the Kremlin he faced problems on a scale far greater than in an established democratic state. While the scale of Putin's victory gave him a mandate for action, his campaign emphasis on consensual goals gave little indication of what he would do to achieve desirable objectives. Any policy a president adopts invites opposition from those expecting to lose out from changes. Conflict is especially likely in the face of a dilemma, when there is something to be said against as well as for any proposed course of action. This chapter examines Vladimir Putin's actions in his first half of his term as president, covering not only what he has done but also how the Russian people evaluate what he has and has not achieved.

Winning the rating war

In office a Russian president seeks popular approval without a visible enemy. Whereas the US president must struggle continually with Congress and the British prime minister faces a periodic challenge from the opposition leader in the House of Commons, the president of Russia is not so challenged. The closest Russia has to a leader of the opposition, Gennady Zyuganov, is a two-time loser in presidential elections. The president depends on his own achievements for popularity or, as Boris Yeltsin showed, unpopularity.

Popularity

Along with lavish spending on political campaigning, Russian political elites have become fascinated with the opinion poll ratings of politicians. The word rating has been imported into Russian, and references to polls are frequent in the media. Whereas Boris Yeltsin had incentives to ignore opinion polls showing his unpopularity, Vladimir Putin can turn to the polls for reassurance, and he has shown an American-style appetite for polls. The Kremlin can use polls in a multiplicity of ways: as a source of psychological reassurance; as feedback showing that its actions are correct because they are popular; and as a means of influencing other politicians to go along with the president because he represents both power and popularity.

President Putin's public rating has been consistently high, a matter of particular concern to a first-term president facing a race for re-election in

2004. Immediately after he became acting president, almost four-fifths of Russians approved Vladimir Putin's performance; only 13 per cent were negative and 11 per cent were don't knows (fig. 9.1). Immediately after the presidential election, Putin's approval rating was just as high. Monthly VTsIOM surveys since have shown that the president's initial rating was not the product of a honeymoon but the start of a sustained period of popularity rare in established democracies. The least high level of approval, 61 per cent, came at the end of June 2000; the following month it was again over 70 per cent and it has consistently remained at that level since March 2001 and, by November, reached a new peak of 80 per cent. At the start of 2002, 75 per cent of the electorate approved Putin's performance (for updating, see *www.RussiaVotes.org*).

Even though the president appoints the government, there is a big gap in the public's evaluation of the two. When VTsIOM asked about both in March 2000, 77 per cent approved of Putin while 44 per cent approved the government of Russia. Since then, the proportion of Russians disapproving the performance of the government has usually been much the same as those approving; the median group are don't knows. The public's ratings of the president and of the government usually go up and down together, but the gap remains. As for the Duma, Russians consistently disapprove its performance by a margin of more than two to one. In July 2000, only 26 per cent approved what the Duma was doing and 56 per cent disapproved; the remainder were don't knows. A year later the figures were virtually the same. Consistent public disapproval of the Duma's performance is exploited by the Kremlin in its relations with Duma members.

Personally, a president can welcome the approval of many who dislike the government of the day and the Duma. However, the failure of his personal popularity to transfer to institutions of government questions the extent to which Vladimir Putin is evaluated as the chief policymaker of government, as opposed to his being a familiar, reassuring and even engaging media personality.

Intensity of commitment

If support comes from fair-weather friends, they will disappear at the first sign of political difficulties. Intensity of commitment is especially important in Russia, because of the absence of established party loyalties that encourage commitment to a party leader who becomes president. Since Vladimir Putin is not a party leader, he is free to appeal to voters with diverse political loyalties and ideologies – but in doing so he also risks spreading commitment thin.

Figure 9.1 PRESIDENT PUTIN FAR MORE POPULAR THAN RUSSIAN GOVERNMENT.

Q. On the whole do you approve or disapprove of the performance of Vladimir Putin as president of Russia?
Q. Do you approve or disapprove of the performance of the government of Russia as whole?

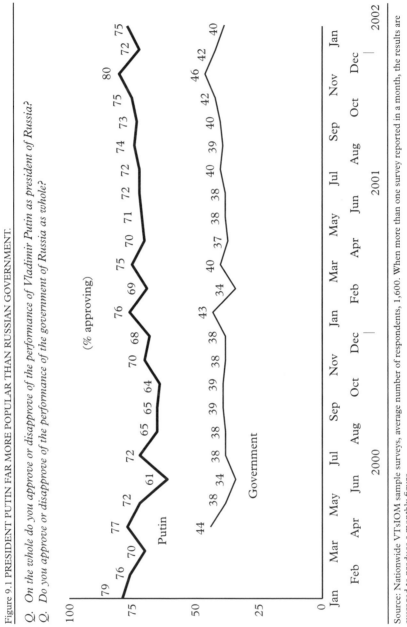

Source: Nationwide VTsIOM sample surveys, average number of respondents, 1,600. When more than one survey reported in a month, the results are averaged to produce a monthly figure.

Figure 9.2 ATTITUDES TOWARD PUTIN POSITIVE BUT LUKEWARM.

Q. What assessment would you make of Vladimir Putin as president, if 1 is the worst and 10 is the best mark?

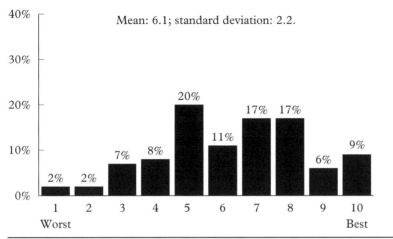

Source: New Russia Barometer X. Nationwide survey, 17 June–3 July 2001. Number of respondents, 2,000.

When the New Russia Barometer asks people to assess President Putin on a scale ranging from worst (1) to best (10), the median Russian consistently gives him a positive rating. However, the commitment lacks the apparent strength implied by the dichotomous choice between approval and disapproval. For example, while 72 per cent stated approval of Putin in June 2001, only 8 per cent gave him the best rating and 56 per cent placed him in the positive half of that scale. Reciprocally, while 22 per cent stated disapproval, only 3 per cent rated Putin at the very bottom of the rating scale. In the tenth NRB survey in summer 2001, the mean rating for Putin was 6.1, slightly above his 5.9 rating immediately after the presidential election. However, there is a wide dispersion of attitudes toward him (fig. 9.2). Russians who are strongly pro-Putin outnumber those who are strongly negative, but both groups are in a minority. Most Russians are inclined to favour Putin but there is little evidence of intense commitment nor is there any evidence of strong dislike.

What explains the variation in the degree to which Russians rate President Putin as good or bad? In his election campaign, Putin appealed for votes as a post-transformation candidate, distancing himself from the Soviet and Yeltsin past. Once in office, voters can judge Putin on the performance of his government rather than in relation to his predecessors. To identify what determines the intensity of commitment to President

Putin, we have analysed the views of the whole of the Russian electorate, and not just those voting for major list parties. This is appropriate since Putin presents himself as president of all the Russian people, whether they voted for or against him or did not vote. Since assessment is on a 1 to 10 scale, multiple regression analysis is the appropriate statistical technique to use to identify significant influences. The first regression analysis had 36 transformation, political ideology and equilibrium influences, including all those reported in the two preceding chapters on Duma and presidential voting plus additional indicators relevant in assessing an incumbent president. We then dropped those influences lacking statistical significance and conducted a second regression analysis with 15 influences that were initially significant at the .05 level or better. It explains 35.7 per cent of the variance in commitment to President Putin, and all

Table 9.1 *Influences on popular rating of President Putin*

Influences on rating of Putin from worst to best

	b	Beta
Equilibrium influences		
Political		
Putin raises world's respect for Russia	58	20
Putin improves social protection	41	16
Kremlin corrupt	−32	−14
Supports actions in Chechnya	27	11
Trusts Federal Security Service	12	09
State television major source of information	25	09
Frequently discusses politics	−16	−07
Economic		
Monthly household income (thousand rubles)	−03	−05
Social		
Pride in Russian citizenship	29	11
Age	01	08
Education level	−05	−05
Political ideology		
Communist	−41	−08
Transformation influences		
Pro-political system in five years	005	10
Pro-current political system	003	07
Hardships sooner or later will benefit	18	06

Variance explained: adjusted R^2 35.7%
(Beta and b values for regression coefficients significant at .01 or better.)

Source: New Russia Barometer X. Nationwide survey, 17 June–3 July 2001. Number of respondents, 2,000. Dependent variable as in fig. 9.2.

the influences reported in tab. 9.1 are significant at the level of .01 or better.

Influences on the degree of commitment to Vladimir Putin differ from those affecting electoral choice (cf. tabs. 7.4, 8.4 and 9.1). Political performance is by far the most important determinant of how people assess Putin, a pattern often found too in assessments of an American president or a British prime minister. Net of other influences, people who think that Putin has raised the world's respect for Russia a lot are likely to give Putin an average rating 1.7 points higher than those who think he has not raised respect at all. Similarly, those who think social protection of the poor has improved a great deal under Putin give him a mean rating more than 1.6 points higher than those who think he has not. Where Putin is perceived as performing badly, his rating falls. Among the 22 per cent of Russians who see the president's staff in the Kremlin as totally corrupt, the average mark of Putin is 1.0 point lower than among the 15 per cent who see Putin's staff as practically free of corruption. Putin's strong identification with national security gives him stronger support from those favouring military action in Chechnya, and his background in the KGB gives him stronger support from those who trust the Federal Security Service, but the differences are not so great as for the previously described influences.

Two contrasting sources of political communication – state television and discussion with friends – are significant for assessing Putin. State television is under continuing pressure to show the president performing well. Among Russians who think state television a very good source of finding out what is going on, Putin's rating is 0.8 higher than among those who think state television a very bad source of information. By contrast with state television, talking politics with friends is today free of pressures from the Kremlin, and people who discuss politics more often are more likely to be opinion leaders in informal networks on which Russians rely. Those who discuss politics often are likely to rate Vladimir Putin half a point lower than those who never talk about politics. Thus, much of the advantage that the president gains from the influence of state television is cancelled out by the criticisms voiced of him by those who talk politics most.

On entering office, Vladimir Putin had the good fortune to inherit an economy that was moving forward from the depths of the ruble collapse of 1998. With a boost from the world price for oil being high, the Russian economy has continued to expand in the first half of his term of office. While Putin was not responsible for the economic upsurge, like any politician he can nonetheless claim credit for it and use it to strengthen his support. This expectation is matched by theories postulating that marginal fluctuations in economic conditions account for marginal fluctuations in presidential popularity in political systems in equilibrium. However, the economic boom has *not* strengthened commitment to Putin. The initial regression analysis included four measures of economic conditions, such as the evaluation of current and future household living conditions. However, only one influence – current income – registered as significant, and its influence was the opposite of what was expected. Russians with a higher income are less likely to be positively committed to President Putin. Net of other influences, Putin's mean rating was one-quarter of a point lower among those with a very high income than with those with a very low income.

Age and education are familiar influences in political systems in equilibrium, and significant for assessments of Vladimir Putin too. His approval is stronger among less educated and older Russians. Among older Russians, the assessment of President Putin is almost two-fifths of a point higher than among Russians who were too young to vote when the first competitive elections were held in the early 1990s. Independent of age, the most educated Russians are likely to have an assessment of Putin one-quarter of a point lower than the assessment of the least educated Russians.

The success of Vladimir Putin in distancing his popularity from divisions due to transformation is demonstrated by 13 of the 16 transformation measures lacking statistical significance in the initial regression analysis. Commitment to Putin was much the same whether people felt freer than before, did or did not favour democracy as an ideal, thought the current system democratic or preferred undemocratic alternatives. Judgments about economic systems past, present and future were of no consequence, and commitment to Putin was also unaffected by whether people preferred state to private ownership, or plenty of goods with high prices in shops or controlled prices and shortages.

Interestingly, the transformation influences that increase commitment to Putin are future-oriented rather than past-oriented. Among those who think that the hardships of transformation will bring positive results to the majority of people in the next five years, the president has a rating 0.5 higher than among those who think that the costs of transformation will never bring benefits. In addition, those who are positive about the political system in the future and also about the current system are also more strongly committed to Putin. Since these transformation influences are about the future rather than the past, they imply that continuing commitment to Putin depends on performance. By contrast, the lower opinion of Putin among those with a Communist ideology is less likely to be altered, one way or another, by future developments.

In established democracies, the approval citizens give an elected leader is a variable, fluctuating up and down during a term of office (Rose, 2001: ch. 6; Stanley and Niemi, 2000). Since the personality of a leader remains constant, fluctuations cannot be explained by personality. Nor can the most attractive or heroic features of a leader prevent a loss of approval when political events affecting the government's performance take an unfavourable turn. In principle, most equilibrium influences are variables that can go up and down; for example, the world's respect for Russia is likely to go down when there is a headline event such as the Kursk nuclear submarine accident and to go up when social protection benefits increase in value. Yet even a big downturn in the public assessment of President Putin would leave him more popular (or at least, less unpopular) than President Yeltsin had been.

Centralizing power

In a political system close to equilibrium, the successor to a disruptive or transforming leader can win political popularity by acting as a stabiliz-ing force, carefully balancing demands from competing groups and pro-nouncing decisions reflecting the lowest common denominator of com-peting interests. Among the already powerful – the oligarchs, the Yeltsin Family and the security services – many hoped that Putin's relative in-experience would make him stabilize a political system in which they were well entrenched. Stories also circulated that Putin would have to go along with established interests because of *kompromat* about illegal activities in which he was alleged to be involved when acting as a liaison between Western businesses and municipal authorities in St Petersburg (Reddaway, 2001: 27ff.). But in the context of Russia at the beginning of the millennium, simply balancing existing interests would maintain an unpopular status quo or even risk the further deterioration of Russia's polity and economy. Putin rejected that role.

As president of the Russian Federation Vladimir Putin holds a strong office in a weak state. Presidential eminence is a mixed blessing, for the activities of government are widely dispersed among many institutions in Moscow and in the regions, each with its own networks and interests. In the name of promoting order, Putin has sought to make himself effective by building a strong state with himself at the centre:

Our state and its institutions and structures have always played an exceptionally important role in the life of the country and its people. For Russians, a strong state is not an anomaly to be gotten rid of. Quite the contrary, it is a source of order and main driving force of any change (Putin, 2000: 214).

However, the state that Putin invokes has never been a rule-of-law state, and in Soviet times it was also an anti-modern state.

The starting point is the need to take command of the Kremlin by appointing and controlling aides so that they follow the president's will rather than going into business for themselves, as members of the Yeltsin Family often did. Second, Putin must make his priorities felt in strategically important government ministries and public agencies, including the Ministry of Finance, the Central Bank, the Defence Ministry and the Federal Security Service. Up to a point, this can be done by appointing new directors or using the threat of the sack to influence officials appointed by the previous government. But there are departmental priorities and interests that do not change at election time: for example, the concerns of the Ministry of Defence with new equipment and soldiers' pay, and of the Finance Ministry with tax collection. There are too many agencies within the executive branch for the president to have time to attend to what each is doing. Many ministries – for example, those concerned with education, labour and health – are involved in the delivery or non-delivery of services that are priorities for tens of millions of Russian households. Third, because Russia is a federal state, responsibility for delivering many public services is in the hands of 89 regions, each of which has its own separately elected governor, its own local priorities and an administrative structure that is a miniature version of the institutional complexities found in Moscow, matching or even exceeding the level of corruption in central government. A Kremlin advisor, Alexander Oslon (2001), has summed up the situation thus: 'It is naive to think that by signing a decree, the president can get results.'

Increasing the Kremlin's grip

Vladimir Putin's political career was not based on campaigning for votes; he reached the top through his skill in manipulating patronage from the underside of the patron–client relationship, initially in the KGB, then in St Petersburg and finally within the Kremlin. Becoming president turned Putin from a protege of the powerful to the chief dispenser of patronage.

Putin's first step as president was to create a team of advisors loyal to himself. The dismissal of President Yeltsin's daughter, Tatyana Dyachenko, from her Kremlin position as an unofficial link with the oligarchs marked the start of his takeover of government. Putin appointed a small number of colleagues from St Petersburg to major posts. He also appointed former colleagues and superiors in the Federal Security Service, explaining, 'I have known them for many years and I trust them. It has nothing to do with ideology. It's only a matter of their professional qualities and personal relationships' (quoted in Gordon, 2000). In addition, Putin turned to his own ends people who had served his predecessor and, wanting to remain in office, were anxious to demonstrate how they could serve him too. In the first instance he kept as his Kremlin chief of staff Alexander Voloshin and as prime minister Mikhail Kasyanov. Later, he appointed a trusted colleague from KGB days, Sergei Ivanov, as defence minister; and named Boris Gryzlov, the first leader of Unity in the Duma, as minister of the interior. The longer he is in the Kremlin the more his appointees, whatever their background, are Putin's men – or very occasionally women, as gender-balancing has yet to reach the top of Russian politics. When Putin appointed Lyubov Kudelina as a deputy defence minister her gender caused a stir inside the Moscow Ring Road.

Presidential appointees were sent a cautionary message by the experience of Pavel Borodin, in charge of state property under President Yeltsin, and the man who gave Putin his first job in Moscow. On becoming acting president, Putin shunted Borodin to responsibility for relations with Belarus. A year later Borodin received a mysterious invitation to attend President Bush's inauguration. On arrival in New York Borodin was arrested on Swiss government charges relating to corruption in the award of contracts for renovating the Kremlin. His answers to interrogation by Swiss prosecutors gave nothing away. In April 2001, Borodin was released from a Swiss prison on bail paid by the Russian government, and given a diplomatic passport so that he is now immune from prosecution when travelling.

The second priority has been to strengthen the centre's grip on the *vertikal*, the relationship between the Kremlin and the 89 regions of the federal state. In the Soviet era, power was centralized through the Communist Party. As the party's authority weakened under Mikhail Gorbachev, regional officials began to go into business for themselves. Making the office of regional governor elected gave it political legitimacy. The Yeltsin government's readiness to negotiate bilateral agreements in more than half of Russia's regions increased the autonomy of individual regions – and led those not so privileged to demand that Moscow generalize such concessions in the name of inter-regional equity. Some regional governments asserted the supremacy of their laws over federal authority and adopted laws contradicting provisions of federal laws or the Constitution of the Russian Federation. Regions claimed privileges in particular over taxation, banking, enterprises and inter-regional tariffs (Solnick, 2000; Stoner-Weiss, 2001b; Huskey, 2001). The breakaway Chechen Republic represented the extreme end of a continuum of separatist practices stretching across the Federation. Decentralization did not bring government closer to the people; it meant that 'most abuses of power in Russia occur on the provincial and local levels' (Fish, 2001: 73).

President Putin has sought to reverse the creeping separatism eroding the authority of central government and in non-Russian regions such as Tatarstan creating khanates threatening the integrity of the Russian

Federation (Sharlet, 2001). He has strengthened the centre's capacity for exercising influence by creating seven federal districts, each with a presidential plenipotentiary to supervise about a dozen regions. The first overlords appointed included two former KGB generals, two army generals and one former general in the Interior Ministry. The presidential representatives are members of the prestigious Security Council in Moscow and can influence federal appointments in their territory. Grouping a number of regions under a single commissar weakens the opportunity for a single governor to co-opt a presidential representative. The Ministry of the Interior and the tax police have also reorganized their field staffs to match the seven military districts of the Russian Federation.

The upper house of Parliament, the Federation Council, has been reorganized. The right of regional governors and the speaker of the regional legislature to sit ex officio in the upper house of the Russian Parliament, the Federation Council, has been abolished by legislation, and this has also cost regional officials their legal immunity from prosecution. Instead, governors and regional legislatures each nominate one full-time representative to the Federation Council. Concurrently, a new Duma law has given the president the right to warn and even dismiss governors deemed to have violated federal laws. As a concession, regional governors have been made members of a newly created State Council, consulting in meetings four times a year. Between meetings the voice of the Council is a Presidium whose members are appointed by the president.

Third, President Putin has paid close attention to the politics of the Duma. Rather than relying on decrees, he has sought to provide a legislative basis for government actions, thereby making Duma members co-responsible for controversial policies. Government ministries and the Kremlin now give detailed attention to draft bills before a presidential initiative is put to the Duma for enactment. Since Unity, the only party with unqualified loyalty to Putin, has barely one-sixth of the votes in the Duma, Putin has cultivated inter-party coalitions. The Kremlin has more often gained votes from People's Deputies and the Zhirinovsky Bloc than support from the Union of Right Forces or Fatherland-All Russia (Remington, 2002). The Kremlin has also been ready to threaten to use its constitutional power to dissolve the Duma if it passed a vote of no confidence, a step that would greatly benefit pro-Putin candidates as long as the president remains popular.

Fourth, President Putin has sought to strengthen support for himself from fuzzy-focus parties without acquiring the obligations and limits to electoral appeal of leadership of a single party. In June 2001, the Duma approved a Kremlin-backed bill making it more difficult for parties to appear on the list ballot. To qualify in the future, a party or bloc of several parties must have at least 10,000 members and branches with 100 members each in at least half the country's 89 regions. It must also submit registration documents prior to the announcement of the election. Independents can continue to nominate candidates in single-member districts.

To reduce the electoral clout of rich critics, the law now limits private contributions to parties to 3,000 rubles per person per year, and parties deemed to have violated this provision can be subject to legal action. Annual state funding is being given all parties or blocs receiving more than 3 per cent of the list or presidential vote or winning at least 12 single-member district seats. Financial restrictions on campaign expenditure are also likely to increase the influence of time given free on television, which is subject to influence by the Kremlin. The law does not prevent parties that failed to win many votes from fighting again, nor does it prevent new parties or blocs of smaller parties being formed.

The merger of parties reduces and simplifies electoral choice. In spring 2001, Unity and Fatherland-All Russia announced they would form a common front to support the legislative programme of President Putin. This marked a major shift by Fatherland-All Russia. Its deputies had often voted against Unity deputies in major Duma votes. In December 2001, the merger of the parties comprising the two blocs was agreed under the name Unified Russia. Immediately, the merger strengthened the pro-Kremlin vote in the Duma, and makes it more difficult for a credible challenge to Vladimir Putin in a bid for re-election in 2004. A VTsIOM poll immediately after the merger showed that, after excluding non-voters and don't knows, Unified Russia was favoured by 32 per cent of list voters, second to the 36 per cent for the Communist Party and well ahead of third-place parties supported by 6 or 7 per cent of voters. However, by April 2002, Communist support had remained high at 37 per cent while voters endorsing the merged party had fallen to 19 per cent. In this mid-term poll, four other parties were also endorsed by at least 5 per cent, sufficient to quality for list seats: Union of Right Forces, the Zhirinovsky Bloc, Yabloko and Women of Russia (for updating, see *www.RussiaVotes.org*). In the Duma, the Kremlin need not rely solely on list parties for support; it can also mobilize votes from biddable representatives sitting for single-member districts.

Selective enforcement of the law

The Russian state is a permeable state, in which leading officials can become part of a network of interests doing deals under a common roof to their private advantage. To create a state that is not dependent on oligarchs for tax revenue and is not exploited by oligarchs for their private benefit requires the creation of a state strong enough to assert the dictatorship of law.

Vladimir Putin approaches law enforcement from a radically different background than lawyers raised in a *Rechtsstaat*. The laws that most concern him are not about protecting the rights of individual citizens or minorities but laws that empower the state to act, especially against those who threaten the powers that be. As a KGB official, Putin was trained to keep Soviet citizens under surveillance with none of the hindrances imposed by doctrines of individual rights. He was also trained to act firmly against anti-state activities, a qualitatively different sort of crime than the purse-snatchings and break-ins that threaten the security of ordinary Russians.

Paradoxically, law enforcement is the first constraint on the president's ambitions to introduce the dictatorship of law. The police, the courts, prosecution officials and prisons are understaffed; their employees are underpaid and often corrupt. They have also been trained to serve the party-state rather than impartially applying the rule of law. The result is that many formal changes authorized by law reform have not been applied in practice. Insofar as rules are applied, many bureaucrats give more attention to procedures than to outcomes, and procedural delays are especially likely to act as a brake on reform measures that disturb bureaucrats and their political superiors. A scholarly review of the problem of reforming the law in Russia is aptly entitled 'The Disjuncture between Legal Reform and Law Enforcement: The Challenge Facing the Post-Yeltsin Leadership' (Gordon B. Smith, 1999a; see also Solomon and Foglesong, 2000; Shelley, 2001).

From the highest office in the land, there is little that a president can do to secure law enforcement on the streets. The inability of the American White House to do anything about crime in Washington, DC, is an example of the limits of top-down influence. There are a multitude of violators, for the Russian Federation has continued the Soviet practice of writing laws and regulations so vague and contradictory that enterprises and public officials routinely break or bend them to get things done. As Boris Berezovsky, an oligarch and Kremlin advisor, has said of the political and financial elite, 'Only those who have been asleep for the past ten years are not at risk of going to jail' (Clover, 2000). Hence, the concern of President Yeltsin and his Family with securing an amnesty for their actions in office. Given these constraints, President Putin can be only selectively involved in enforcing the law. With a super-abundance of law-breakers to pursue, the hand of the Kremlin falls selectively on those whom it deems to have '*failed the loyalty test*' (Brown, 2001c: 48; italics in the original).

President Putin has used selective law enforcement to punish or intimidate oligarchs and the media. The brunt of punishment has been felt by two media oligarchs who have opposed him politically. Boris Berezovsky, nicknamed 'Godfather of the Kremlin', controlled ORT, nominally a state-owned television station, and an oil company, Sibneft (Klebnikov, 2000). Berezovsky forfeited his immunity from prosecution by resigning from the Duma shortly after his election in 1999, and announcing the formation of an anti-Putin movement. When federal prosecutors sought to interview Berezovsky about his foreign currency profits from Aeroflot, the state airline, he fled abroad, claiming he was a victim of political persecution. Backers of the Kremlin took control of ORT television. Another Berezovsky-owned station, TV6, offered employment to displaced journalists critical of the Kremlin. In January 2002, in response to a lawsuit against it by an oil company pension fund that was a minority shareholder, a Russian court ordered the liquidation of TV6. Berezovsky charged that this showed that there was 'an emerging authoritarian power which does not want Russia's citizens to know what is happening in the country' (Cottrell, 2002b).

Vladimir Gusinsky was owner of Media-Most and NTV, which broadcast *Kukly*, a puppet show satirizing Putin, and attacked Putin on Chechnya. Within eight weeks of the election, masked tax police and security forces raided the office of Media-Most and a month later Gusinsky was held for three days in the notoriously unhealthy Butyrka prison. In June Gusinsky agreed to cede control of NTV in exchange for the cancellation of criminal charges and debt claims, and fled to Gibraltar, where he repudiated the agreement as coerced. In April 2000, Gazprom, the state gas monopoly that had loaned Media-Most $300 million, used this debt to take control of NTV and two newspapers that criticized the government, *Itogi* and *Segodnya*. Media-Most journalists resigned in protest, claiming the move was a Kremlin-sponsored attack on the freedom of the press.

There has also been selective targeting of individual journalists. Putin (2000: 173) has described Andrei Babitsky's critical reporting of the war in Chechnya from the field as 'much more dangerous than firing a machine gun'. In January 2000, Babitsky was arrested in Chechnya by Russian forces and two weeks later handed over in front of television cameras to unidentified Chechens in exchange for several Russian prisoners. Subsequently Babitsky was brought by Chechens to Dagestan, where Russian officials arrested and imprisoned him again. In December 2001, Grigory Pasko, a journalist who had disclosed that the Russian Navy was dumping nuclear waste in the Sea of Japan, was sentenced to four years in prison for treason. Other investigative journalists pursuing stories displeasing to oligarchs or the Kremlin have been physically assaulted and even murdered. The effect has been to encourage 'self-censorship in the central mass media' (Brown, 2001a: 553).

The selective use of law enforcement has been explained by one of Putin's backers as a way of giving oligarchs the message 'you are not to meddle in politics' and making the political situation in the country 'considerably more quiet and controllable' (Ulyanov, 2001). For example, companies associated with Vladimir Potanin and Anatoly Chubais have been investigated for irregularities during privatization, and tax inspectors visited Lukoil, the massive auto producer AvtoVaz and Sibneft. In a six-minute meeting, the government used its 38 per cent share in Gazprom to stage a boardroom coup, placing a Putin protege in charge of an enterprise accounting for 15 per cent of Russia's export earnings and 20 per cent of its tax revenues. The boardroom coup at Gazprom also gave Putin's forces control of NTV (Saivetz, 2000). When Putin met 18 leading Russian oligarchs in July 2000, he told them they were expected to abide by the law in the future. The implicit amnesty for past wealth was confirmed in October, when the deputy procurator told the Duma that there would be no further investigation of irregularities in the 'loans for shares' privatization of enterprises rich in natural resources. However, in January 2002, Russian prosecutors arrested two leading executives in the Gazprom network as part of an investigation into stripping the company's owners, which include the Russian state, of assets. In the circumspect words of Anatoly Chubais, 'Oligarchs now understand that clean business earns them money' (Jack, 2001a).

When wielding power, Putin has shown a politician's skill in exploiting ambiguity. For example, while President Yeltsin was unable to agree a new national anthem with a Communist-controlled Duma, President Putin has done so. The new anthem premiered on New Year's Eve 2001 offered something for everybody. It has anodyne references to Mother Russia, to forests and to fields. It hymns 'Russia our holy country' which is 'protected by God'. Although the anthem contains no verbal references to Lenin and Stalin, all but the completely tone-deaf can hear that its melody is the same as the old Soviet anthem approved by Stalin. The same man, Sergei Mikhalkov, wrote words for the Stalinist anthem, the de-Stalinized Soviet anthem and the new anthem that President Putin has approved.

President Putin has shown a KGB agent's skill in exploiting the vulnerabilities of others. In moving against selected oligarchs unpopular with many of their business competitors as well as vastly unpopular with the Russian people, President Putin has sent a message familiar in Soviet times: the Kremlin is watching you. If you step out of line you risk loss of office, criminal investigations, loss of property, and arrest or exile.

Large categories of powerholders, such as governors, bankers and generals, have not been deprived of their positions. However, they have been
leaned on as encouragement to go along with the Kremlin if they wish
to continue prospering. While select individuals are vulnerable to such
treatment there remains institutionalized opposition to even-handed enforcement of the dictatorship of law. As Stephen Holmes (2000: 52) has
argued:

> Putin can selectively break the backs of some so-called oligarchs while promoting
> others, but which banker-industrialists will support him if he indiscriminately and
> simultaneously launches a confiscatory attack on them all? The shape of Putin's
> Russia will probably depend less on the new president's private intentions, be
> these liberal or illiberal, than on the bargains he will have to make to obtain the
> political support he so plainly requires.

Disciplining wild capitalism

The command economy of Soviet days was disorderly, because the numbers entered to monitor fulfilment of the plan did not match what state
enterprises were doing. The economic system that followed has brought
into the open corruption and lawlessness, and created opportunities for
amassing great wealth. In his millennium address, Vladimir Putin (2000:
212) declared that he wanted to put an end to the stateless ideal of a
market economy promoted by Western economic advisors:

> The experience of the 1990s demonstrates vividly that merely experimenting with
> abstract models and schemes taken from foreign textbooks cannot assure that our
> country will achieve genuine renewal without any excessive costs. The mechanical
> copying of other nations' experience will not guarantee success.

An unexpected consequence of the collapse of the ruble in August 1998
is that it acted as shock therapy promoting economic growth. The fall of
the foreign exchange value of the ruble reduced the importation of foreign
goods, creating an opportunity for Russian firms to sell more to domestic
consumers, to invest in producing more and better goods and to increase
exports. An economic recovery began in 1999, President Yeltsin's last
year in office (EBRD, 2001a: 15). Inflation more than halved and interest rates did likewise, although both still remain in double-digit figures. In
Vladimir Putin's first two years in office, the boom has gathered momentum as the official rate of economic growth has remained high, increasing
tax revenue needed to pay pensions and reduce the government's debt. It
has also made it easier for employers to pay wages to their workers. The
tenth NRB survey in July 2001 found that 63 per cent of employees had
been paid regularly throughout the past year, compared to 37 per cent in
1998.

Economic statistics designed for an economy in equilibrium do not tell the whole story about an economy in transformation. The appearance of a Russian boom has owed much to the high price of oil in world markets. Official accounts omit transactions that enterprises choose to make off the books, whether in hard currency, in cash or in barter. They take at face value the transactions that enterprises put into accounts that are used by tax collectors. In such circumstances, it is possible for national income accounts to show the economy growing in aggregate while many Russian enterprises are still engaged in value-subtracting activities that are obstacles to the creation of a market economy (cf. Gaddy and Ickes, 2001a; Senokosov and Skidelsky, 2001).

While the economy is in better shape than four years earlier, it is not yet Putin's Germanic ideal of an orderly *Nationalwirtschaft* (national economy) that contributes to strengthening both state and society. It is still a disorderly economy in which entrepreneurs have opportunities to make money outside or inside the law or by a combination of both. The Kremlin has sought to strengthen its grip on government agencies and the oligarchs by reducing the transfer of state property into private hands and by using state shares in companies in mixed ownership to put pressure on those who have benefited most from *nomenklatura* privatization. It is seeking to reduce the loophole licences and regulations that give legal authority for private enrichment and for public officials to solicit bribes. It is also giving a higher profile to the work of the State Audit Chamber, now directed by Sergei Stepashin, Putin's predecessor as prime minister.

Paralleling the logic of Ronald Reagan, the Putin government has sponsored legislation cutting taxes in order to increase the number of Russians paying taxes and the total sum it collects. Income tax is now lower than anywhere in the OECD world, a flat rate of 13 per cent, thereby reducing the benefit to taxpayers of evading taxation and the bribes that tax officials can extract from would-be evaders. Tax legislation has also been used to strengthen the *vertikal*. A larger portion of tax revenue is henceforth due to central government than to the regions. Clarification of Russian rights of ownership to land now make it possible for owners to sell their land or borrow money against it to start a business. As a political compromise, the new land law does not create a market in agricultural land, which in Soviet times was vested in public authorities or cooperatives. Foreigners can now buy commercial land – but not land in border areas or territories deemed specially relevant to national security.

New prospects for domestic growth are an incentive for new rich Russians to repatriate money from their foreign bank accounts to invest in Russia, but the enforcement of the law against selected oligarchs is an incentive for rich Russians to keep earnings abroad. Official statistics show an increase in Russian investment in the Russian economy, but percentage figures can be misleading when the starting point is low. Foreign investors remain wary, especially those who were burnt by the collapse of the ruble in August 1998, and who are worried about the insecurity of property rights. Foreign investments are subject to selective enforcement of planning permissions, building codes and local taxes, and tax collectors can take more money from foreign firms with few political friends than from Russian firms. An upbeat story in an American magazine, *Business Week*, lists actions that Putin's government is taking to reduce corruption and encourage foreign investment and concludes, 'This cleanup will take years. But at least it's starting' (Starobin and Belton, 2002).

When an International Monetary Fund mission visited Moscow to offer additional financial support in return for commitments to further reform, the Putin government rejected its offer, preferring to run the economy its own way. To demonstrate its readiness to do without IMF conditions, it has used revenues generated by the economic recovery to reduce its debt to the IMF by more than a third in two years. However, the size of the debt legacy is such that it will take up to 20 years to repay all its foreign debts (Lopez-Claros and Zadornov, 2002: 114; cf. fig. 1.3). If oil prices enter the bust phase of a boom-and-bust cycle, the payment of debt interest and much else will again present a challenge.

The Russian people have very different priorities for public expenditure than do foreign lenders. When a June 2001 VTsIOM survey asked what state money should be spent on first and foremost, people were quick to name several examples, but paying back lenders was rarely mentioned:

Health	69%
Social protection	54%
Education	52%
Defence	28%
Law and order	27%
Culture and leisure	20%
Debt interest	10%

Going international – before and after September 11

By the time Boris Yeltsin left office, Russia appeared as the sick man of Eurasia. *Izvestiya* commented:

Russia must get used to the idea that the West no longer considers it either the great white hope or the black hole of the global map. It is no longer afraid of our rockets or the so-called restoration of Communism. We are neither better nor worse than Mexico, Brazil or Poland (quoted in Whittell, 2001).

As an unashamed patriot who prided himself on learning 'patriotism and love for the Motherland' in the KGB (quoted in Warren, 2001), Vladimir Putin has sought to regain international respect for his country. In his first year in office, he made 18 trips abroad. Careful preparation and a readiness to ingratiate himself with foreigners enabled Putin to project a different image of his country than Boris Yeltsin did when staggering across the international stage. Putin has encouraged closer links with neighbouring states such as Iran, with whom Russia has a contract to supply $7 billion in armaments. Putin's travels were not intended to promote friendship for its own sake, but to promote Russia's national interest. As Nikolai Ulyanov (2001) has explained:

With Putin at the helm, Russia started pursuing a new policy, one that more resembled the Soviet-era policy. In the world, Russia has its own national interests, quite often at variance with American interests, and Russia intends to resolutely and consistently uphold its interests.

The intersecting interests of the Russian state reflect a combination of geopolitical, security and economic influences different from those on European Union countries and those on the United States. Nowhere is this more evident than in Chechnya. President Putin has proclaimed it a just war in defence of the integrity of the Russian state against terrorists and insurrection. The measures used in Chechnya – bombing and tank assaults – have been war measures rather than measures to promote civil order. The forceful military response of President Putin in Chechnya has been noted by leaders in the other 20 ethnic republics of the Russian Federation. Putin has dismissed criticisms of military actions from the Council of Europe as unwarranted meddling in Russia's domestic affairs and described American complaints about the bombing of Chechnya as hypocritical in view of its 1999 bombing campaign against Serbia.

Most Russians have supported military action in Chechnya but the longer the fighting has continued, the lower the level of support. In March 2000, the month Putin was elected president, VTsIOM found that 70 per cent favoured military action against Chechnya and 22 per cent favoured negotiations. By April 2002 the proportion in favour had fallen to 34 per cent, and 58 per cent now favoured negotiations. Expectations for the future are increasingly pessimistic. In January 2000 only 24 per cent thought the war would continue for many years. By July 2001, 61 per cent of Russians expected the war to drag on indefinitely.

The description of post-Soviet successor states as 'the near abroad' emphasizes the many ties, historical, political, economic and family, that link the Russian Federation with its neighbours in the Commonwealth of Independent States (CIS). Putin's view is that 'He who doesn't regret the break-up of the Soviet Union has no heart; he who wants to revive it in its previous form has no head' (quoted in Rutland, 2000: 342). His priority is to achieve closer relations with other states of the CIS. In this he has the support of public opinion; in the tenth New Russia Barometer 90 per cent endorsed stronger ties between other CIS countries and Russia. The opportunities and incentives for Russian influence in the CIS are substantial.

Although the Russian economy is weak by European standards, it is relatively strong by comparison with successor states to the south and east (EBRD, 2001a). Moreover, Russia's population makes its aggregate resources far greater. Most CIS countries have populations ranging from 3 million to 7 million. By the standards of the European Union, only Ukraine would be considered a big country, and its population is barely a third that of the Russian Federation. The geopolitical position of Russia adds to its influence in the CIS, for proven oil reserves are of little value to a CIS state if it has no means of delivering oil to hard currency markets. If energy-rich landlocked countries in Central Asia sought other routes for reaching hard currency markets, they would require huge amounts of capital to replace dependence on the Russian Federation with dependence on another neighbour, such as Turkey or Iran. Countries that lack such energy resources, such as Ukraine, depend on Russia for energy supplies. Putin recognizes the linkage between economic dependence and political dependence. Former prime minister Viktor Chernomyrdin, whose Soviet career was in the gas industry, has been named ambassador – or, as some put it, viceroy – to Ukraine.

Capitalizing on September 11

Shortly after the second Chechen War broke out, Vladimir Putin used a prescient analogy seeking to engage American understanding in a contribution to the *New York Times*:

I ask you to put aside for a moment the dramatic news reports from the Caucasus and imagine something more placid. Ordinary New Yorkers or Washingtonians, asleep in their homes. Then, in a flash, hundreds perish in explosions at the Watergate or at an apartment complex on Manhattan's West Side. Thousands are injured, some horribly disfigured. Panic engulfs a neighbourhood, then a nation.

Russians do not have to imagine such a calamity. More than 300 of our citizens in Moscow and elsewhere suffered that fate earlier this year when bombs detonated by terrorists demolished five apartment blocks. To Americans these scenarios must seem rather far-fetched (Putin, 1999).

Putin emphasized that Chechen fighters received funds from abroad, citing American intelligence sources identifying Osama bin Laden as helping to finance Chechen fighters. He explicitly linked this with the New York bombing of the World Trade Center basement in 1993. Putin's conclusion was simple: 'No government can stand idly by when terrorism strikes' (ibid.).

After suicide bombers attacked the World Trade Center and the Pentagon on September 11, 2001, Putin's analogy no longer seemed farfetched. Putin interpreted the attack as showing a convergence of national interests: 'The US–Russian relationship is not a zero-sum game any longer' (Fidler and Jack, 2001). He was quick to pledge support to President Bush in what was described as a common war against terrorist enemies linked to Afghanistan. The White House recognized the coincidence of interest. Although there was no question of a military alliance – Russia had suffered a disastrous defeat in an eight-year war in Afghanistan begun in 1979 – Washington wanted cooperation to secure bases in Uzbekistan and Tajikistan for use on Afghanistan's northern flank, and Russian intelligence drawing on years of experience in the field there. Putin has also used the anxiety generated by the attack to secure Duma enactment of a law giving him broad powers to declare martial law in a part or the whole of the Russian Federation in the event of aggression. If martial law is declared, political parties and other organizations must suspend any activities deemed to undermine the defence and security of the state.

Al-Qaeda gave Washington and Moscow a joint interest in fighting terrorism in Central Asia. In November 2001, President Putin made a well-orchestrated trip to Washington and to Ground Zero in New York, and was a guest at the Bush ranch in Texas. Putin sought Washington's cooperation on the military front, pressing Bush not to develop a national missile defence system involving repudiation of the 1972 Anti-Ballistic Missile Treaty and offering to disband politically obsolete Russian bases in Cuba and Vietnam. Putin also raised questions about the future of NATO, historically an anti-Soviet alliance. The two presidents discussed without commitment the idea that in some form Russia could become associated with NATO. Putin also lobbied for the normalization of trade between the two countries, and American support for Russia's application to join the World Trade Organization.

The limits of good will were shown a month after Putin's American trip, when President Bush notified Moscow that the United States was withdrawing from the Anti-Ballistic Missile Treaty in order to develop a new missile defence system. In January 2002, the State Department issued statements that showed Washington still feels free to criticize domestic

Russian actions. It denounced human rights violations in Chechnya and called for the continued independence of TV6, the one major Russian television station perceived as free to criticize the government.

Hardliners in the Russian defence establishment have criticized Putin for conceding too much and extracting too little from Washington. In the words of Gennady Zyuganov, 'Gorbachev ditched the party, Yeltsin destroyed the Soviet Union, and today we are giving up the geopolitical space that Russia has been defending for almost 1,000 years' (Cottrell, 2002a). General Yury Baluyevsky has led delegations to Washington in search of a new military security treaty. The goal of the defence establishment in Russia is to secure a treaty that gives the Russian Federation equal status with the United States, and also imposes treaty obligations on the United States government. But, in the view of Henry Kissinger, Moscow cannot expect to achieve these demands: 'Putin knows that Russia will be too weak to sustain a strategic competition with the US' (Thomson, 2002).

While Russians have been divided about supporting American actions in Afghanistan, there is broad public support for President Putin making common cause with the United States when there are common interests (tab. 9.2). Four-fifths see the terrorist attack of September 11 as threatening all humanity, including Russia, and most see Putin's support for the American fight against terrorism as a means of reducing criticism of Russian actions in Chechnya. Only a third see the United States as just as big a threat to Russia as the Taleban movement. Russians are often indifferent to issues that stir up the political elite. When VTsIOM asked what effect the American withdrawal from the Anti-Ballistic Missile Treaty would have on Russian–American relations, 55 per cent said it would make no difference or had no opinion.

Russians are abandoning the idea that a Third World War would be between Russia and the United States; only 17 per cent see this as a possibility, with or without Muslim engagement. A majority see a Third World War as most likely to involve the United States and Muslim countries. Of those foreseeing such a clash of civilizations, just over half believe Russia would side with the United States and just under half see Russia remaining neutral. The desire to disengage from international conflict is also shown by Russian attitudes toward NATO. Only 14 per cent favour joining NATO and a similar minority favour a military alliance with ex-socialist countries. The majority favours a strategy of co-operation with NATO or strict non-alignment.

In Moscow, old guard military and diplomatic officials want Putin to do more in foreign affairs, even giving the subject the overriding importance it had in Cold War days. However, this has a political danger, for the

Table 9.2 *After September 11 Russian views of cooperation with USA*

	%
1. *Terrorist attack*	
Concern of all humanity	80
Internal US affair	15
Don't know	5
2. *Taleban*	
A threat to world	50
No bigger threat than USA	32
Don't know	18
3. *Support for military action of the USA and Britain in Afghanistan*	
Definitely support	20
Somewhat support	32
Somewhat oppose	24
Definitely oppose	14
Don't know	10
4. *Most important reason for Putin's support of USA*	
Reduce criticism of Russia in Chechnya	44
Terrorists a threat to humanity	35
Win economic help for Russia	10
Don't know	11
5. *Who would a Third World War be between?*	
US, Russia against Muslims	29
US vs. Muslims, Russia neutral	26
US, allies vs. Muslims, Russia	9
US, allies vs. Russia, allies	8
Don't know	28
6. *If there was a NATO–Muslim conflict, should Russia*	
Remain strictly neutral	54
Join, give moral support to NATO	29
Give moral support to Muslims	5
Don't know	12
7. *As for NATO, best policy in Russia's interest is*	
Admission	14
Cooperation	30
Non-alignment	28
Alliance with ex-socialist countries	13
Don't know	15

Sources: VTsIOM. Nationwide surveys. Approximate number of respondents in each survey, 1,600. Fieldwork for first and sixth questions: 24–29 September 2001; second, fourth and fifth questions, 26–29 October 2001; third and seventh questions, 23–26 November 2001.

more time and effort that the president invests in international affairs, the less attention he can give to the first priority of ordinary Russians, domestic issues. When a Public Opinion Foundation poll asked Russians to explain the phrase 'Russia's national interests', 36 per cent had never heard the term and an additional 27 per cent had no idea of what it meant (strana.ru, 2001). If asked, most Russians are prepared to express an opinion about foreign policy issues. However, opinions about foreign policy have virtually no influence on how Russians vote (White, Munro and Rose, 2002).

Putin's limited impact on Russians

A president facing the challenges of Russia needs to make an impact on society, if he is to maintain domestic popularity and an international reputation too. Insofar as politics concern ordinary Russians, what counts is the way that government deals with domestic problems that affect their everyday lives. While most Russian people continue to approve of Putin, they are still waiting for hard evidence of progress on domestic policies. Recognizing this, the president used a New Year message to the Russian people on the eve of 2002 to admit, 'Not everything we planned has been done. So far there are more unresolved things than achievements' (quoted in Center for Defense Information, 2002).

Not much change yet

The tenth New Russia Barometer asked people how much change they had noticed since Vladimir Putin had become president. While relatively few Russians see conditions worsening, most do not see things getting better (tab. 9.3). More than three-fifths see no change in the level of crime; the remainder are divided almost equally into those seeing crime falling and those seeing crime on the increase. Crime in the bureaucracy remains a problem too, for an absolute majority of Russians see no change in the indifference that Russian public officials show to the rule of law. Likewise, the median group sees no increase in order in society. Insofar as people see changes in inflation, more Russians believe it has got worse than better, underscoring the difference between official statistics reporting the rate of annual inflation falling and popular concern with the cumulative effect of inflation over several years. Social protection of the poor is the one major issue where a majority see conditions improving under Vladimir Putin.

To a limited extent, Vladimir Putin's presidency has changed attitudes toward political institutions. The departure of Boris Yeltsin from the

Table 9.3 *Impact of President Putin on Russian society*

Q. How much has the election of Vladimir Putin as president changed the situation of this country compared to that under his predecessor?

	Improved %	Same %	Worse %
Reducing crime	20	63	17
Keeping prices from rising	25	46	29
Equality of all, including public officials, before the law	37	56	7
Introducing order in society	46	46	8
Social protection of the poor	55	35	10

Source: New Russia Barometer X. Nationwide survey, 17 June–3 July 2001. Number of respondents, 2,000.

Kremlin has increased trust in the presidency. Whereas an average of 27 per cent said they trusted the presidency when Yeltsin was in office, after 18 months of President Putin, 50 per cent now express trust in the presidency. Changes in attitudes toward the regime are less, but also positive. The seventh New Russia Barometer found that 36 per cent gave a positive evaluation of the current system of government (fig. 3.6). In the tenth NRB survey, the percentage positive rose to 47 per cent, and the median respondent was neutral rather than negative about the new regime.

Future expectations and risks

In a system in transformation, the future is about hopes or fears rather than about a continuation of current experience. Given popular dissatisfaction with current economic conditions, Putin's best strategy is to promise that people will fare better in the future and, since the future is uncertain, optimistic claims cannot be disproved. However, claims that fly in the face of popular experience and expectations will be dismissed as political hot air.

Expectations of future governance have become more positive under President Putin. When the first NRB survey asked in 1992 what people expected of the new political system in five years, 50 per cent were positive. As experience of the new regime accumulated, positive expectations fell and then rose again. By spring 1998, future political expectations were positive among 49 per cent. By the tenth NRB survey in summer 2001, 62 per cent were optimistic. Since one in six Russians has no

Table 9.4 *Expectations of future reforms*

Q. What do you expect for yourself and your family from reforms in the following areas?

	Good	No difference	Don't know	Bad
	(% replying)			
Pensions	42	24	17	17
Education	36	32	19	14
Military	33	38	18	11
Courts	31	32	26	11
The economy	30	28	20	21
Taxation	28	29	24	19
Domestic energy	20	20	13	47
Cutting bureaucracy	19	30	37	14

Source: VTsIOM. Nationwide survey, 22–25 June 2001. Number of respondents, 1,600. Good: combines answers saying only good or more good than bad. Bad: combines answers saying more bad than good or only bad. Don't know category includes responses of persons who have not heard of the reform.

definite view of the political future, those positive outnumber those negative about future governance by a margin of three to one.

When asked what they expect from reforms now being undertaken by the government, Russians tend to be neutral or negative (tab. 9.4). A majority expect that reforms introduced in education, taxation, bureaucratic regulations, the courts and the military will make no difference to their lives or don't know if this will be the case. There is widespread disagreement about the personal impact of economic reforms. The largest group see no prospect of change or don't know if economic reforms will have an impact. The highest expectations are expressed about pensions, a well-publicized campaign pledge of President Putin. A total of 42 per cent expect pensions to improve under Putin's presidency, and only 17 per cent expect further deterioration. However, nearly half are fearful of increases in the cost of domestic heating.

The future is also full of risks, unwelcome events such as a flood or an aeroplane crash that may *or* may not happen, but if they did could heap blame on governors. At any given moment, the danger of a risk becoming realized is low. Since Russia's governors have lots to worry about here and now, they can ignore hypothetical events, and many may not come to pass, such as wars between the Russian Federation and other CIS states following the dissolution of the Soviet Union. However, Mikhail Gorbachev spectacularly underestimated the risks – to himself and to the Soviet system – of introducing perestroika and glasnost. Since the

Table 9.5 *Risks – familiar and unfamiliar*

Q. Let's consider some things that might happen in this country in the next few years. How likely do you think it would be that:

	Likely	Maybe	Not very likely	Not at all
	%	%	%	%
Heating costs would be so high we couldn't heat our house properly in winter	26	50	21	3
There would be a big HIV-AIDS epidemic threatening millions of Russians	21	50	24	5
Fighting would break out in another mostly non-Russian region besides Chechnya	13	54	30	4
There would be another nuclear power station explosion like Chernobyl	9	46	38	7

Source: New Russia Barometer X. Nationwide survey, 17 June–3 July 2001. Number of respondents, 2,000.

probability of a risk being realized increases with time, the issue is not whether a plane crash or a flood will ever occur, but when and where it will happen – and who will be held responsible whenever it does.

To assess the extent of anxieties, the tenth New Russia Barometer asked people how much risk they think there is of disasters striking Russian society (tab. 9.5). The biggest anxiety is that the cost of energy may rise so much that people could not afford to heat their houses in winter: a quarter think this is likely to happen, and half think it may happen. Currently, the government keeps the domestic price of energy at one-tenth that of world markets; thus, the tenth New Russia Barometer found 71 per cent never went short of heating in the previous year, and only 6 per cent often did so. However, Putin's government has publicly announced it is considering moving domestic heating costs toward world levels.

An HIV-AIDS epidemic is the second greatest anxiety; more than two-thirds see this as probable or possible. Here too, there are realistic grounds for concern, since the new regime has continued the Soviet practice of ignoring public health problems such as drug abuse, prostitution and promiscuity which contribute to the spread of HIV-AIDS. When briefed on demographic evidence of a declining population of men of military and working age, President Putin's response was not to ask about preventive measures but to inquire, 'How do we replace them?' The United Nations' HIV-AIDS programme reports that new diagnoses of the disease have doubled in Russia each year since 1998. The risk of an epidemic is increased by the Russian Ministry of Health refusing hundreds of millions of dollars in foreign grants to purchase drugs to combat AIDS and tuberculosis. Russian officials have objected to donor conditions that drug purchases are subject to quality control and open competitive tender, thus reducing the scope for corruption in their purchase. The Orthodox Church has also opposed public education to reduce risks of infection from drug use (Jack, 2001b; Dyer and Jack, 2001).

Soviet development of nuclear energy has left a legacy of ageing nuclear power stations, waste dumps and military facilities scattered throughout the Russian Federation and the near abroad. Given the fatal fall-out of an uncontrolled release of nuclear energy, engineers have developed sophisticated safety measures to protect against this risk. However, Russia has been less successful than Western nations in implementing nuclear safety measures. When an accident at a nuclear power station at Chernobyl in Ukraine was mishandled in 1986, there was an immediate loss of life and winds spread radiation westward, causing long-term loss of life to many thousands (Egorov et al., 2000). The accidental sinking of the Kursk nuclear submarine in August 2000 did not harm civilian life, but the delayed response of President Putin reminded people of the government's historic disregard for protecting Russian lives. The tenth New Russia Barometer found that 55 per cent think another Chernobyl may occur.

Chechens are not the only ethnic minority in the Russian Federation, and NRB surveys ask whether people think there is a substantial threat to the country's security from people of non-Russian nationality. When the tenth NRB survey asked about a second Chechnya elsewhere in the Russian Federation, 67 per cent thought it might happen. When asked about the possibility of ethnic conflict before the first Chechen war, in 1993, a total of 64 per cent thought this might happen.

The risks to which President Putin is exposed – from Chechnya to nuclear power stations – are only possibilities; forecasts of disasters such as an HIV-AIDS epidemic may turn out to be exaggerated or not disrupt the Kremlin. As long as Vladimir Putin can remain popular by continuous campaigning, he can be confident of election to a second term. But as long as the rule of law is enforced selectively and the health of the Russian people continues to decline, then Vladimir Putin will find himself governing a weak state and an unhealthy society.

Steely assurance

Halfway through Vladimir Putin's first term in office it is unrealistic to pronounce an assessment of his achievements for, as he himself has emphasized, many of the goals that he hopes to achieve remain in the future, and those that are a decade hence are well outside the constitutional limit of his time in office. Nonetheless, enough time has passed, and the president has been generous enough with statements, for people to form a judgment on what has been seen to date.

President Putin sees himself, and is seen, as subject to multiple constraints. The first is the legacy from the past, a legacy that he neither attacks nor praises, but refers to as a way of explaining to the Russian people the scale of the problems at hand and the amount of time required to set them right. Second, he is also constrained by the institutions and processes of the Russian state, and by the way in which bureaucrats are accustomed to behave, ignoring at their convenience the rule of law, whether expressed in a constitutional provision or in a publicly declared presidential directive. The public concurs in discriminating between Vladimir Putin the man and the state that he heads. The former commands far more trust and regard than does the latter. Third, the president is also constrained by the calendar and the clock: there are so many problems that cry out for attention yet so little time to deal with them. For example, the pressures of time are such that he is unlikely to have any time to spend in the average month on such potentially threatening issues as HIV-AIDS. While there are political incentives to invest time and energy in dealing with problems such as unemployment, if there is little that the Kremlin can do to make an impact in an economy still operating partly in the shadows and only in part through recognized institutions, then the arguments against involvement are greater still.

In campaigning for the presidency, Putin cultivated ambiguities, as in his commitment to promote the dictatorship of law. Awkward issues were fudged and statements showed inclinations pointing in very different directions, a conscious attempt to appeal to voters facing different ways. The result was a candidate's image and a winning electoral coalition that appeared fuzzy or unfocused because of its gaps and inconsistencies. As president, Vladimir Putin has had to act in ways that give substance to campaign slogans and, as he would be the first to emphasize, his priorities as a Russian governing in a Russian context are not to be reduced to familiar Anglo-American labels.

Together, Vladimir Putin's activities as a campaigner and a governor have emphasized steely assurance. The assurance is evident in the maintenance of extraordinarily high approval in public opinion polls. The ratings are not based on personality; as an ex-KGB employee Putin is far less outgoing and ready to reveal himself than are politicians of other backgrounds. Nor is assurance based on performance to date, for the foregoing tables show that most Russians have not yet seen positive gains under President Putin. There is no claim to ideological correctness in the assurance that Putin seeks to offer, nor does he claim the charisma needed to level the mountains of obstacles that confront the government. The assurance that he offers is that the future will be more orderly than the past decade and a half. And in a disorderly society that is no small achievement.

If there are any doubts about what Putin offers, there is plenty of evidence of the steel of Putin's determination. Chechens have felt this in its most brutal form. The media oligarchs who attacked Putin have felt the full force of the selective enforcement of the law, and other oligarchs have seen, from that example, that it is imprudent to cross the Kremlin and expose yourself to the cutting edge of presidential powers. The magnetism that Putin has exerted on Duma politicians has been based on power, and the patronage that it offers to loyalists, and not on personality.

The dilemma facing Vladimir Putin is that he wants to be a French-style *étatiste* leader in a society without a modern state like that of the Fifth French Republic or even the nineteenth-century empire of Napoleon III. In a rule-of-law state, a president can exercise constitutional powers effectively, because decisions made by leaders are carried out by bureaucratic officials. However, in Russia officials have a considerable capacity to frustrate edicts from on high. The result is that measures proclaimed by President Putin to establish order may not be effective. As Boris Yeltsin showed, frustration can lead the president to exert *vlast* to get what he wants, whether it is tax revenue from a company owned by oligarchs or political acquiescence from journalists wanting to print evidence of misgovernment. But to substitute dictatorship for law weakens rather than strengthens the attempts at founding a modern state in Russia.

10   In search of an equilibrium

The period of unpredictable transformation in Russia now appears to be coming to a close. Decisions taken a decade ago cannot easily be reversed; the probability that next year will be similar to this year is far greater in 2002 than it was in 1992. Political inertia makes incremental change more likely. However, settling down can be interpreted in several ways – putting a stop to a deteriorating situation; maintaining the status quo; or laying foundations for progress.

A chronicle of Russia in the past decade is full of shock events affecting everyday life. A sequence of shocks encourages the view that Russian politics is one damned thing after another, that there is no rhyme or reason in events as each shock is independent of what went before. In statistical terms, this can be described as a random walk, an apt metaphor for the pillar-to-post lurches of Russian government under Boris Yeltsin. In such a situation, the churning of politicians, policies and resources does not produce improvement nor does it lead to deterioration. Cumulatively, a random walk goes nowhere. From the perspective of the ordinary Russian, going nowhere is preferable to becoming worse off. Yet any sequence of events over ten years, 120 months and 3,652 days is bound to form a pattern of some kind (Rose, 2002a).

The spectre haunting Russia is not that of a return to Communism or a turn toward fascist nationalism; it is the risk of going nowhere. The conditions in which the Russian people find themselves today are unsatisfactory, but after a decade of change it is easier to stay on the path that the country's governors have been following than to turn back or to turn in another direction. Insofar as the government of the Russian Federation is already in equilibrium, President Putin is presiding over the consolidation of an incomplete democracy. The challenge facing Vladimir Putin is how to avoid Russia becoming mired in a low-level equilibrium trap.

The shortcomings of the Russian state today are not the result of popular demand for misrule; they are due to the failure of political elites to supply the normal institutions of a modern state. The Russian state is strong enough that hundreds of thousands of tons of oil can be regularly delivered to the West in return for billions of dollars of hard currency paid to new rich Russians. But it is not strong enough to collect taxes routinely and deliver wages monthly to school teachers and nurses. In the words of *Novaya gazeta*, 'Our state is not weak. It is irresponsible' (quoted in Peel, 2000).

The Russian ideal of a normal society is much the same as that of citizens living in democratic modern states. When asked in the tenth NRB survey to describe a normal society, 90 per cent or more describe it as a society in which government does not interfere with the everyday lives of its citizens, public officials treat ordinary people fairly, there is no fear of crime on the streets, money does not lose its value due to inflation, everybody who wants to work can find a job and there are opportunities to improve one's living conditions. However, 93 per cent think that Russia today is not a normal society.

There is a very broad consensus about the chief obstacles to Russia becoming a normal society: blame is placed on the state (fig. 10.1). Two-thirds say that the state's failure to enforce the law and government corruption are major obstacles to normal life; low wages and unemployment, also deemed responsibilities of the state, are the second major obstacle. One-quarter place blame on the legacy from Soviet times or transition to the market economy. Logically, the national culture defines what is normal (or at least, expected) in a society. However, Russians do not see their current conditions as culturally determined. National traditions, the way ordinary people behave and popular resistance to change are each seen as major obstacles by one in ten. Democracy is least likely to be blamed for the failure of Russia to be normal.

The gap between the ideal of normality and the current state of Russia can be a challenge to action or it can produce resigned acceptance of whatever is. Vladimir Putin accepts the challenge. But whether his actions will lead to Russia becoming a normal society, or at least making progress toward becoming a normal society, depends on popular response. Determination to change is evident in the Kremlin, but resistance to change is also evident within government and in the country. An equilibrium can be arrived at by Putin succeeding in improving governance so that the Russian state is both democratic and modern. Or an equilibrium can be arrived at by a lowering of expectations by governors and governed producing acceptance of the status quo, however undesirable it is deemed. This chapter draws on the tenth New Russia Barometer survey to show what ordinary Russians make of what Vladimir Putin has done – and how Russia is settling down after more than a decade of upheavals.

Figure 10.1 CHIEF OBSTACLES TO RUSSIA BECOMING A NORMAL SOCIETY.

Q. What do you think is the biggest obstacle to Russia becoming a normal society? And the second biggest?

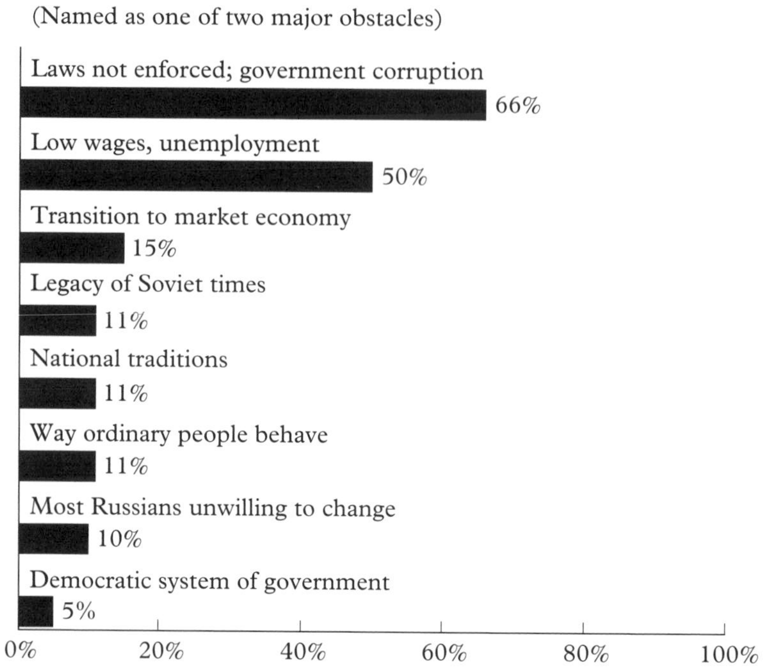

(Named as one of two major obstacles)

Laws not enforced; government corruption
66%

Low wages, unemployment
50%

Transition to market economy
15%

Legacy of Soviet times
11%

National traditions
11%

Way ordinary people behave
11%

Most Russians unwilling to change
10%

Democratic system of government
5%

0%   20%   40%   60%   80%   100%

Source: New Russia Barometer X. Nationwide survey, 17 June–3 July 2001. Number of respondents, 2,000. Base for percentages: the 93 per cent saying country not yet a normal society.

The rule of law in short supply

Many deficiencies of government can be blamed on events outside the control of governors, for example a downturn in the world economy, drought causing crop failure or terrorist attacks. However, governors cannot avoid responsibility for the rule of law, because law is a unique product of government. Public officials are not only expected to lay down laws but also to follow them. But this is not the way in which elected officeholders and bureaucrats behave in the Russian Federation today.

Although Russia has an elaborate set of state security institutions, these institutions are principally designed to protect the state rather than to enforce the law against public officials. Security institutions can spy on citizens and intimidate unfriendly journalists, civic activists and politically awkward oligarchs (Knight, 2000a; Mendelson, 2000). When the tenth

New Russia Barometer asked what people think are the priorities of the FSB (formerly the KGB, Vladimir Putin's bureaucratic home), 19 per cent see it as primarily defending authorities from criticism; 20 per cent see it as defending society against threats to national security; and 61 per cent think it does both. Given these beliefs, Russians hesitate to engage in political activities that might attract the attention of the FSB; they protect their civil liberties by not exercising them.

The Soviet doctrine of socialist legality stressed that the end justified the means, and officials of the party-state practised what Marxism-Leninism preached. However, most Russians do not accept this view. The tenth New Russia Barometer asked whether the FSB should be able to do whatever it deems necessary, even if this meant breaking laws protecting individual rights and freedoms. In reply, 40 per cent opposed this, and 38 per cent thought extreme means should be used only in exceptional cases. Barely a fifth of Russians endorsed the FSB doing whatever it wanted whenever it wanted.

Corruption in public life is palpable evidence of the absence of the rule of law, and every Russian household is vulnerable to its effects. More than two-thirds see institutions of government as corrupt. The chief difference is the degree to which institutions are considered corrupt (fig. 10.2). Two of the services regarded as most corrupt – the police and local government – are those about which people are most likely to have first-hand knowledge. The Kremlin and the FSB, viewed as less corrupt, are quite remote from ordinary people, but so too is the Duma, which 77 per cent of respondents saw as corrupt.

In a *Rechtsstaat*, bureaucratic requirements to fill out forms to request services may cause annoyance or inefficiency, but such procedures maintain equity and honesty in administration. In Russia, they do not. Discretion in enforcing the law gives public officials opportunities for extracting money from those who have a direct interest in the enforcement or non-enforcement of the law. Once established in a government post, an official can extract payments from businesses for not enforcing rules that an enterprise wants waived, or for doing their job promptly, for example clearing goods from customs that retailers need to sell before they go stale or out of fashion.

The simplest way for ordinary people to avoid corruption is to avoid contact with public officials; 72 per cent of Russians report that they have had no such contact in the past year. Among those who did have contacts, only 4 per cent said they got what they wanted without difficulty; 10 per cent did not get what they wanted; 4 per cent used connections or gave a present or cash to secure their aim; and 9 per cent experienced delays and inconvenience. In sum, five-sixths of Russians having dealings

Figure 10.2 PERCEPTION OF CORRUPTION OF PUBLIC OFFICIALS.

Q. How common do you think bribe-taking and corruption are in:

(Percentage saying somewhat or totally corrupt)

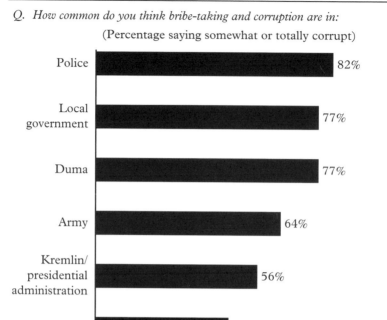

Source: New Russia Barometer X. Nationwide survey 17 June–3 July 2001. Number of respondents, 2,000.

with officials found them inefficient, frustrating or corrupt. When asked whether it would be acceptable to give money to a public official to get what was wanted, 46 per cent thought it would be all right and 54 per cent said it would not.

Ordinary Russians vulnerable to crime on the street or break-ins at home (fig. 3.3) do not look to the state to enforce the law. When asked what people should do if they feel unsafe on the street, more than three-quarters advise going out as little as possible after dark or having other people with you when you do so. Almost as many advise going out with a fierce dog and almost half think it would be prudent to carry a knife or even a gun for protection. Less than one in five expect that complaining to the police would be helpful. Self-protection rather than police protection is also seen as the best way to make one's home safe from thieves.

Incentives to crime and corruption could be countered by the certainty of punishment. However, the certainty that exists today is that violations of the law will *not* be punished. When asked how likely it is that the courts punish those who break the law, only 20 per cent think it probable or very likely that public officials who take bribes will be punished and 27 per cent expect courts to punish businessmen involved in bribery. By contrast, 53 per cent expect those who break into houses or commit robbery on the streets will be punished. If a Russian wants to escape punishment for making money by acting outside the law, he or she is better advised to get a government job than a gun.

In an established market economy, businesses can rely on contracts being carried out by those who sign them. This is not the case in Russia. In the private sector, *arbitrazh* courts have been created to deal with commercial disputes without direct state involvement. Yet even if a company gets a favourable judgment, enforcement is slow and uncertain. Delays can make a verdict meaningless if a firm goes bankrupt while waiting for a debt to be paid. After substantial field research, Kathryn Hendley (1999: 99) concludes 'The experience of Russian managers has taught them not to count on law as a mechanism for maximizing an enterprise's interests. Believing in the usefulness of law would require an enormous leap of faith.' When a business has difficulty in getting paid, it usually turns to informal negotiations rather than to courts of law in an effort to get paid. Political contacts can be mobilized to make debtors pay up or to get banks to extend credit. If these measures fail, businesses can turn to private protection agencies, including the Russian *mafiya*. Private supply and demand of services can achieve an equilibrium of sorts, but doing so weakens the authority of the state and reduces the tax revenues needed to strengthen it (Frye, 2000: 155ff.).

An hourglass not a civil society

The Soviet system denied the existence of civil society, that is, institutions that could represent the political interests of individual citizens and groups. Instead, the Communist Party organized top-down institutions to promote the party line and mobilize mass support for whatever the party-state decreed. In response, ordinary Russians insulated themselves as best they could from the intrusive reach of the party-state through informal ties with trusted friends and relatives. The result was an hourglass society, with numerous horizontal ties between elites at the top of Soviet society and strong horizontal ties among informal groups at the base of society. However, contact between top and bottom was minimized (Shlapentokh, 1989: ch. 1; Rose, 1995b).

Strong horizontal but weak vertical ties

In Robert Putnam's (1993) theory of social capital, strong face-to-face ties in informal groups at the base of society are meant to spill upwards, creating trust in representative institutions of civil society and thus making democracy work. The New Russia Barometer has documented strong ties at the base of society. When people are asked if they can discuss personal matters with family or friends, 93 per cent identify someone they can talk to about important matters. Informal ties help people cope with the disruptions of transformation. Whereas more than four-fifths of unemployed Russians do not get benefits from the government's social protection services, 78 per cent feel confident that they could borrow as much as a week's wages from their informal social protection system of friends and relatives. In addition, 58 per cent have someone outside their immediate household who would help look after them if they fell ill.

However, the hourglass legacy of Soviet times does not lead to the conversion of strong horizontal ties into the vertical links that Putnam assumes will follow and will help make civil society effective. People who are known in horizontal face-to-face relations are trusted by 57 per cent of Russians, 22 per cent are neutral and the remainder distrustful. But in reply to the follow-up question, asking if most people in the country can be trusted, only 32 per cent agreed that they could, and 41 per cent actively distrust most people, with the remainder neutral.

For a society with an educated, largely urban population, Russia has an extraordinarily low level of membership in institutions of civil society. To secure an accurate count of organizational membership, one cannot turn to official figures that were grossly inflated by the party-state and are now out of date. The tenth New Russia Barometer explicitly asked people *Do you belong to any of the following types of organizations?*:

	Members
Sport or recreation group	4%
Housing bloc, neighbourhood association	2%
Musical, literary or art group	2%
Charitable organization	0.5%
Political party	0.5%
None	91%

A separate question about church attendance found 9 per cent saying they went to church at least once a month. Given that the Russian Orthodox Church supported the state in Soviet times as well as under the tsar, it is not an institution of civil society.

Every society divides into groups with distinctive political interests that can be represented by institutions of civil society. For example, industrial enterprises represent managers and employees; banks represent the financial community; and television stations claim to speak on behalf of their viewers as well as to them. However, those who speak on behalf of institutional interests are not elected; the editors of newspapers, university professors and directors of major enterprises are appointed. Moreover, most institutions that represent interests do not have individual members as do self-governing choirs or tennis clubs. A business association has business enterprises as its constituent members and the television programmes that viewers watch are selected by producers and controllers of television networks.

The disjunction between institutions and those on whose behalf they speak is illustrated by attitudes toward trade unions, which are intended to represent specific groups of employees. In the total adult population, 52 per cent are employed. Of this total, half do not have a union at their place of work, and, where there is a union, more than one-fifth are not union members. Altogether, 20 per cent of Russian adults are members of a trade union. When members are asked whether they trust union officials at their place of work to represent their interests, two-thirds of union members do so. When asked whether national trade union officials can be trusted to look after their interests, only two-fifths of union members do so. In all, only one-quarter of union members and 5 per cent of Russian adults trust both local and national officials to represent the views of workers.

Institutions do not need a mass membership to exercise political influence. This is obviously the case for institutions within government, such as the Constitutional Court and the Federal Security Service. When asked about the influence of varied institutions on Russian life, a majority name elected officials – the president and governors – and non-elected bankers as having significant influence. More than two-fifths think television is influential, and the same percentage name the Federal Security Service. A third or more attribute substantial influence to directors of industrial enterprises, to newspapers and to the Army. Elected representatives – whether described collectively as Duma members or political parties or as individual representatives in single-member districts – are ranked low in influence (fig. 10.3).

If institutions claim to represent broad-based interests in society, they should have a broad base of trust. However, a majority of Russians do not trust major civil and political institutions. The institutions most likely to be trusted, or least likely to be distrusted, are President Putin,[1] the Army and regional governors[2] (fig. 10.3). The security services, the

---

[1] Trust in the president reflects personal rather than institutional characteristics. In the tenth NRB survey, 50 per cent said they trusted the president, whereas in the final NRB survey under President Yeltsin only 14 per cent trusted the president.

[2] On a seven-point scale, respondents choosing the mid-point, four, are sceptical. Sceptics are the median respondents for trust in the Army and in regional governors. For all other institutions in figure 10.3, an absolute majority express positive distrust, that is, a reply of one to three on a seven-point scale.

Figure 10.3 INSTITUTIONS: INFLUENCE WITHOUT TRUST.

Q. To what extent do you trust each of these institutions to look after your interests?
Q. How much influence do you think each of the following groups has on Russian life today?

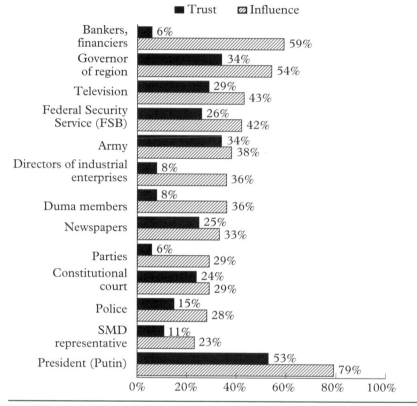

Source: New Russia Barometer X. Nationwide survey, 17 June–3 July 2001. Number of respondents, 2,000. Trust and influence figures represent those giving a rating of five to seven on a seven-point scale.

Constitutional Court, television and newspapers are each trusted by about one-quarter of the population. Representative political institutions are especially distrusted: only 6 per cent trust political parties, 8 per cent trust Duma members generally and 11 per cent trust the Duma representative for their district. Directors of major enterprises and the police are equally distrusted.

Major institutions are more likely to be considered influential than to be trusted (fig. 10.3). The gap is greatest for bankers and financiers; 59 per cent see them influencing Russian life but they are trusted by only

6 per cent. The second biggest deficit is registered by Duma members and directors of industrial enterprises; each group is deemed influential by 36 per cent but trusted by only 8 per cent. The gap is also substantial for regional governors, who are deemed influential by more than half, but trusted by only one-third of the citizenry. The gap is also great for political parties; relatively few think political parties have influence and even fewer find parties trustworthy.

In the uncivil context of a state without the rule of law, Russians are not using new-found freedoms to be politically active. Instead, people are turning their backs on the state, showing 'idiotization', the conscious rejection of the obligations of the model citizen in a civic democracy (cf. Nodia, 1996: 26).

An absence of accountability

Competitive party elections are central to accountability in a democratic modern state, and Russians value elections. After the third Duma election and second presidential ballot, when the tenth New Russia Barometer asked respondents what they thought of elections with a big choice both of candidates and parties for the Duma, and of candidates for the presidency, 79 per cent endorsed competitive elections. It is especially noteworthy that endorsement of elections is found not only among those voting for winners. A majority of those voting for losing candidates and a majority of non-voters are also in favour of elections. However, most Russians do not think that election winners act as if they were accountable. When the tenth NRB survey asked *Do you think having elections regularly makes government do what ordinary people want?*, two-thirds replied that governors are not at all or not much interested in doing what ordinary people want, while only 5 per cent think governors usually do what people want and the remaining 29 per cent think this is to some extent so. In the absence of accountability, elections do not produce a complete democracy.

The constitution establishes horizontal accountability within government, that is, institutions that to some extent can act as checks on other institutions of government. At the national level, the separate election of the president and the Duma creates two competing institutions with electoral legitimacy, albeit they have unequal powers. To determine the extent to which people think the president ought to have unchecked powers, the New Russia Barometer asks: *Do you think the president of Russia should have the right to suspend the Duma and introduce presidential rule by decree if he considers that necessary?* Under President Yeltsin, the proportion of Russians willing to endorse unchecked presidential rule was always low, averaging only 18 per cent. Since Vladimir Putin has become president, the proportion prepared to endorse decree powers rose to 81 per cent in the tenth New Russia Barometer. NRB surveys ask the complementary question: *Do you think the Duma should have the right to stop the president taking decisions that it considers wrong?* Even though the Duma is widely distrusted, under President Yeltsin an average of 64 per cent endorsed the Duma being able to act as a check on the president. Under Putin a bare majority continue to endorse the Duma's power to check the president: in the tenth NRB survey 51 per cent favoured this.

Federalism provides additional checks on centralized power. Whereas President Putin believes in the supremacy of the Kremlin at the top of the vertical hierarchy of government, Russians are divided about who ought to have the last word in disputes between the regions and the Kremlin. In reply to a question about who should have the last word when there is a dispute between a regional governor and the federal government, 57 per cent favoured the federal government having the final word as against 43 per cent wanting the governor to have the final word.

That politicians should check each other is a central principle of the United States Constitution, and it was explicitly incorporated into the 1949 German Constitution to act as a bulwark against a return to the totalitarianism of Hitler's regime. However, without a means of promoting cooperation, a separation-of-powers system is vulnerable to rancorous disputes leading to reciprocal vetoes on action. In established democracies, political parties give politicians incentives to cooperate in making public policy and to help voters identify whom to hold accountable for what they like or dislike.

As previous chapters have shown, Russia's political elite avoids vertical accountability for government because political parties do not appear on all three national ballots. The vacuum that parties leave is filled by a plethora of independent candidates in half the Duma seats and for the presidency. The list PR ballot forces voters to choose a party, but it also leads those elected to look to party managers for re-election rather than to the people who voted for them, because re-election depends primarily on being given a high position on the party's list, rather than being placed in a low position which guarantees defeat even if the party easily passes the PR threshold. The supply of a floating choice of parties from one election to the next further inhibits accountability.

For vertical accountability to be effective, parties must be present where voters live. Given both party list and independent Duma members, the tenth New Russia Barometer asked its nationwide sample to name those parties that were active in their region. Almost half did not know of any parties active locally and an additional sixth positively replied that there were none (fig. 10.4). Even though the Communist Party has a

Figure 10.4 LOW VISIBILITY OF PARTIES WHERE VOTERS LIVE.

Q. Which of the parties and factions in the Duma participate actively in the political life of your region? (Can name more than one.)

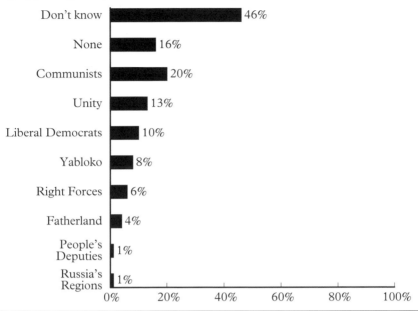

Source: New Russia Barometer X. Nationwide survey, 17 June–3 July 2001. Number of respondents, 2,000.

long-established brand name and contested a relatively large number of SMD districts, only one-fifth see it as active locally. Even though virtually every citizen knows that Vladimir Putin is president, the party with which he is most often associated, Unity, has registered its presence locally with only 13 per cent of the electorate. Two parties that have fought each Duma and presidential election – the Liberal Democratic Party of Vladimir Zhirinovsky and Yabloko, the party of Grigory Yavlinsky – are visible to only 10 per cent and 8 per cent of the electorate respectively.

In theory Duma members representing single-member districts should, like members of the United States Congress, publicize their name and activities in order to win re-election by exploiting the advantages of incumbency. However, Duma representatives from single-member districts do not publicize successfully their name and what they are doing. In the NRB survey taken 18 months after the 1999 election, only 21 per cent of citizens could correctly name their SMD Duma representative. Given the readiness of Duma members elected from single-member districts to migrate between Duma fractions or to join a non-ballot party in Moscow, voters have even more difficulty in ascertaining the Duma fraction to which they are nominally linked by the independent decision of their SMD representative.

The absence of party accountability is even greater at the regional level. The chief elected office is that of governor. A big majority of governors are elected as independent candidates. Incumbency is a bigger asset than a party label, and governors do make an effort to be known. In the tenth NRB survey, 84 per cent could correctly name their regional governor. This is acceptable to the Kremlin, because it is far easier to negotiate with the winner of a gubernatorial election than to pick a winner in advance and organize campaigns in 89 regions. Vladimir Putin's experience of losing his job after organizing an unsuccessful bid for re-election by the mayor of St Petersburg illustrates the penalties that are imposed on those who back losers. Elections to regional legislatures show even fewer signs of partisan accountability; only 10 per cent of regional legislature members are candidates of major parties in the Duma. While practices differ from region to region, the normal pattern is that the governor uses patronage and pressure to create a malleable regional legislature, and those under the governor's roof exercise power with little accountability to citizens of the region and sometimes with limited regard to the rule of law as well (Stoner-Weiss, 2001a; Slider, 2001).

The weakness of vertical accountability has led Lilia Shevtsova (2000: 37) to charge that Vladimir Putin heads a 'constitutional electoral autocracy', a variation on the Latin American model of presidential rule characterized as 'delegative democracy' (O'Donnell, 1994). Shevtsova's phrase recognizes that, by winning a constitutionally valid election, Putin has the right to the highest position in the state. But it also emphasizes that he is not accountable to anyone, except to the electorate in a bid for re-election in 2004, and thereafter not even to the electorate, since a second-term president cannot run again. But the term autocrat suggests a person who rules by himself, and this exaggerates the power that any one individual can wield within so complex a system of government as that of the Russian Federation. However, the horizontal checks and balances that the constitution imposes and that are reinforced by the political self-interest of officeholders do not encourage vertical accountability to the electorate.

Elections without accountability create a situation that a Russian can characterize as 'They pretend to represent us; we pretend to support them.' When the ninth NRB survey asked people how the change from the Communist regime to the present has affected the influence of people like themselves on government, only 19 per cent said that it had increased. By contrast, 52 per cent felt they have no more influence on government today than before and 29 per cent actually say that their influence on government has decreased.

Matching supply and demand

Russians are now free to voice demands for democratic government in a modern state, but political elites have yet to supply this. Although Russia now has free elections, in the absence of political accountability, institutions of civil society and the rule of law, it is not a modern state and therefore it cannot be a complete democracy.

As individuals, Russians have gained in personal freedom from the weakness of a state that had sought to control what they did and said, and millions have taken advantage of this fact. But collectively, everyone in Russian society is disadvantaged by the state's inability to prevent crime in the streets and corruption in government. Competition for power and advantage among elites strengthens and enriches the winners, but it is of little advantage to the majority of citizens, who are bystanders in struggles for spoils.

Problems of supply

Russia's challenge to President Putin goes far beyond the need to win re-election; it is to make Russia a modern state. He inherited a very mixed legacy: electoral competition and individual freedom were well entrenched but government was in the hands of officials with a vested interest in ignoring or exploiting the law. Nothing was done to create political parties holding governors accountable to the electorate. To describe Putin's task as rebuilding the state underestimates its scale. Rebuilding was appropriate in post-1945 Germany, because the Federal Republic was heir to institutions of a *Rechtsstaat*; the replacement of the Nazi regime with free elections could therefore make the Bonn Republic a democratic as well as modern state. In his millennium address, Putin (2000: 210) recognized the gravity of the challenge facing him, a prospect inspiring a 'mixture of hope and of fear'.

Although Vladimir Putin has raised trust in the presidency of the Russian Federation, he has not raised its democratic credentials. When Russians are asked to place the new regime on a ten-point scale from complete dictatorship to complete democracy, the mean score in 1998 was 5.3, almost exactly at the midpoint (fig. 3.5). When the question was repeated three years later, the mean score remained nearly the same, 5.5. The median Russian sees the regime today as equidistant between dictatorship and democracy.

For Vladimir Putin, strengthening the Russian economy is a goal almost equal to strengthening the state. However, the legacy of 70 years of a command non-market economy is a great burden. The most optimistic prospect that Putin (2000: 213) can offer is:

> It will take us approximately fifteen years and an 8 per cent annual growth of our Gross Domestic Product to reach the per capita GDP level of present-day Portugal or Spain, which are not among the world's industrial leaders.

However, there is no empirical justification for assuming that the official Russian economy could grow at 8 per cent a year for a decade and a half. Official figures have only recorded that rate for one year, 2000; the preceding and following year the Russian economy grew at a rate of little more than 5 per cent annually. If the average growth rate of 6.3 per cent for the period 1999–2001 was sustained indefinitely, it would take Russia at least 25 years to catch up with the current living standard of Portugal (cf. World Bank, 2001: 45). In his April 2002 State of the Union message, Putin ordered officials to raise the rate of growth, as if Russia were still a command economy.

Even if Russia caught up with Portugal's current living standard, it would still lag far behind other European Union countries economically, for their economies are growing too. At its historic rate of growth, the Portuguese standard of living will double before Russia gets to where Portugal is today. If comparison is made between Russia and economies of East Central European countries now negotiating membership in the European Union, its gap with the Czech Republic, Hungary and Poland is less than Portugal, but it is nonetheless real. After initial shocks in the early 1990s, East Central European economies started expanding while the Russian economy continued to contract and then stagnate. Admission to the European Union will promote the political and economic integration in Europe of ex-Soviet dominated countries and increase institutional barriers between them and Russia.

Problems of demand

Given elite indifference to creating a modern state, what of popular demand? Russians do not aspire to a utopian goal; the journey to and from socialism has shown how great are the costs of pursuing an impossible ideal. Instead, Russians aspire to a normal life, not in terms of what was *normalno* under Leonid Brezhnev or Boris Yeltsin, but a normal life as it is conceived by Europeans or Americans. However, the context in which Russians aspire to a normal life is radically different.

Although Russia can claim to be a major power in the world, that does not make it a European power. The tsarist empire was built by expansion into Central Asia and eastwards more than to the west. St Petersburg was founded by Tsar Peter the Great to open the country to the West, but for most of the twentieth century it bore the name of Lenin. In any event it has only 8 per cent of the population of the Russian Federation. In his autobiography, Vladimir Putin, a proud son of St Petersburg, found life in Dresden in the 1980s, at that time a Soviet-bloc rather than a European city, much better than life at home. The same was true of his wife, who was born in Kaliningrad, which belonged to a different world than the East Prussian city formerly on that site, Königsberg, the home of Immanuel Kant.

When the tenth NRB survey asked whether people thought Russia's future lies with Western Europe or in closer ties with Slavic neighbours such as Belarus and Ukraine, 68 per cent saw Russia more closely linked with other post-Soviet states as against one-third seeing its future linked more with Western Europe (fig. 10.5). There are good historical, linguistic and cultural reasons why Russians should see the country's future more closely linked with Belarus and Ukraine. But the readiness of people to endorse links with these countries raises questions about how deeply Russians are committed to becominga modern and democratic state,

Figure 10.5 WHERE DOES RUSSIA'S FUTURE LIE?

Q. Some say that Russia's future lies with the countries of Western Europe. Others think it lies with Slavic countries such as Ukraine and Belarus. Which is closer to your view?

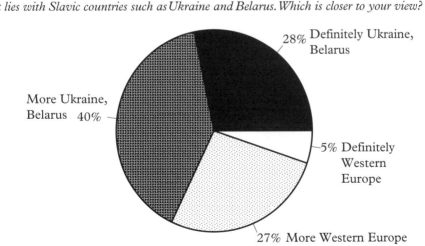

Source: New Russia Barometer X. Nationwide survey 17 June–3 July 2001. Number of respondents, 2,000.

since Ukraine is even more corrupt than the Russian Federation, and Belarus is following the path of post-Soviet Central Asian states in rejecting free and fair elections.

In a country undergoing both economic and political transformation, democracy can be valued either as an end in itself or as an instrumental means to other ends. If the demand is unconditional, then the performance of government will not weaken commitment to that goal. However, if democracy is valued instrumentally, then this weakens demand or makes it contingent on circumstances. Therefore, the tenth NRB survey asked Russians whether they saw democracy as preferable under all conditions or whether its desirability depends on circumstances. In reply, only 29 per cent say democracy is best in all circumstances, while 34 per cent think that authoritarian government is sometimes better (fig. 10.6). The largest group −37 per cent – say that the typeof government that

Figure 10.6 RUSSIAN SUPPORT FOR DEMOCRACY QUALIFIED.

Q. Which of the following statements do you agree with most?
    a. Democracy is preferable to any other kind of government.
    b. In some situations an authoritarian government can be preferable to a democratic one.
    c. It doesn't matter to people like me whether we have a democratic or a non-democratic government.

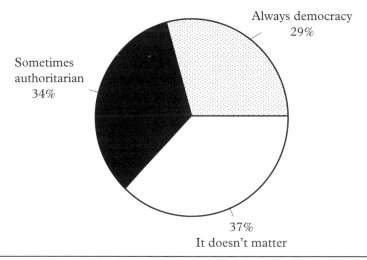

Source: New Russia Barometer X. Nationwide survey, 17 June–3 July 2001. Number of respondents, 2,000.

the country has doesn't make any difference to people like themselves. Russians thus show themselves much less committed to democracy as an end in itself than do peoples in other continents where new regimes have been created. In four Mediterranean countries – Spain, Portugal, Italy and Greece – an average of 81 per cent believe that democracy is always preferable, and in seven African countries this view is endorsed by 75 per cent (Morlino and Montero, 1995: 236; Bratton and Mattes, 2001). The instrumental view that Russians have of democracy is consistent with Russian views of a democratic system as offering both freedom and economic welfare. It is also consistent with Vladimir Putin pursuing the dictatorship of law by whatever means the Kremlin chooses.

The demand for democratic governance is further weakened if people believe it is unsuitable for their country. In the past, many scholars have argued that this is the case for Russia. In addition to asking for evaluations of democracy as an ideal and of the current regime, the tenth NRB survey also asked the extent to which democracy is thought suitable for Russia. There is no consensus among Russians on this point. While 30 per cent are inclined to think democracy is very suitable for Russia, choosing the three highest points of the scale, 25 per cent are inclined to think it is completely unsuitable. The plurality of Russians are in the middle; the mean score on the 10-point scale is 5.6.

The demand for a modern state is weakened if people think that very little can be done to strengthen the rule of law because corruption is inevitable. Insofar as this is the case, public awareness of corruption will not lead to a demand to clean up government but to a helpless shrug of the shoulders or even a readiness to profit by ignoring the law. The tenth NRB survey probed the extent to which corruption is deep-rooted by asking *Would you say the level of corruption in government today is mainly*:

An eternal Russian problem	31%
Product of Communist past	6%
Result of new system of government	25%
A combination of all of these	37%

Two-thirds see corruption as an eternal problem of Russia unaffected by the nature of the regime or even made worse by what happened in the Communist past or by changes since. Hardly anyone thinks corruption was simply due to Communism and is thus likely to decline with the dying out of its legacy, and a quarter think that corruption is a product of the Russian Federation. The extent to which blame is apportioned for lawless governance is less important than the cumulative effect: most Russians regard a corrupt state as part of the eternal order of things rather than a problem that can be solved.

A new equilibrium?

Equilibrium is about adaptation. When the Russian Federation was launched there were many predictions that people would refuse to adapt to the abandonment of Soviet-style welfare, and, if the new regime did not cushion the shock of transformation, public protests would threaten its survival (e.g. Przeworski, 1995). Initially, a big majority of Russians shared this expectation. In January 1992, the first NRB survey found that 93 per cent thought mass demonstrations were likely in protest against inflation, 81 per cent in protest about the political situation and 76 per cent thought demonstrations likely in protest against rising unemployment.

Inflation, unemployment and political turbulence have given Russians ample cause to demonstrate in the streets, but they have shown no taste for such protests. Instead, Russians have tried to adapt to the treble shocks of transformation and, even though a big majority have not yet succeeded in doing so, most people are still trying. When the tenth New Russia Barometer asked *How have the big changes in society since Soviet times affected you?*, only 17 per cent said they would never be able to adjust to the new Russia. A third indicated that they had already adapted. The largest group, 49 per cent, are still trying to adapt.

An equilibrium is the end point in a long-term process of adjustment. The greater the adjustment required, the longer it is likely to take to achieve stability, however that term is defined. To endure this process requires patience. Russians have lots of patience, in the original sense of the word, suffering without protest and without expecting that difficulties will necessarily be overcome. Revolutionaries such as Lenin were patient, pursuing their endeavours for more than a quarter-century before they could see some fruits of their efforts (Rose, 1997). The monolithic power of the Leninist party-state encouraged patience too. Vladimir Shlapentokh (2001: xi) prefaces his book, *A Normal Totalitarian Society*, with the statement that, while living within a system that he hated, he and his friends adapted through what were literally flights of fancy:

We kept our conclusions about the system strictly to ourselves. In these years, we dreamed of leaving the Soviet Union, a fantasy that seemed as feasible as a voyage to Mars. We even invented a code name for this enterprise: the Dzungarian Gate, a mountain passage from Soviet Central Asia to China's Xinjiang Province.

Life in the Russian Federation continues to draw on a vast reservoir of patience. The shocks of transformation, for better and for worse, have made many Russians uncertain about whether their lives will ever become normal. When the tenth New Russia Barometer asked *How long do you think it will be before Russia becomes a normal society?*, 50 per cent say it is difficult to know. Those who have a definite expectation are divided: 9 per cent think Russia is already normal, 32 per cent think it will be normal within a decade and 9 per cent think Russia will never become normal.

A stable equilibrium can arise through a revolution of falling expectations, in which people reduce their hopes of what the future will bring and accept that whatever good the future brings may come later rather than sooner. Hope deferred generates neither frustration nor despair, but patience. When asked how long it will take before a majority of people benefit from transformation, only one in ten believe this will never come and even fewer think it will happen within President Putin's term of office (fig. 10.7). After the disappointments and uncertainties of a decade, like Chekhov's *Three Sisters*, most Russians keep on hoping that transformation will eventually prove worthwhile.

A political equilibrium is stable but not static; incremental alterations continue to occur, but they do not radically alter the system. The turnover of generations is a familiar example of incremental change and generational change can influence popular support for the regime. Consistently NRB surveys find that younger adults are more positive toward the new regime than are older people. In the tenth NRB survey, among those aged 60 or above, only 32 per cent were positiveabout the new regime while,

Figure 10.7 PATIENCE – WITH OR WITHOUT MUCH HOPE.

Q. Do you think that the big changes since Soviet times, which have imposed so many hardships, will bring positive results to the majority of people of this country sooner or later?

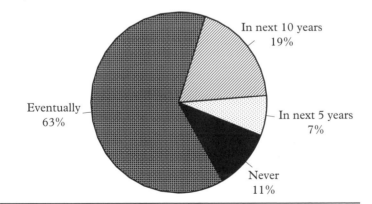

Source: New Russia Barometer X. Nationwide survey, 17 June–3 July 2001. Number of respondents, 2,000.

among those aged 18 to 29, 57 per cent were positive about the new regime. Older Russians are least likely to endorse democracy as preferable to any other kind of government, while a plurality of younger Russians think democracy is always best. In reply to a key question about the market – whether it is better to have lots of goods in shops and high prices, or low prices and few goods and shortages – 76 per cent of older Russians choose the shortages of a command economy while 67 per cent of younger Russians favour window-shopping in a market economy. Insofar as these views are maintained or increase among each new cohort of Russian adults, support for the new regime will gradually increase. But since the adult population changes at the rate of only about 2 per cent a year, it will take another generation before enough of today's young Russians move into middle age and become representative of society as a whole.

A political equilibrium can be disrupted abruptly. The readiness of ordinary Russians to distance themselves from a distrusted state rather than to demand reforms shows that a revolution from below is unlikely. The actions of Mikhail Gorbachev show that elite initiatives can disrupt an equilibrium, and so did Boris Yeltsin's, but their fates are a caution to Vladimir Putin about the risks of attempting too much too quickly with too little support from political elites. However, necessity can force abrupt changes, as the 1998 ruble crisis illustrates. The Russian Federation remains vulnerable to imperative pressures to finance public expenditure and to repay foreign debts. Yet crises can be opportunities as well as threats, as Vladimir Putin demonstrated in response to the September 11 terrorist attack on the United States.

Settling down differently

The disequilibrium between ideals and reality can be closed by lowering aspirations or by improving performance. The danger facing Russia today is that the new regime settles into a low-level equilibrium trap, in which elections give voters a choice of who rules but rulers fail to produce a modern state. In such circumstances, most people will evade or avoid the state when it suits their convenience, and exploit it when that is possible. As long as government respects individual freedom and people can get by economically, the political system will be in an equilibrium of sorts. While this is not what most Russians want, it is what political elites have shown they can supply.

There are already signs of people adjusting political evaluations to conform with experience. When the New Russia Barometer asked people to evaluate the regime at the beginning of 1992, only 14 per cent were positive. When the question was repeated in 2001, there were 47 per cent positive about the current regime. The passive acceptance of the new regime is shown by 33 per cent endorsing both the new system of government as well as the pre-perestroika regime.

On entering office, President Putin pledged himself to introducing the dictatorship of law. If he succeeds, this will contribute substantially to making Russia a modern state – provided that the emphasis is on law rather than dictatorship. The demand for order in Russia is so great that whatever President Putin imposes will gain widespread support – if it works. To succeed, President Putin does not have to take control of Russian society but of Russian government. First of all, he must replace the selective enforcement of the law and apply the rule of law to all who act in its name.

When Vladimir Putin argues that the Russian state should be the main driving force of any change, he is true to its history. If the transformation from the Soviet party-state to the Russian Federation reduces the pressures of an anti-modern state without establishing the institutions and procedures that support a modern state, life will go on. Major enterprises will sometimes pay taxes on time – and sometimes they will not. Teachers and nurses will sometimes be paid on time and sometimes not. A majority will still rely on informal and second economy activities to eke out their existence. Disputes between Moscow and regional governments will not be about how the law should be interpreted but whether and to what extent laws are to be applied. Financiers will sometimes look to the market to make money, and sometimes look to the state.

Russia is settling down differently. The Russian people have accepted that there is no turning back to the past. There is a resigned acceptance that this is the only government that Russia is likely to have in the foreseeable future. The longer the Russian Federation persists, for better *and* for worse, the more likely a consensus is to develop in favour of an electoralist regime without order as a lesser evil than an undemocratic anti-modern state. Up to a point, this can be described as consolidating the regime, inasmuch as the current system is recognized as 'the only game in town'. But Russia's political elite has yet to demonstrate that they are playing a game that is in accord with the rules of a democratic modern state.

Appendix A
New Russia Barometer samples

The following New Russia Barometer surveys are referred to in the text:

Year		Date	Number of respondents
1992	I	26 January–25 February	2,106
1993	II	26 June–22 July	1,975
1994	III	15 March–9 April	3,535
1995	IV	31 March–19 April	1,943
1996 i	V	12–31 January	2,340
1996 ii	VI	25 July–2 August	1,599
1998	VII	6 March–13 April	1,904
2000 i	VIII	13–29 January	1,940
2000 ii	IX	14–18 April	1,600
2001	X	17 June–3 July	2,000

Nine of the ten surveys were conducted by VTsIOM, the Russian Centre for Public Opinion Research; NRB III was conducted by MNENIE Opinion Service. Exceptionally, the first NRB survey in winter 1992 excluded rural areas, which, according to Goskomstat, accounted for 26.7 per cent of the 1987 Russian population. Comparison of urban and rural respondents in NRB II showed that, except for a few obvious variables such as occupation, the results of NRB I were not biased by the absence of rural respondents.

Respondents are selected by a multi-stage, stratified sample. For example, in the tenth NRB survey the Russian Federation was first stratified into ten large regions by seven social, economic and infrastructure attributes. Each region was assigned interviews in proportion to its share of the population, using Goskomstat estimated population statistics for the year 2000. At the second stage, each region was stratified according to the status of administrative units, characteristics of the population and whether units were autonomous republics of the Russian Federation. Moscow and St Petersburg were included independently. The total number of interviews within a region was determined proportionate to population. At the third stage, urban and rural districts were selected on a probability proportionate to population basis. At the fourth stage, each district was stratified by population characteristics: for example, villages within a rural district or a ward or electoral precinct within a city. A total of 42 different regions (*subyekt*) of the Russian Federation with 33 oblast centres, 42 other cities and towns and 31 villages were included in the sample. Within these units, 195 primary sampling units were selected and assigned to interviewers. The average interviewer had taken part in more than ten previous VTsIOM surveys. Within each primary sampling unit, households were selected by a random route method, in which the interviewer called at every *n*th house. At each household one individual was selected as a respondent on the basis of a sex by age by education grid. VTsIOM field supervisors verified 299 interviews directly with respondents.

When the number of interviews is about 1,600, respondents are selected by a multi-stage nationwide random sample, but the number of sampling points is reduced. In the ninth NRB survey, for example, a total of 27 oblast centres, 31 cities and towns and 25 villages were included, with 160 primary sampling units.

Questionnaires are checked by the Organization Department of VTsIOM and entered for computer analysis there. Comparison of the results is made with Goskomstat population statistics, which were estimates, since no Russian census had been carried out since 1987, and as appropriate VTsIOM calculates weights by age, education or gender. Analysis of the data was carried out at the Centre for the Study of Public Policy, University of Strathclyde, using SPSS statistical programs. The effects of weighting on key political, economic and social data are examined and lack any substantial significance. In years in which the starting age for the adult sample was 15, respondents aged 15 to 17 were excluded from analysis. For further details, see Rose 2002b.

Appendix B
Coding of independent variables

Appendix Table B. *Coding of independent variables*

Variables used in multi-variate analyses in tables 7.4, 8.4 and 9.1.

		NRB VIII 2000		NRB IX 2000		NRB X 2001	
		Mean	SDev.	Mean	SDev.	Mean	SDev.
Voted in presidential election:							
For personality	0=No, 1=Yes	na		.29	.45	na	
For man of power	0=No, 1=Yes	na		.06	.23	na	
For policies	0=No, 1=Yes	na		.24	.43	na	
Former CPSU member	0=No, 1=Yes	.11	.31	.10	.30	na	
Rating of past political system	−100 to +100	36	52	31	55	34	50
Rating of current political system	−100 to +100	−11	55	−13	51	−2	50
Rating of future political system	−100 to +100	25	48	26	44	20	50
President can rule by decree	1=Completely disagree to 4=Completely agree	2.72	.95	2.83	.91	3.15	.83
Trust in police	1=No trust to 7=Complete trust	2.88	1.75	2.97	1.63	2.70	1.61
Trusts Federal Security Service	1=No trust to 7=Complete trust	na		na		3.33	1.75
Rating Yeltsin's performance	1=Lowest, 10=Highest	2.99	2.03	2.13	1.51		

Rating Putin's performance	1=Lowest, 10=Highest	5.78	2.46	5.91	2.24	6.10	2.24
Kremlin corrupt	1=Not at all to 4=Totally corrupt	na		na		2.63	.99
Putin raises world respect for Russia	1=Respect fallen to 4=Risen greatly	na		na		2.91	.79
Putin improves social protection	1=Much worse, 3=The same, 5=Much better	na		na		3.45	.89
Frequently discusses politics	1=Never to 4=Very often	na		na		2.51	.97
Current system is dictatorial or democratic	1=Complete dictatorship 10=Complete democracy	5.29	2.12	5.29	1.89	5.49	2.01
Dictatorship the only way out	1=Completely disagree to 4=Completely agree	2.00	1.02	2.24	.96	2.04	1.03
Feels close to political party	1=Yes 0=No	.49	.50	.55	.50	na	
Governor supported Putin in presidential election	1=Yes 0=No	na		.44	.56	na	
Has a preferred political outlook	1=Yes 0=No	.65	.48	.60	.49	.66	.48
Political outlook:							
Pro-market	1=Yes 0=No	.18	.38	.26	.44	.25	.43
Great power patriot	1=Yes 0=No	.07	.25	.07	.26	.04	.19
Communist	1=Yes 0=No	.24	.43	.17	.37	.29	.45
Supports action in Chechnya	1=Completely oppose to 4=Completely support	2.94	.92	3.15	.80	2.42	.93
Expects Russian victory in Chechnya	1=Yes 0=No	.45	.49	na		.21	.41
Priority problem: Chechnya	1=Yes 0=No	na		.39	.49	na	
Household income last month	100 to 10,000 rubles	1970	1706	1947	1465	3303	2451

(cont.)

Appendix Table B (*cont.*)

Variables used in multi-variate analyses in tables 7.4, 8.4 and 9.1.

		NRB VIII 2000		NRB IX 2000		NRB X 2001	
		Mean	SDev.	Mean	SDev.	Mean	SDev.
Past household economic situation	1=Much better now, 3=Same, 5=Much better past	3.37	1.49	3.55	1.38	3.22	1.44
Current household economic situation	1=Very bad to 4=Very good	1.97	.68	2.03	.73	1.89	.65
Future household economic situation	1=Much better now, 3=Same, 5=Much better future	3.16	.94	3.32	.88	3.13	.97
Rating of past economic system	−100 to +100	47	43	45	46	44	46
Rating of current economic system	−100 to +100	−27	54	−30	51	−12	51
Rating of economic system in future	−100 to +100	14	53	16	51	16	53
Communist regime blamed for economic problems	1=Not at all to 4= A lot	2.51	.93	2.30	.97	na	
Businessmen blamed for economic problems	1=Not at all to 4= A lot	2.22	.89	2.36	.85	na	
Private ownership better	1=Definitely state to 4=Definitely private	1.98	.96	1.77	.87	1.92	.92
Prefers low prices, shortages to lots of goods, high prices in shops	1=Definitely lots of goods, 4=Definitely low prices	2.56	.98	2.40	.95	2.46	1.00
Hardships sooner or later will benefit	1=Never to 4=In next five years	na		na		2.22	.73

Variable	Coding	Mean	SD	Mean	SD	Mean	SD
Priority problem: inflation	0=No 1=Yes	na		.40	.49	na	na
Priority problem: unemployment	0=No 1=Yes	na		.35	.48	na	na
Age	18 to 90	44	17	45	18	45	18
Gender	0=Male, 1=Female	.54	.50	.54	.50	.54	.50
Education	1=Elementary or less, 10=Postgraduate	5.06	2.53	5.05	2.58	5.05	2.62
Attendance at religious services	1=Never, 3=A few times a year, 5=Weekly or more often	1.73	.99	1.80	.99	1.93	1.05
Town size	0=Village 10=>1 million	4.77	3.79	4.73	3.80	4.87	3.82
Socio-economic status	1=Lowest 10=Highest	3.96	2.15	4.96	2.17	4.24	2.15
Pride in Russian citizenship	1=No pride to 4=Very proud	3.19	.92	3.06	.80	2.79	.90
Consider self European	1=Not European, 4=Certainly European	2.51	.99	2.68	.99	2.54	1.04
State TV useful in deciding vote	1=No use to 4=Very useful	2.49	1.05	2.62	.98	2.67	.81
Own experience useful in deciding vote	1=No use to 4=Very useful	3.14	.94	3.45	.72	na	

*na=variable not available in data set.

References

Anderson, Barbara A., and Silver, Brian D., 1986. 'Infant Mortality in the Soviet Union: Regional Differences and Measurement Issues', *Population and Development Review*, 12, 4, 705–38.

Anderson, Eugene N., and Anderson, Pauline R., 1967. *Political Institutions and Social Change in Continental Europe in the Nineteenth Century*. Berkeley: University of California Press.

Anon., 2000. 'And the Winner Is?', *Moscow Times*, special issue, 9 September.

Aslund, Anders, 1995. *How Russia Became a Market Economy*. Washington, DC: Brookings Institution.

Bartolini, Stefano, 2000. 'Franchise Expansion'. In Richard Rose, ed., *The International Encyclopedia of Elections*. Washington, DC: CQ Press, 117–30.

Berlin, Isaiah, 1958. *Two Concepts of Liberty: An Inaugural Lecture*. Oxford: Clarendon Press.

Blasi, Joseph R., Kroumova, Maya, and Kurse, Douglas, 1997. *Kremlin Capitalism: Privatizing the Russian Economy*. Ithaca: Cornell University Press.

Bonnell, Victoria E., and Breslauer, George W., eds., 2001. *Russia in the New Century*. Boulder, CO: Westview Press.

Boutenko, Irene A., and Razlogov, Kirill E., 1997. *Recent Social Trends in Russia 1960–1995*. Montreal: McGill-Queen's University Press.

Boxer, Vladimir, and Hale, Henry, 2000. 'Putin's Anti-Campaign Campaign', *AAASS NewsNet*, May, 10–11.

Bratton, Michael, and Mattes, Robert, 2001. 'Africans' Surprising Universalism', *Journal of Democracy*, 12, 1, 107–21.

Bratton, Michael, and Walle, Nicolas van de, 1997. *Democratic Experiments in Africa*. New York: Cambridge University Press.

Breslauer, George W., 1978. 'On the Adaptability of Soviet Welfare-State Authoritarianism'. In Karl W. Ryavec, ed., *Soviet Society and the Communist Party*. Amherst: University of Massachusetts Press, 3–25.

  2001. 'Personalism versus Proceduralism: Boris Yeltsin and the Institutional Fragility of the Russian System'. In Bonnell and Breslauer, 2001, 35–58.

  2002. *Gorbachev and Yeltsin as Leaders*. New York: Cambridge University Press.

Brown, Archie, 1994a. 'The Brezhnev Era, 1964–1982'. In Brown, Kaser, and Smith, 1994, 122–5.

  1994b. 'Social Control and Social Development: The Emergence of Civil Society'. In Brown, Kaser, and Smith, 1994, 459–61.

1996. *The Gorbachev Factor*. Oxford: Oxford University Press.

2000. 'Transnational Influences in the Transition from Communism', *Post-Soviet Affairs*, 16, 2, 177–200.

ed., 2001a. *Contemporary Russian Politics: A Reader*. Oxford: Oxford University Press.

2001b. 'From Democratization to Guided Democracy', *Journal of Democracy*, 12, 4, 35–41.

2001c. 'Vladimir Putin and the Reaffirmation of Central State Power', *Post-Soviet Affairs*, 17, 1, 45–55.

Brown, Archie, Kaser, Michael, and Smith, Gerald S., eds., 1994. *The Cambridge Encyclopedia of Russia and the Former Soviet Union*. Cambridge: Cambridge University Press.

Buiter, Willem H., 2000. 'Challenges of the Second Transition Decade in Russia', *Transition* (Washington, DC: World Bank/William Davidson Institute/SITE), August–October, 24–6.

Bunce, Valerie, 1995a. 'Paper Curtains and Paper Tigers', *Slavic Review*, 54, 4, 979–87.

1995b. 'Should Transitologists Be Grounded?', *Slavic Review*, 54, 1, 111–27.

Butler, D. E., and Stokes, Donald E., 1974. *Political Change in Britain*. London: Macmillan, 2nd edn.

Campbell, Angus, Converse, P. E., Miller, W. E., and Stokes, D. E., 1960. *The American Voter*. New York: John Wiley.

Carnaghan, Ellen, 2001a. *Have Your Cake and Eat It Too: Tensions Between Democracy and Order Among Russian Citizens*. Glasgow: University of Strathclyde Studies in Public Policy No. 352.

2001b. 'Thinking about Democracy: Interviews with Russian Citizens', *Slavic Review*, 60, 2, 336–66.

Center for Defense Information, 2002. 'Interfax Carries "Text" of Putin's New Year Message', *CDI Russia Weekly*, No. 187, *www.cdi.org/russia*, 4 January.

Central Electoral Commission, 1996. *Vybory deputatov Gosudarstvennoi dumy 1995* [Elections of Deputies to the State Duma 1995]. Moscow: Ves' mir.

2000a. *Vybory deputatov Gosudarstvennoi dumy Federal'nogo sobraniya Rossiiskoi federatsii 1999: elektoral'naya statistika* [Elections of Deputies to the State Duma of the Federal Assembly of the Russian Federation 1999: Electoral Statistics]. Moscow: Ves' mir.

2000b. *Vybory prezidenta Rossiiskoi federatsii 2000: elektoral'naya statistika* [Elections of the President of the Russian Federation 2000: Electoral Statistics]. Moscow: Ves' mir.

2000c. *Vybory prezidenta Rossiiskoi federatsii 26 marta 2000 goda* [Elections of the President of the Russian Federation, 26 March 2000]. *www.fci.ru/prez2000/default.htm*.

Churchill, Winston, 1947. *Parliamentary Debates*, House of Commons. London: HMSO, 11 November, col. 206.

Clark, John, and Wildavsky, Aaron, 1990. *The Moral Collapse of Communism: Poland as a Cautionary Tale*. San Francisco: ICS Press.

Clem, Ralph S., and Craumer, Peter R., 2000. 'Spatial Patterns of Political Choice in the Post Yel'tsin Era: The Electoral Geography of Russia's 2000 Presidential Election', *Post-Soviet Geography and Economics*, 41, 7, 465–82.

Clover, Charles, 2000. 'Kremlin Accused of Persecuting the Rich', *Financial Times*, 17 July.

Cohen, Ira J., 1985. 'The Underemphasis on Democracy in Marx and Weber'. In R. J. Antonio and R. M. Glassman, eds., *A Weber–Marx Dialogue*. Manhattanville: Kansas State University Press, 274–95.

Colton, Timothy, and Hough, Jerry F., eds., 1998. *Growing Pains: Russian Democracy and the Election of 1993*. Washington, DC: Brookings Institution.

Colton, Timothy J., and McFaul, Michael, 2000. 'Reinventing Russia's Party of Power: "Unity" and the 1999 Duma Election', *Post-Soviet Affairs*, 16, 3, 201–4.

Connor, Walter D., 1988. *Socialist Dilemmas: State and Society in the Soviet Bloc*. New York: Columbia University Press.

Conquest, Robert, 1990. *The Great Terror: A Re-assessment*. London: Pimlico.

Converse, Philip E., 1964. 'New Dimensions of Meaning for Cross-Section Sample Surveys in Politics', *International Journal of Social Science*, 16, 1, 19–34.

Cottrell, Robert, 2002a. 'Putin's Risky Strategy', *Financial Times*, 12 February.

   2002b. 'Russian Court Puts TV Station out of Business', *Financial Times*, 11 January.

Daalder, Hans, 1995. 'Paths Toward State Formation in Europe'. In H. E. Chehabi and Alfred Stepan, eds., *Politics, Society and Democracy: Comparative Studies in Honor of Juan J. Linz*. Boulder, CO: Westview Press, 113–30.

Dahl, Robert A., 1971. *Polyarchy: Participation and Opposition*. New Haven: Yale University Press.

   1998. *On Democracy*. New Haven: Yale University Press.

Derksen, Wilfred, 2002. 'Elections around the World', *www.electionworld.org*, 14 January.

Diamond, Larry, 1999. *Developing Democracy: Toward Consolidation*. Baltimore: Johns Hopkins University Press.

Downs, Anthony, 1957. *An Economic Theory of Democracy*. New York: Harper & Brothers.

Duverger, Maurice, 1954. *Political Parties*. New York: John Wiley.

Dyer, Geoff, and Jack, Andrew, 2001. 'Russia Warned of "Huge" Aids Epidemic', *Financial Times*, 29 November.

Eberstadt, Nicholas, 1999. 'Russia: Too Sick to Matter?', *Policy Review*, 95, 3–24.

EBRD [European Bank for Reconstruction and Development], 2000. *Transition Report 2000*. London: EBRD.

   2001a. *Transition Report 2001*. London: EBRD.

   2001b. *Transition Report Update, April 2001*. London: EBRD.

Egorov, Nikolai N., Novikov, Vladimir M., Parker, Frank L., and Popov, Victor K., ed., 2000. *The Radiation Legacy of the Soviet Nuclear Complex: An Analytical Overview*. London: Earthscan/IIASA.

Elster, Jon, Offe, Claus, and Preuss, Ulrich K., 1998. *Institutional Design in Post-Communist Societies: Rebuilding the Ship at Sea*. New York: Cambridge University Press.

Emmons, Terence, 1983. *The Formation of Political Parties and the First National Elections in Russia*. Cambridge, MA: Harvard University Press.

European Institute for the Media, 2000. *Monitoring the Media Coverage of the March 2000 Presidential Elections in Russia: Final Report.* Düsseldorf: European Institute for the Media.

Fidler, Stephen, and Jack, Andrew, 2001. 'High Hopes', *Financial Times*, 12 November.

Finer, S. E., 1997. *The History of Government.* Oxford: Oxford University Press, 3 vols.

Fish, M. Steven, 1995. *Democracy from Scratch: Opposition and Regime in the New Russian Revolution.* Princeton: Princeton University Press.

2001. 'Putin's Path', *Journal of Democracy*, 12, 4, 71–8.

Fitzpatrick, Sheila, 1999. *Everyday Stalinism. Ordinary Life in Extraordinary Times: Soviet Russia in the 1930s.* New York: Oxford University Press.

Flora, Peter, and Alber, Jens, 1981. 'Modernization, Democratization and the Development of Welfare States in Western Europe'. In P. Flora and A. J. Heidenheimer, eds., *The Development of Welfare States in Europe and America.* New Brunswick, NJ: Transaction Publishers, 37–80.

Freeland, Chrystia, 2000. *Sale of the Century: The Inside Story of the Second Russian Revolution.* London: Little, Brown.

Frisby, Tanya, 1998. 'The Rise of Organised Crime in Russia: Its Roots and Social Significance', *Europe–Asia Studies*, 50, 1, 27–49.

Frye, Timothy, 2000. *Brokers and Bureaucrats: Building Market Institutions in Russia.* Ann Arbor: University of Michigan Press.

Fukuyama, Francis, 1992. *The End of History and the Last Man.* New York: Free Press.

Gaddy, Clifford W., and Ickes, Barry W., 1999. 'A Simple Four-Sector Model of Russia's Virtual Economy', *Post-Soviet Geography and Economics*, 40, 2, 79–97.

2001a. 'Stability and Disorder: An Evolutionary Analysis of Russia's Virtual Economy'. In Bonnell and Breslauer, 2001, 103–23.

2001b. 'The Virtual Economy and Economic Recovery in Russia', *Transition* (World Bank), February–March, 15–19.

Gaidar, Yegor, 1999. *Days of Defeat and Victory.* Seattle: University of Washington Press.

Gibson, James L., 2001. 'The Russian Dance with Democracy', *Post-Soviet Affairs*, 16, 2, 129–58.

Goble, Paul A., 1995. 'Chechnya and Its Consequences', *Post-Soviet Affairs*, 11, 1, 23–7.

Gorbachev, Mikhail, and Mlynar, Zdenek, 2002. *Conversations with Gorbachev: On Perestroika, the Prague Spring and the Crossroads of Socialism.* New York: Columbia University Press.

Gordon, Michael, 2000. 'Putin, in a Rare Interview, Says He'll Use Ex-KGB Aides to Root out Graft', *New York Times*, 24 March.

Gregory, Frank, and Brooke, Gerald, 2000. 'Policing Economic Transition and Increasing Revenue: A Case Study of the Federal Tax Police Service of the Russian Federation, 1992–1998', *Europe–Asia Studies*, 52, 3, 433–55.

Grossman, Gregory, 1977. 'The "Second Economy" of the USSR', *Problems of Communism*, 26, 5, 25–40.

Gurr, T. R., 1970. *Why Men Rebel*. Princeton: Princeton University Press.

Hale, Henry, 2000. 'The State of Democratization in Russia in Light of the Elections', Program on New Approaches to Russian Security, Policy Memo No. 119, *www.fas.harvard.edu/~ponars/POLICY%20MEMOS/Hale119.html*, April, 4 March 2002.

Hamilton, Alexander, Madison, James, and Jay, John, 1948. *The Federalist Papers*. New York: Modern Library edn, No. 51.

Hanson, Philip, and Bradshaw, Michael, 2000. *Regional Economic Change in Russia*. Cheltenham: Edward Elgar.

Hedlund, Stefan, 1999. *Russia's 'Market' Economy: A Bad Case of Predatory Capitalism*. London: UCL Press.

Hellman, Joel S., 1998. 'Winners Take All: The Politics of Partial Reform in Postcommunist Transitions', *World Politics*, 50, 203–34.

Hendley, Kathryn, 1999. 'Rewriting the Rules of the Game in Russia: The Neglected Issue of the Demand for Law', *East European Constitutional Review*, 8, 4, 89–95.

Hirschman, Albert, 1963. *Journeys toward Progress: Studies of Economic Policy-Making in Latin America*. New York: Twentieth Century Fund.

Holmes, Stephen, 2000. 'Introduction: Putin's Russia', *East European Constitutional Review*, 9, 1/2, 51–2.

Hough, Jerry, 1988. *Russia and the West*. New York: Simon and Schuster.

Huntington, Samuel P., 1991. *The Third Wave: Democratization in the Late Twentieth Century*. Norman: University of Oklahoma Press.

Huskey, Eugene, 1990. 'Government Rulemaking as a Brake on *Perestroika*', *Law and Social Inquiry*, 15, 3, 419–32.

    1992. 'From Legal Nihilism to *Pravovoe gosudarstvo*: Soviet Legal Development 1917–1990'. In Donald D. Barry, ed., *Toward the Rule of Law in Russia?* Armonk, NY: M. E. Sharpe, 23–42.

    2001. 'Political Leadership and the Center–Periphery Struggle: Putin's Administrative Reforms'. In Archie Brown and Lilia Shevtsova, eds., *Gorbachev, Yeltsin, Putin: Political Leadership in Russia's Transition*. Washington, DC: Carnegie Endowment for International Peace, 113–42.

IFES [International Foundation for Election Systems], 2000. *Parliamentary and Presidential Elections in Russia, 1999–2000*. Moscow and Washington, DC: IFES.

Jack, Andrew, 2000. 'Putin Picks Kasyanov as Premier of Russia', *Financial Times*, 11 May.

    2001a. 'A Better Class of Baron', *Financial Times*, 2 December.

    2001b. 'Moscow Bars World Bank Health Loan', *Financial Times*, 8 June.

Jay, Antony, ed., 2001. *The Oxford Dictionary of Political Quotations*. Oxford: Oxford University Press, 2nd edn.

Johnson, Juliet, 2000. *A Fistful of Rubles: The Rise and Fall of the Russian Banking System*. Ithaca: Cornell University Press.

    2001. 'Path Contingency in Postcommunist Transformations', *Comparative Politics*, 33, 3, 253–74.

Johnson, Simon, and Loveman, Gary, 1995. *Starting Over in Eastern Europe: Entrepreneurship and Economic Revival*. Cambridge, MA: Harvard Business School Press.

Jowitt, Ken, 1992. *New World Disorder: The Leninist Extinction.* Berkeley: University of California Press.

Karatnycky, Adrian, Motyl, Alexander, and Schnetzer, Amanda, eds., 2001. *Nations in Transit 2001: Civil Society, Democracy and Markets in East Central Europe and the New Independent States.* New York: Freedom House.

Karl, Terry Lynn, 2000. 'Electoralism'. In Richard Rose, ed., *The International Encyclopedia of Elections.* Washington, DC: CQ Press, 95–6.

Karl, Terry Lynn, and Schmitter, Philippe C., 1995. 'From an Iron Curtain to a Paper Curtain', *Slavic Review*, 54, 4, 965–78.

Katsenelinboigen, A., 1977. 'Coloured Markets in the Soviet Union', *Soviet Studies*, 29, 1, 62–85.

Keenan, Edward, 1986. 'Muscovite Political Folkways', *Russian Review*, 45, 115–81.

King, Charles, 2000. 'Post-Postcommunism: Transition, Comparison and the End of "Eastern Europe"', *World Politics*, 53, 1, 143–72.

King, David, 1997. *The Commissar Vanishes: The Falsification of Photographs and Art in Stalin's Russia.* Edinburgh: Canongate.

Klebnikov, Paul, 2000. *Godfather of the Kremlin: Boris Berezovsky and the Looting of Russia.* New York: Harcourt, Brace.

Klecka, William R., 1980. *Discriminant Analysis.* Beverly Hills, CA: Sage Series in Quantitative Applications in the Social Sciences, 07-001.

Klingemann, Hans-Dieter, 1999. 'Mapping Political Support in the 1990s: A Global Analysis'. In Pippa Norris, ed., *Critical Citizens: Global Support for Democratic Government.* Oxford: Oxford University Press, 78–99.

Knight, Amy, 2000a. 'The Enduring Legacy of the KGB in Russian Politics', *Problems of Post-Communism*, 47, 4, 3–15.

2000b. 'Hit First and Hit Hard: Putin's Outlook Exposed', *Times Literary Supplement*, 9 June, 4–5.

Koestler, Arthur, 1940. *Darkness at Noon.* London: Jonathan Cape.

Kornai, Janos, 1992. *The Socialist System: The Political Economy of Communism.* Princeton: Princeton University Press.

Korsunsky, Vladimir, 1999. 'Putin prizval k Edinstvu' [Putin calls to Unity], *Kommersant*, 25 November.

Korzhakov, Alexander, 1997. *Boris Yeltsin ot rassveto do zakata* [Boris Yeltsin from dawn to dusk]. Moscow: Interbook.

Kullberg, Judith, 2001. *The Post-Totalitarian Game: Structure and Agency in Transitions from Communism.* Glasgow: University of Strathclyde Studies in Public Policy No. 353.

Ledeneva, Alena, 1998. *Russia's Economy of Favours: Blat, Networking and Informal Exchange.* Cambridge: Cambridge University Press.

2001. *Unwritten Rules: How Russia Really Works.* London: Centre for European Reform.

Levada, Yury, 2001. 'Homo Praevaricatus: Russian Doublethink'. In Brown, 2001a, 311–22.

Lier, John D., and Lambroza, Shlomo, eds., 1992. *Pogroms: Anti-Jewish Violence in Modern Russian History.* Cambridge: Cambridge University Press.

Lieven, Anatol, 1998. *Chechnya: Tombstone of Russian Power.* New Haven: Yale University Press.

Linz, Juan J., 2000. *Totalitarian and Authoritarian Regimes*. Boulder, CO: Lynne Rienner Publishers.

Linz, Juan J., and Stepan, Alfred, 1996. *Problems of Democratic Transition and Consolidation: Southern Europe, South America and Post-Communist Europe*. Baltimore: Johns Hopkins University Press.

Lipset, S. M., and Rokkan, Stein, eds., 1967. *Party Systems and Voter Alignments*. New York: Free Press.

Lopez-Claros, Augusto, and Zadornov, Mikhail M., 2002. 'Economic Reforms: Steady as She Goes', *Washington Quarterly*, 25, 1, 105–16.

Ma, Shu-Yun, 2000. 'Comparing the Russian State and the Chinese State: A Literature Review', *Problems of Post-Communism*, 47, 2, 3–12.

McFaul, Michael, 2000. 'Russia under Putin: One Step Forward, Two Steps Back', *Journal of Democracy*, 11, 3, 19–33.

2001. *Russia's Unfinished Revolution*. Ithaca: Cornell University Press.

Marer, Paul, Arvay, Janos, O'Connor, John, Schrenk, Martin, and Swanson, Daniel, 1992. *Historically Planned Economies: A Guide to the Data*. Washington, DC: World Bank.

Mendelson, Sarah E., 2000. 'The Putin Path: Civil Liberties and Human Rights in Retreat', *Problems of Post-Communism*, 47, 5, 3–12.

Meslé, F., Shkolnikov, V., and Vallin, J., 1992. 'Mortality by Cause in the USSR in 1970–1987: The Reconstruction of Time Series', *European Journal of Population*, 8, 281–308.

Miller, Arthur H., and Klobucar, Thomas F., 2000. 'The Development of Party Identification in Post-Soviet Societies', *American Journal of Political Science*, 44, 4, 667–85.

Mishler, William, and Rose, Richard, 2001, 'Political Support for Incomplete Democracies: Realist vs. Idealist Theories and Measures', *International Political Science Review*, 22, 4, 303–20.

Mishler, William, and Willerton, John P., 2000. *The Dynamics of Presidential Popularity in Post-Communist Russia: How Exceptional Is Russian Politics?* Glasgow: University of Strathclyde Studies in Public Policy No. 335.

Montgomery, Isobel, 2001. 'Georgy Shakhnazarov', *Guardian* (London), 28 May.

Morlino, Leonardo, and Montero, José Ramon, 1995. 'Legitimacy and Democracy in Southern Europe'. In R. Gunther, P. N. Diamandouros, and H.-J. Puhle, eds., *The Politics of Democratic Consolidation: Southern Europe in Comparative Perspective*. Baltimore: Johns Hopkins University Press, 231–60.

Moser, Robert G., 2001. 'The Consequences of Russia's Mixed-Member Electoral System'. In M. S. Shugart and M. P. Wattenberg, eds., *Mixed-Member Electoral Systems: The Best of Both Worlds?* Oxford: Oxford University Press, 494–518.

Munro, Neil, and Rose, Richard, 2001. *Elections in the Russian Federation*. Glasgow: University of Strathclyde Studies in Public Policy No. 344.

Myers, A. R., 1975. *Parliaments and Estates in Europe to 1789*. London: Thames & Hudson.

Neumann, Iver B., 1996. *Russia and the Idea of Europe*. London: Routledge.

Nodia, Ghia, 1996. 'How Different Are Postcommunist Transitions?', *Journal of Democracy*, 7, 4, 15–29.

Nove, Alec, 1975. 'Is There a Ruling Class in the USSR?', *Soviet Studies*, 27, 4, 615–38.

OECD [Organization for Economic Cooperation and Development], 1993. *OECD Health Systems: Facts and Trends, 1960–1991*. Paris: OECD Health Policy Studies, No. 3, vol. I.

OSCE [Organization for Security and Cooperation in Europe], 2000. *Final Report. Russian Federation: Presidential Election 26 March 2000*. Warsaw: Office for Democratic Institutions and Human Rights/OSCE Election Observation, 19 May.

O'Donnell, Guillermo, 1994. 'Delegative Democracy', *Journal of Democracy*, 5, 1, 55–69.

Olson, Mancur, 2000. *Power and Prosperity: Outgrowing Communist and Capitalist Dictatorships*. New York: Basic Books.

Oslon, Alexander, 2001. 'A Pollster's Perspective on the Putin Phenomenon', summary of lecture given at Kennan Institute, Washington, DC, *wwwics.si.edu/kennan/reports/2001/oslon.htm*, 9 March.

Oversloot, Hans, and Verheul, Ruben, 2000. 'The Party of Power in Russian Politics', *Acta Politica*, 35, 2, 123–45.

Owen, Thomas C., 1997. 'Autocracy and the Rule of Law in Russian Economic History'. In Sachs and Pistor, 1997, 23–40.

Pallotta, Gino, 1976. *Dizionario politico e parlamentare*. Rome: Newton Compton Editori.

Peel, Quentin, 2000. 'A President Torn between Progress and Order', *Financial Times*, 5 September.

polit.ru, 1999. Gubernatorskii pasyans: tablitsa politicheskoi aktivnosti gubernatorov [Governors' Patience: Table of Governors' Political Activism], *www.polit.ru/documents/112556.html*, 24 September.

    2001. Lenta Novostei [News Band], *www.polit.ru/documents/435446.html*, 16 August.

Pridham, Geoffrey, 2001. 'Uneasy Democratizations – Pariah Regimes, Political Conditionality and Reborn Transitions in Central and Eastern Europe', *Democratization*, 8, 4, 65–94.

Przeworski, Adam, 1995. *Sustainable Democracy*. New York: Cambridge University Press.

Przeworski, Adam, Alvarez, Michael, Cheibub, Jose Antonio, and Limongi, Fernando, 1996. 'What Makes Democracies Endure', *Journal of Democracy*, 7, 1, 39–55.

Putin, Vladimir, 1999. 'Why We Must Act', *New York Times*, 14 November.

    2000. *First Person*, with N. Gevorkyan, N. Timakova and A. Kolesnikov. London: Hutchinson.

    2001a. 'Annual Address to the Federal Assembly'. In BBC Monitoring Service, 'Text of Russian President's Annual Address to Federal Assembly', *Johnson's Russia List* No. 5185, *www.cdi.org/russia/johnson/5185.html*, 4 April.

    2001b. 'Transcript of Interview with Russian President Vladimir Putin by Various US Journalists'. Moscow, 18 June. Russian-Studies@Jiscmail.ac.uk.

Putnam, Robert D., 1993. *Making Democracy Work*, with Robert Leonardi and Raffaella Y. Nanetti. Princeton: Princeton University Press.

Reddaway, Peter, 2001. 'Will Putin Be Able to Consolidate Power?', *Post-Soviet Affairs*, 17, 1, 23–44.

Reddaway, Peter, and Glinski, Dmitri, 2001. *The Tragedy of Russia's Reforms: Market Bolshevism against Democracy*. Washington, DC: United States Institute of Peace.

Reese, Roger R., 2000. *The Soviet Military Experience: A History of the Soviet Army, 1917–1991*. London: Routledge.

Reich, Gary W., 2001. 'Coordinating Party Choice in Founding Elections: Why Timing Matters', *Comparative Political Studies*, 34, 10, 1237–63.

Remington, Thomas F., 2000. 'Notes on Duma Deputy Survey, 2000'. Atlanta: Emory University, duplicated.

   2002. 'Putin's Legislative Strategy'. In Dale Herspring, ed., *The Putin Regime*. Lanham, MD: Rowman Littlefield.

Remnick, David, 2000. 'Letter from Moscow: The Black Box', *New Yorker*, 27 March, 40–50.

Robinson, Neil, 2001. 'The Myth of Equilibrium: Winner Power, Fiscal Crisis and Russian Economic Reform', *Communist and Post-Communist Studies*, 34, 423–46.

Roeder, Philip G., 1993. *Red Sunset: The Failure of Soviet Politics*. Princeton: Princeton University Press.

Rose, Richard, 1992a. 'Escaping from Absolute Dissatisfaction: A Trial-and-Error Model of Change in Eastern Europe', *Journal of Theoretical Politics*, 4, 4, 371–93.

   1992b. 'Toward a Civil Economy', *Journal of Democracy*, 3, 2, 13–26.

   1995a. 'Adaptation, Resilience and Destitution: Alternative Responses to Transition in the Ukraine', *Problems of Post-Communism*, 42, 6, 52–61.

   1995b. 'Russia as an Hour-Glass Society: A Constitution without Citizens', *East European Constitutional Review*, 4, 3, 34–42.

   1996a. 'Ex-Communists in Post-Communist Societies', *Political Quarterly*, 67, 1, 14–25.

   1996b. *What Is Europe? A Dynamic Perspective*. New York and London: Longman.

   1997. 'How Patient Are People in Post-Communist Societies?', *World Affairs*, 159, 3, 130–44.

   1999a. 'Living in an Antimodern Society', *East European Constitutional Review*, 8, 1/2, 68–75.

   1999b. 'The Long and the Short of the Transformation in Central Europe'. In R. Andorka, T. Kolosi, R. Rose, and G. Vukovich, eds., *A Society Transformed: Hungary in Time–Space Perspective*. Budapest: Central European University, 179–204.

   2000a. 'A Supply-Side View of Russia's Elections', *East European Constitutional Review*, 9, 1/2, 53–9.

   2000b. 'Uses of Social Capital in Russia: Modern, Pre-Modern and Anti-Modern', *Post-Soviet Affairs*, 16, 1, 33–57.

   2001. *The Prime Minister in a Shrinking World*. Oxford and Boston: Polity Press.

2002a. 'A Decade of Change But Not Much Progress'. In Donald W. Kelley, ed., *Decade of Post-Communism*. Fayetteville: University of Arkansas Press.

2002b. *A Decade of New Russia Barometer Surveys*. Glasgow: University of Strathclyde Studies in Public Policy No. 360.

Rose, Richard, and Carnaghan, Ellen, 1995. 'Generational Effects on Attitudes to Communist Regimes: A Comparative Analysis', *Post-Soviet Affairs*, 11, 1, 28–56.

Rose, Richard, and McAllister, Ian, 1990. *The Loyalty of Voters*. London: Sage Publications.

Rose, Richard, and Mishler, William, 1998. 'Negative and Positive Partisanship in Post-Communist Countries', *Electoral Studies*, 17, 2, 217–34.

Rose, Richard, Mishler, William, and Haerpfer, Christian, 1998. *Democracy and Its Alternatives: Understanding Post-Communist Societies*. Oxford: Polity Press and Baltimore: Johns Hopkins University Press.

Rose, Richard, Munro, Neil, and White, Stephen, 2000. 'How Strong is Vladimir Putin's Support?', *Post-Soviet Affairs*, 16, 4, 287–312.

2001. 'Voting in a Floating Party System: The 1999 Duma Election', *Europe–Asia Studies*, 53, 3, 419–43.

Rose, Richard, and Shin, Doh Chull, 2001. 'Democratization Backwards: The Problem of Third-Wave Democracies', *British Journal of Political Science*, 31, 331–54.

Rose, Richard, Shin, Doh Chull, and Munro, Neil, 1999. 'Tensions between the Democratic Ideal and Reality: South Korea'. In P. Norris, ed., *Critical Citizens: Global Support for Democratic Governance*. Oxford: Oxford University Press, 146–65.

Rose, Richard, and Tikhomirov, Evgeny, 1993. 'Who Grows Food in Russia and Eastern Europe?', *Post-Soviet Geography*, 34, 2, 111–26.

1996. 'Russia's Forced-Choice Presidential Election', *Post-Soviet Affairs*, 12, 4, 351–79.

Rudden, Bernard, 1994. 'The Soviet Political System: Constitution'. In Brown, Kaser, and Smith, 1994, 366–73.

Rustow, Dankwart A., 1955. *The Politics of Compromise: A Study of Parties and Cabinet Government in Sweden*. Princeton: Princeton University Press.

1970. 'Transitions to Democracy', *Comparative Politics*, 2, 337–63.

Rutland, Peter, 2000. 'Putin's Path to Power', *Post-Soviet Affairs*, 16, 4, 313–54.

Ryabov, Andre, 2001. 'Yeltsin's Elite Retains Leading Positions in Government', *Segodnya*, 20 March.

Sachs, Jeffrey D., and Pistor, Katharina, eds., 1997. *The Rule of Law and Economic Reform in Russia*. Boulder, CO: Westview Press.

Saivetz, Carol R., 2000. 'Russian Foreign Policy Free-Lancing: The Cases of Lukoil, Gazprom and Rosvooruzheniye', *Post-Soviet Affairs*, 16, 1, 25–31.

Sakwa, Richard, 1996. *Russian Politics and Society*. London: Routledge, 2nd edn.

Sapir, Jacques, 2001. 'The Russian Economy: From Rebound to Rebuilding', *Post-Soviet Affairs*, 17, 1, 1–22.

Schmitter, P. C., and Karl, Terry Lynn, 1994. 'The Conceptual Travels of Transitologists and Consolidologists: How Far to the East Should They Attempt to Go?', *Slavic Review*, 53, 1, 173–85.

Schumpeter, Joseph A., 1952. *Capitalism, Socialism and Democracy*. London: George Allen & Unwin, 4th edn.

Seabright, Paul, ed., 2000. *The Vanishing Rouble: Barter Networks and Non-Monetary Transactions in Post-Soviet Societies*. Cambridge: Cambridge University Press.

Senokosov, Yuri and Skidelsky, Edward, eds., 2001. *The Russian Economy Today*. Moscow and London: Moscow School of Political Studies/Centre for Post-Collectivist Studies Russia on Russia Paper No. 6.

Sharlet, Robert, 2001. 'Putin and the Politics of Law in Russia', *Post-Soviet Affairs*, 17, 3, 195–234.

Shelley, Louise, 2001. 'Crime and Corruption'. In White, Pravda, and Gitelman, 2001, 239–53.

Shevtsova, Lilia, 1999. *Yeltsin's Russia: Myths and Reality*. Washington, DC: Carnegie Endowment for International Peace.

    2000. 'Can Electoral Autocracy Survive?', *Journal of Democracy*, 11, 3, 36–8.

    2001. 'From Yeltsin to Putin: The Evolution of Presidential Power'. In Archie Brown and L. Shevtsova, eds., *Gorbachev, Yeltsin, Putin: Political Leadership in Russia's Transition*. Washington, DC: Carnegie Endowment for International Peace, 67–112.

Shlapentokh, Vladimir, 1989. *Public and Private Life of the Soviet People*. New York: Oxford University Press.

    1995. 'Russian Patience: A Reasonable Behaviour and a Social Strategy', *Archives Européennes de Sociologie*, 36, 2, 247–80.

    2000. 'A Normal System? False and True Explanations for the Collapse of the USSR', *Times Literary Supplement*, 15 December.

    2001. *A Normal Totalitarian Society: How the Soviet Union Functioned and How It Collapsed*. Armonk, NY: M. E. Sharpe.

Shleifer, Andrei, and Treisman, Daniel, 2000. *Without a Map: Political Tactics and Economic Reform in Russia*. Cambridge, MA: MIT Press.

Simon, Janos, 1998. 'Popular Conceptions of Democracy in Postcommunist Europe'. In S. H. Barnes and J. Simon, eds., *The Postcommunist Citizen*. Budapest: Erasmus Foundation and Institute for Political Science, Hungarian Academy of Sciences, 79–116.

Skilling, H. Gordon, and Griffiths, Franklyn, eds., 1971. *Interest Groups in Soviet Politics*. Princeton: Princeton University Press.

Slider, Darrell, 2001. 'Politics in the Regions'. In White, Pravda, and Gitelman, 2001, 147–70.

Smith, Gordon B., 1999a. 'The Disjuncture between Legal Reform and Law Enforcement: The Challenge Facing the Post-Yeltsin Leadership'. In Smith, 1999b, 101–22.

    ed., 1999b. *State-Building in Russia: The Yeltsin Legacy and the Challenge of the Future*. Armonk, NY: M. E. Sharpe.

    2001. 'Russia and the Rule of Law'. In White, Pravda and Gitelman, 2001, 108–27.

Smith, Stephen S., and Remington, Thomas F., 2001. *The Politics of Institutional Choice: The Formation of the Russian State Duma*. Princeton: Princeton University Press.

Smyth, Regina A., 2001. 'Elections, Parties and State Development'. Washington, DC: Paper to the annual conference of the American Association for the Advancement of Slavic Studies, 15–18 November.

Solnick, Stephen L., 1998. *Stealing the State: Control and Collapse in Soviet Institutions*. Cambridge, MA: Harvard University Press.

2000. 'Is the Center Too Weak or Too Strong in the Russian Federation?' In Valerie Sperling, ed., *Building the Russian State*. Boulder, CO: Westview Press, 137–56.

Solomon, Peter H. Jr, and Foglesong, Todd S., 2000. *Courts and Transition in Russia: The Challenge of Judicial Reform*. Boulder, CO: Westview Press.

Stanley, Harold W., and Niemi, Richard G., 1994. *Vital Statistics on American Politics*. Washington, DC: CQ Press, 4th edn.

2000. *Vital Statistics on American Politics 1999–2000*. Washington, DC: CQ Press.

Starobin, Paul, and Belton, Catherine, 2002. 'Cleanup Time in Russia', *Business Week*, 14 January.

Stoner-Weiss, Kathryn, 2001a. 'Central Governing Incapacity and the Weakness of Political Parties: Russian Democracy in Disarray', unpublished typescript, 30 November.

2001b. 'The Limited Reach of Russia's Party System: Underinstitutionalization in Dual Transitions', *Politics and Society*, 29, 3, 385–414.

strana.ru, 2001. 'Russians Identify National Interests with Nation's International Authority' (19 April). In CDI Russia Weekly No. 150, 20 April: *www.cdi.org/russia/150.html*.

Summers, Lawrence H., 1991. 'Lessons of Reform for the Baltics'. Indianapolis: paper to Hudson Institute Conference, 29 October.

TACIS [Technical Assistance to the Commonwealth of Independent States], 2000. 'Affiliations of Regional Heads and the Regional Perspective'. Moscow: European Union Project for Capacity Development on Election Monitoring Briefing Document No. 3, 7 March.

Thomson, Robert, 2002. 'Lunch with the *FT*: Henry Kissinger', *Financial Times*, 19 January.

Tikhomirov, Vladimir, 2001. 'Russian Debt Problems in the 1990s', *Post-Soviet Affairs*, 17, 3, 262–84.

Transparency International, 2001. *Perception of Corruption Index*. Berlin: *www.transparency.de*.

Treisman, Daniel, 1999. *After the Deluge: Regional Crises and Political Consolidation in Russia*. Ann Arbor: University of Michigan Press.

Ulyanov, Nikolai, 2001. 'During the Past Year Putin Has Prepared the Country for Serious Economic Reforms'. No. 146. CDI Russia Weekly 23 March *www.cdi.org/russia/146.html*, translated from *www.strana.ru*.

Vachudova, Milada Anna, 2000. 'EU Enlargement: An Overview', *East European Constitutional Review*, 9, 4, 64–9.

Ware, Robert Bruce, 2000. 'Who Stole Russia's Election?', *Christian Science Monitor*, 18 October.

Warren, Marcus, 2001. 'Spies Doing a Bad Job, Says Former KGB Man Putin', *Daily Telegraph*, 22 June.

Webb, Beatrice, and Webb, Sidney, 1937. *Soviet Communism: A New Civilization*. London: printed for trade union subscribers, 2nd edn.

Weber, Max, 1947. *The Theory of Social and Economic Organization*. Glencoe, IL: Free Press.

1973. *Wirtschaft und Gesellschaft*. Tübingen: J. C. B. Mohr, 5th edn.

Wedel, Janine, 1998. *Collision and Collusion: The Strange Case of Western Aid to Eastern Europe, 1989–1998*. New York: St Martin's Press.

White, Stephen, 1979. *Political Culture and Soviet Politics*. London: Macmillan.

White, S., Pravda, Alex, and Gitelman, Zvi, eds., 2001. *Developments in Russian Politics*. Basingstoke: Palgrave, 5th edn.

White, Stephen, Rose, Richard, and McAllister, Ian, 1997. *How Russia Votes*. Chatham, NJ: Chatham House.

White, Stephen, Munro, Neil, and Rose, Richard, forthcoming. 'Parties, Voters and Foreign Policy'. In Vicki L. Hesli and William M. Reisinger, eds., *The 1999–2000 Elections in Russia*. New York: Cambridge University Press, ch. 3.

Whittell, Giles, 2001. 'Putin's Authority Leaves Russia in the Cold', *The Times*, 17 April.

Winiecki, Jan, 1988. *The Distorted World of Soviet-Type Economics*. London: Routledge.

World Bank, 1997. *The State in a Changing World*. Washington, DC: World Bank.

2001. *World Bank Atlas 2001*. Washington, DC: World Bank.

Yeltsin, Boris, 1994. *The Struggle for Russia*. New York: New York Times Books.

1999. Speech on Russian television, 31 December. In LegacyRus.com, 2002, 'President Boris Yeltsin's Resignation Address, 12/31/1999', *Legacy Rus Library Level 9*, *www.legacyrus.com/library/RussianBank/YeltsinResignation Address.htm*, n.d., 4 March.

2000. *Midnight Diaries*. London: Weidenfeld and Nicolson.

Z [Martin Malia], 1990. 'To the Stalin Mausoleum', *Daedalus*, 119, 1, 295–344.

Zisk, Kimberly Martin, 2001. 'Institutional Decline in the Russian Military: Exit, Voice and Corruption'. In Bonnell and Breslauer, 2001, 35–58.

Index

Abramovich, Roman, 136
accountability, 46ff., 101–17, 118–40,
  227ff.
Africa, 53
against all, voting, 137, 177
age, 155, 194
agriculture, 18, 155
anti-modern state, *see* state
anxieties of Russians, 214f.
army in politics, 29f., 78f., 209, 222, 226
Austria, 52
Aven, Peter, 36

Babitsky, Andrei, 201
Baluyesky, Yury, 209
barter, 71f.
Belarus, 56ff., 233
Berezovsky, Boris, 50, 113, 124, 136,
  175, 200f.
Berlin Wall, 24
biznesmen, 32f., 226
Bolsheviks, market, 33
Borodin, Pavel, 197
Breslauer, George, 28
Brezhnev, Leonid, 20f., 62f.
Brown, Archie, 60
Bunce, Valerie, 11
Bush, President George W., 208

Camdessus, Michel, 7
car ownership, 64f., 73
Chechnya, 96–100, 151–3, 175,
  206f., 215
Chekhov, Anton, 14, 237
Chernobyl nuclear accident, 48, 214f.
Chubais, Anatoly, 38, 83f., 114
Churchill, Winston, 77
civil society, 43ff., 223ff.
class and voting, 154f., 183
Clinton, President William, 38, 50
Commonwealth of Independent States
  (CIS), 206f., 233

Communist Party of the Russian
  Federation, 4f., 31f., 91ff., 104–17,
  119–40, 142–63, 170ff., 198f.,
  229
Communist Party of the Soviet Union,
  18ff., 78
Congress of People's Deputies, 28ff.
connections (*blat*), 69f.
consolidation of incomplete democracy,
  10, 43, 58f., 218ff.
constitution, 26ff., 52, 89, 102
Constitutional Court, 226
consumer goods, 73f.
coping economically, 34f., 72ff.
corruption, 43–60, 63, 212f., 220ff.,
  235
Council for Mutual Economic Assistance
  (COMECON), 54
coup, failed, 25
crime, 68f., 222ff.; *see also* order,
  corruption

Dagestan, 96, 179
Dahl, Robert, 10
debts of Russian state, 32–40, 205
democracy defined, 4f., 41–60, 74–81,
  145f., 234ff.
destitution, 73
dictatorship, 3f., 76ff., 233ff.
dictatorship of law, 3f., 60
double-think, 4, 21
Dresden, life of Putins in, 232
Dudintsev, Vladimir, 4
Duma, 30, 88, 106–17, 118–40, 141–65,
  198f., 222, 226f.
Dyachenko, Tatiana, 82, 196
Dzhabrailov, Umar, 173

economy, command, 32–40, 64ff.
economy in transformation, 33–40, 66–74,
  146ff., 203ff., 232
education and voting, 155, 194